Studies in the History of Medieval Religion

VOLUME X

GILDS IN THE MEDIEVAL COUNTRYSIDE

Social and Religious Change in Cambridgeshire c.1350–1558

This is a study of religious gilds in Cambridgeshire, from their apparent proliferation in the mid-fourteenth century to their dissolution under Edward VI. It explores their failure to return during the Catholic revival of Mary I's reign. Gilds, or fraternities, reflected the social hierarchies of their communities: local gentry acted as patrons, and below them an oligarchy of wealthier tenants exercised control through manorial, gild and parish office. Fraternities benefited their members by fostering mutual charity in life and commemoration after death; they made substantial contributions to the parish through the organisation of religious devotions and the maintenance of additional priests, and, in social and economic terms, through the ownership of land, animals and other corporate amenities such as gildhalls.

Dr Bainbridge examines lay responses to changing devotional and doctrinal patterns; the inter-relation of the religious and the secular; and the differing roles of gilds in rural and urban parishes, and in the densely settled shire of Cambridge and the sparsely populated fens of the Isle of Ely. Her study is based on the returns to the 1388–9 survey of religious gilds and surviving gild records, and a sample of about two thousand wills provides the context; manorial records, poll-tax returns and letters patent give further information on the communities in which they flourished.

Dr VIRGINIA BAINBRIDGE teaches at St Hilda's College, Oxford.

Studies in the History of Medieval Religion

ISSN 0955–2480

General Editor Christopher Harper-Bill

GILDS IN THE MEDIEVAL COUNTRYSIDE

Social and Religious Change in Cambridgeshire c.1350–1558

VIRGINIA R. BAINBRIDGE

THE BOYDELL PRESS

First published 1996
The Boydell Press, Woodbridge

ISBN 0 85115 617 7

The Boydell Press is an imprint of Boydell & Brewer Ltd
PO Box 9, Woodbridge, Suffolk IP12 3DF, UK
and of Boydell & Brewer Inc.
PO Box 41026, Rochester, NY 14604–4126, USA

A catalogue record for this book is available
from the British Library

Library of Congress Cataloging-in-Publication Data
Bainbridge, Virginia R. (Virginia Rosalyn), 1961–
Gilds in the medieval countryside : social and religious change in Cambridgeshire, c. 1350–1558 / Virginia R. Bainbridge.
p. cm. – (Studies in the history of medieval religion, ISSN 0955–2480 ; v. 10)
Includes bibliographical references and index.
ISBN 0–85115–617–7 (hardback: alk. paper)
1. Confraternities – England – Cambridgeshire – History.
2. Cambridgeshire (England) – Church history. I. Title.
II. Series.
BX808.5.G7B35 1996
267'. 1824265–dc20 96–4785

This publication is printed on acid-free paper

Printed in Great Britain by
Boydell & Brewer Ltd, Woodbridge, Suffolk

Contents

Maps

Sororibus Meis
In Umbra Historiae

This book is produced with the assistance of
a grant from Isobel Thornley's Bequest to
the University of London

Acknowledgements

It gives me great pleasure to acknowledge and thank the many people who have contributed to the successful completion of this project: first and foremost my supervisor Dr Caroline Barron, for her unfailing support and kindness.

Dr David d'Avray, Dr Brenda Bolton, Dr Clive Burgess, Frances Devereux, Professor Barrie Dobson, Father Simon Hobbes, Dr Beat Kümin, Kay Lacey, Dr Michael Lane, Bill Liddell, Felicity Knowlson, Stephanie Macek, Dr Joanna Mattingley, Christina McConnell, Beverley McHainch, Ruby Norris, Dr Dorothy Owen, Dr W.M. Palmer, Dr Alice Prochaska, Dr Susan Reynolds, Dr Miri Rubin, Professor the Earl Russell, Raphael Samuel, Dr Peter Scott, Dr Bob Scribner, Judy Snowball, Professor Doctor Matthieu Spiertz and Marieke Spiertz, Dr Jane Selby, Bridget Taylor, Dr Bill Tighe, Tim Wales: mentors and friends over the years. All the staff and members of Royal Holloway and Bedford New College History Department;* the Institute of Historical Research;* Birkbeck Centre for Extra-Mural Studies; Regent's College; the Paleography Room, Senate House Library; London University Central Research Fund;* the British Federation of Women Graduates;* the Ecclesiastical History Society;* the Max-Planck-Institut für Geschichte, Göttingen, Germany;* St Deiniol's Library, Hawarden, Wales;* Cambridge University Library Department of Manuscripts; Cambridgeshire County Record Office; Parish Studies Group; the Tuesday Group; All Saints' Church Margaret Street; Central Training Division Greater London Council: all my colleagues and students, especially my class at Ilford WEA 1989–93, who have shared with me the excitement of the journey into the past: and all my friends for their love.

I would also like to thank the Ecclesiastical History Society for permission to include Chapter 4, a previous version of which has appeared as 'The Medieval Way of Death', in *Prophecy and Eschatology*, Studies in Church History Subsidia x, Oxford 1994, ed. Michael Wilks; the general editor of the Victoria History of the Counties of England for permission to include Map 1; Dr John McCann, formerly of the Historic Buildings Division of Essex County Council, for permission to include Map 2; and the County Archivist of Cambridgeshire for permission to use the map of Cambridgeshire parishes as the basis for Map 3.

* Scholarships from these bodies have aided the competion of this project.

Abbreviations

ACE	Archdeaconry Court of Ely, Original Wills 1513–1558, Ely Dioceasan Archives
Bateson	Mary Bateson, ed., *Cambridge Gild Records*, Publns Camb. Antiq. Soc., no. 39, Cambridge 1903
BIHR	*Bulletin of the Institute of Historical Research*
BL	British Library
Camb.	Cambridge
Cambs.	Cambridgeshire
Cambs. & Hunts. Arch. Soc.	*Transactions of Cambridgeshire and Huntingdonshire Archaeological Society*
CCRO	Cambridgeshire County Record Office
CUL	Cambridge University Library
East Anglian	*The East Anglian, or Notes and Queries* on subjects connected
N & Q	with the counties of Suffolk, Cambridgeshire, Essex and Norfolk
ECC	Ely Consistory Court, Original Wills, 1485, 1503–58, Ely Diocesan Archives
EcHR	*Economic History Review*
EDA	Ely Diocesan Archives, Cambridge University Library
EETS	Early English Text Society
EHD	*English Historical Documents*
EHR	*English Historical Review*
HMSO	Her Majesty's Stationery Office
JEH	*Journal of Ecclesiastical History*
KCC	Wills proved under the peculiar jurisdiction of King's College Cambridge, registered in Ledger Book 1, 1449–1558, King's College Cambridge
Palmer	W.M. Palmer, 'Village Gilds of Cambridgeshire', *Cambs. & Hunts. Arch. Soc.* i, 1902, 330–402; and separately printed, Ely 1904
P&P	*Past and Present*
PCC	Cambridgeshire wills proved under the jurisdiction of the Prerogative Court of Canterbury, 1383–1558, Public Record Office
PRO	Public Record Office

Proc. Camb. Antiq. Soc.	Proceedings of Cambridge Antiquarian Society
Publns Camb. Antiq. Soc.	Publications of Cambridge Antiquarian Society
SCH	*Studies in Church History*
TRHS	*Transactions of the Royal Historical Society*
Toulmin Smith	Joshua Toulmin Smith, ed., *English Gilds*, EETS, original series, no. 40, London 1870; 2nd impression 1892
VCC	Original wills proved under the peculiar jurisdiction of the Vice-Chancellor's Court, Cambridge University 1521–58, Cambridge University Library
VCH Cambs.	*Victoria History of the County of Cambridgeshire*
WCR1	Wisbech Corporation Records, vol. 1, The Register of Holy Trinity Gild, Wisbech and Fenland Museum
WFM	Wisbech and Fenland Museum, Wisbech, Cambridgeshire

1

Ideology and Historiography: Modern Images of Medieval Gilds

Medieval gilds have fascinated generations of historians. There has been an academic literature on gilds in Germany since the seventeenth century. In England antiquarian studies were produced from the eighteenth century, and the great wave of enthusiasm for them throughout Europe in the late nineteenth and early twentieth centuries produced the great classics of English gild scholarship. *English Gilds* by Joshua Toulmin Smith, *The Gild Merchant* by Charles Gross, *The Parish Gilds of Medieval England* by Herbert Westlake and *The English Craft Gilds* by Stella Kramer are still the only general surveys in their field.[1] All the English gild historians of this period worked within the empirical tradition of historical writing, and yet all approached the subject with their own ideologies, using their work to explore the preoccupations of their own times.

Westlake was writing under the inspiration of the Oxford Movement for the revival of Catholic worship in the Church of England. This was extremely influential in pioneering a new approach to the remnants of medieval English Catholicism, its liturgy and rituals, institutions such as gilds which provided religious services for their members, and its physical remains, the medieval parish churches. Until the mid-nineteenth century antiquarian authors had stressed the chronology of the fabric and the tombs and monuments of local dignitaries, an attitude which still prevails today.[2] All cultural memory of the liturgical symbolism and practical use of these religious spaces

1 S. Loggon, *A History of the Brotherhood or Guild of the Holy Ghost in the Chapel of the Holy Ghost near Basingstoke in Hampshire*, Reading 1742, is an example of antiquarian gild scholarship; *English Gilds*, ed. J. Toulmin Smith, EETS, original series 40, London 1870, with an introduction by L. Toulmin Smith and an essay 'On the History and Development of Gilds and the Origin of Trade Unions', by L. Brentano. See Brentano, p. clx for reference to 17th-century German gild literature; C. Gross, *The Gild Merchant: A Contribution to British Municipal History*, 2 vols, Oxford 1890, reissued 1927; H.F. Westlake, *The Parish Gilds of Medieval England*, London 1919; S. Kramer, *The English Craft Gilds: Studies in their Progress and Decline*, New York 1927.

2 See, for example, N. Pevsner and others, *The Buildings of England*, 60 vols, London and Harmondsworth 1951–84; *VCH England*, London c.1900–date. For a more sympathetic

by the parish, gild and other groups of laymen had been erased, first by the influence of the apologists for the post-Reformation establishment, and later through the agnostic influence of the Enlightenment. Organs such as *The Ecclesiologist* contributed to the development of Victorian gothic architecture and church restoration.[3] The Arts and Crafts Movement was an additional influence on the study of medieval craftsmen and their products,[4] and general public interest in the romance of the Middle Ages led many authors to write popular works on everyday religious and social life before the Reformation.[5] Westlake's study of the parish gilds was among the more scholarly of these.[6]

It was in this atmosphere that the vicars of All Saints Church, Cambridge, set up gilds dedicated to St Agnes in 1878 and All Saints in 1889. Like their medieval predecessors, members of St Agnes Gild (mostly women) took an oath and met regularly, in their case for tea rather than ale as in past times, and the 1889 minutes of All Saints Gild reveal it to have been a refoundation of one originally begun in 1871, which had fallen into abeyance. These gilds, however, had a distinctly didactic flavour. They were led by the clergy and met for devotional instruction and communion. At the 1889 meeting of All Saints Gild, the Reverend Todd gave an address on the history of the gild and the characteristics of 'Church Gilds as now established', dividing their work into four branches: to assist individual devotion; to make collective devotion; to foster more frequent communion; and to increase involvement in parish work. Such gilds, despite their ancestry, were clearly of their time.[7]

The work of Toulmin Smith emerged from ideological traditions which were no less strong and no less concerned with roots and origins. His volume concentrated on the English ordinances of the fourteenth-century gilds. It was published by the Early English Text Society, itself a part of the movement

approach to medieval Catholicism, see F. Bond, *Dedications and Patron Saints of English Churches: Ecclesiastical Symbolism: Saints and Their Emblems*, London 1914.

3 *The Ecclesiologist*, Cambridge Camden Society, London 1841–68. Ironically, many physical remains of gild and chantry chapels were destroyed by the Victorians in their 'gothicisation' programme; C. Platt, *The Parish Churches of Medieval England*, London 1981, 116, argues that gild chapels took up a large proportion of the space in Coventry St Michael's and Holy Trinity, as was the case in many medieval parish churches.

4 J.C. Cox and A. Harvey, *English Church Furniture*, London 1907; F. Bond, *Screens and Galleries in English Churches*, London 1908.

5 For example the *Antiquary's Books* series published by Methuen in the early 1900s, including Abbot Gasquet, *Parish Life in Medieval England*, London 1908, esp. ch. 12, 'Guilds and Fraternities'.

6 See also H.F. Westlake, 'The Parish Gilds of the Later Fourteenth Century', *Transactions of St Paul's Ecclesiological Society* viii, 1917–20, 99–110. It must be noted that Westlake's analysis here is not systematic, but rather consists of anecdotal musings on the subject.

7 CCRO, P20/24/1–7 esp. 1, 2, Records of St Agnes and All Saints' Gilds; C. Walford, *Gilds: Their Origins, Constitution, Object and Later History*, London 1879, new and enlarged edn 1888, 260–1, on the 19th-century revival of religious gilds under the influence of the Oxford Movement.

to explore the development of the English language inspired by that great pride in nationhood which characterised the Victorian era. The quest for the roots of nationhood led to the study of constitutional history, the origins of institutions as the embodiment of national identity. The study incorporated both the evolution of central organs of government,[8] and the history of collective activity and self-regulation among free men. Toulmin Smith was dismissive of the 'simple piety' which informed the gilds' religious activities, and was concerned instead with 'how the ancient principle of association more than one thousand years' old had been in use as a living practice among the common folk'.[9] He was concerned primarily with what he termed 'social' gilds. Gross and Kramer too explored the role of other 'voluntary associations' in medieval society through their studies of the merchant and craft gilds. Political changes in the course of the nineteenth century, the increase in state intervention through the growth of bureaucracy and local government, the development of parliamentary democracy and the Trade Union Movement, against a background of liberal and socialist ideologies, as well as vast economic and social changes, brought to the fore the study of the English tradition of freedom as embodied in the collective institutions of the past.[10] The era of the common man demanded the study of those groups to which he had belonged in previous eras, and among them the medieval gilds.

Toulmin Smith's work was published posthumously, and the preface was written by a German scholar, Lujo Brentano.[11] Brentano's essay describes the origin and varieties of medieval gilds, religious, merchant, and craft gilds, as forerunners of the trade unions. As Sidney and Beatrice Webb pointed out, Brentano made no explicit claim that the ancestry of the trades unions lay in the gilds, other than through the juxtaposition of this material. As the Webbs saw it there was no connection between the employers' organisations of the medieval period, and the working men's organisations of the nineteenth century, other than their shared objectives, to maintain certain standards of living for their members.[12] Nevertheless the idea that the origins of the trades union lay in the medieval gilds became widespread and was taken up in such works as George Unwin's *The Gilds and Companies of London.* He discussed the fourteenth-century political conflicts between merchant and

8 W. Stubbs, *Select Charters Illustrative of English Constitutional History*, 1st edn, Oxford 1870; W. Stubbs, *Constitutional History of England*, 3 vols, Oxford 1874–8, 2nd and 3rd edns, 1878–80.

9 Toulmin Smith, see Introduction by L. Toulmin Smith, xxix.

10 F.W. Maitland, *Township and Borough*, Cambridge 1898; S. and B. Webb, *English Local Government*, 10 vols, London 1906–29.

11 Toulmin Smith, xlix–cxcix, 'On the History and Development of Gilds and the Origin of Trades-Unions', an essay by L. Brentano, also separately printed. See esp. section V, clxv–cxcix.

12 S. and B. Webb, *The History of Trade Unionism*, 1st edn, London 1894, 2nd edn, 1920, 12–21.

craft gilds in terms of class struggle, and attempted to trace the links between the gilds and the trade unions.[13]

Brentano was writing within the tradition of German medieval scholarship, which had contributed so much to English constitutional history.[14] In searching for the origins of English 'nationhood', Toulmin Smith and his contemporaries had found this in the Germanic tribesmen, as described by Caesar and Tacitus, transmitted through those who had settled in England in successive waves from the fifth century, particularly the Angles and the Saxons.[15] According to Stubbs 'the polity developed by the German race on British soil is the purest form of their primitive instinct'.[16] German historians had developed the 'Genossenschafttheorie': a theory of communal activity and relationships, the obligations of men bound together in mutual fellowship in political community, town, village or gild. Maitland's understanding was that 'The new theory was to be philosophically true, scientifically sound, morally righteous, legally implicit in codes and decisions, practically convenient, historically destined, genuinely German, and perhaps exclusively Germanistic.'[17] Indeed according to George Unwin, Lujo Brentano 'may be said to have inaugurated the scientific study of the English Gild'.[18] However, not all were convinced of the impartiality of what he wrote. Brentano was contradicted by an additional introduction by another English scholar, Toulmin Smith's daughter Lucy, and by a set of notes prefacing his essay, which suggest that there had been some controversy with his editor F.J. Furnivall over its contents. The conflicts seem to have arisen from nationalistic and anti-Catholic sentiment on Furnivall's behalf.[19]

Furnivall was suspicious that Brentano had termed those gilds without specific trade and craft associations 'religious' as in continental historiography, rather than 'social' gilds after Toulmin Smith, because he was a Roman Catholic. Furnivall asked him to warn the readers of this so that they might

13 G. Unwin, *The Gilds and Companies of London*, London 1908. See Preface and ch. xviii, 'From Gild to Trade Union', for the influence of Brentano's work.

14 G. Waitz, *Deutsche Verfassungsgeschichte*, 8 vols, Kiel 1844–78; L. Brentano, *Die Arbeitergilden Der Gegenwart*, 2 vols, Leipzig 1871–2; W. Stubbs, *Constitutional History*, i, ch. 1, discusses his relationship with the German tradition of scholarship; O.G. Oexle, '*Die Mittelalterliche Zünfte als Forschungsproblem: ein Beitrag zur Wissenschaftsgeschichte der Moderne*', *Blätter für Deutsche Landesgeschichte* 118, 1982, 1–77.

15 Stubbs, *Constitutional History*, i, chs 1–4.

16 Stubbs, *Constitutional History*, i, ch. 10.

17 O. Giercke, *Political Theories of the Middle Ages*, translated with an introduction by F.W. Maitland, Cambridge 1922, Introduction, xxv; O. Giercke, *Das Deutsche Genossenschaftsrecht*, 3 vols, Berlin 1868–81; O. Giercke, *Die Genossenschaftstheorie und die Deutsche Rechtsprechung*, Berlin 1887; O. Giercke, *Community in Historical Perspective: A Translation of Selections from Das Deutsche Genossenschaftsrecht* (The German Law of Fellowship) Principally from Volume i, translated by M. Fisher and ed. A. Black, Cambridge 1990.

18 Unwin, *The Gilds and Companies of London*, Preface, v.

19 Toulmin Smith, Notes, lvii–lx.

be aware of his prejudices. Furnivall himself was a part of the Whig tradition of English historiography, with its deep-rooted suspicion of Catholicism. Raphael Samuel and others have described the historical opposition of the secular branch of the socialist movement to organised religion.[20] Socialism was a major inspiration to the development of economic history, and the underlying anti-Catholic sentiments which informed much of this work precluded a balanced understanding of the role of religion in medieval society. Westlake and other Roman- or Anglo-Catholic writers sought to redress this balance by representing the Middle Ages as a 'golden age' of Christian faith. Brentano, it must be noted, was not among these authors.

Furthermore, evidence of the tension between the Germanic origins of English institutions and English nationalistic pride is expressed in Furnivall's complaint that Brentano did not stress adequately that England was the birthplace of the gilds. English historians at this time were anxious to assert that England did indeed possess the 'purest form' of Germanic institutions. Furnivall here was pointing to the four sets of Anglo-Saxon Gild Statutes, the earliest surviving gild constitutions in Europe, as evidence of this.[21] This evidence may now be seen as the chance survival of documentation, rather than proof of the absence of such institutions elsewhere. It is with the Anglo-Saxon gilds that all English authorities of this time begin their exploration of the history of English gilds.

George Unwin related the evolution of modern organs of government from the gilds, to that potent historical force, 'progress'. 'We can there watch in all its successive phases that transformation of social forces into political forces, which is the very essence of what we call progress.'[22]

The influence of Darwinian ideas on the scientific study of history may be perceived in this preoccupation with the origin and continuity of apparently similar institutions. In his book *Two Thousand Years of Gild Life* the Reverend J. Malet-Lambert describes the analysis of various types of gild as

> a task which may be compared with the one which confronts the student of biology in his attempt to classify and trace the connection of the various organs of animals and plants in the light of the modern theory of evolution.[23]

He traced gild type institutions from Plato's association of the Muses to nineteenth-century Kingston-upon-Hull, briefly taking in the gilds of China, India and Turkey on his picturesque journey. This methodological approach

20 *Disciplines of Faith*, ed. J. Obelkevich, L. Roper and R. Samuel, London 1987, Introduction, 3–9.

21 *Diplomatarium Anglicum Aevi Saxonici*, ed. B. Thorpe, London 1865, Preface xvi–xvii, 605–17; *EHD*, i, c.500–1041, ed. D. Whitelock, 2nd edn, London 1979, 382–3, 603–7.

22 Unwin, *The Gilds and Companies of London*, 12.

23 Rev. J. Malet-Lambert, *Two Thousand Years of Gild Life*, Hull 1891, ch. 1, 'Sociological Theories as to the Origin of the Gilds', 11.

has its limitations, as it can yield only superficial similarities between often unrelated institutions. Nevertheless it is still followed today, as in Anthony Black's 1984 volume *Gilds and Civil Society*.[24] He uses the same model of continuity to trace these 'liberal institutions', the expression of 'the community of labour', from the early Middle Ages to the twentieth century through the political philosophy of the medieval jurists, Thomas Aquinas, Marsiglio of Padua and Jean Bodin, to Hegel, Giercke, Durkheim and others. These examples illustrate the temptation to trace an exact genealogy of the gild. This approach is largely the product of a confusion within nineteenth- and early twentieth-century English historiography. As may be seen from the titles and contents of their books, the early gild historians applied the name gild to a number of very different social groups. Unwin and Westlake treated all previous gild forms as the antecedents of those of the later Middle Ages, which were the subjects of their studies.[25] Other writers were more sophisticated. They divided the genus *gildae* into a variety of species: Brentano into early gilds, religious or social gilds, town, merchant and craft gilds; Gross into clerical, socio-religious, trade gilds, merchant, craft, and artisan.[26] These divisions corresponded to what they perceived as metamorphoses of the basic gild form, to fulfil various different functions over the course of the Middle Ages. It is clear from the sources that *gild* was used by contemporaries interchangeably with other terms to describe a variety of institutions; in England *ars*, *fraternitas*, *confraternitas* and brotherhood; in France *ghilde*, *confrérie*, *charité*; in Italy *arte*, *scuole*, *confraternitas*; in Germany *zunfte*, *gild*, *brüderschaft*; to name but a few. The use of the term *gild* in the nineteenth century, however, was far more widespread and more indiscriminate, and has persisted to the present day as the accepted translation of many disparate medieval English and continental terms.[27] The most useful definition of gild seems to be club or society: alternatively, gilds may be compared with the committee of today.[28]

Charles Gross rejected the theory that medieval gilds were derived from the Romans or Scandinavians, any more than the Roman *collegia* were derived from the Hebraic *essenes*; 'every age has forms of association peculiar to itself, which have grown up spontaneously. It is not necessary to see the germ of the gilds in any antecedent age or institution.'[29] Gabriel le Bras, a later commentator, writes 'la confrérie n'est pas une institution propre au Christianism.

24 A. Black, *Gilds and Civil Society in European Political Thought from the Twelfth Century to the Present*, London 1984.

25 Unwin, *The Gilds and Companies of London*, esp. chs I and II; Westlake, esp. chs I and II.

26 Gross, *The Gild Merchant*, 176.

27 I am grateful to Dr Susan Reynolds for clarifying this point.

28 S. Reynolds, *Kingdoms and Communities in Western Europe 900–1300*, Oxford 1984, 70; G.H. Martin, 'The English Borough in the Thirteenth Century', *TRHS*, 5th series xiii, 1963, 123–44, esp. 126.

29 Gross, *The Gild Merchant*, i, 176.

Elle se retrouve dans toutes les civilisations passées et presentés'.[30] As it is common for men and women to bond together for mutual purposes in all societies, what is important is not to seek continuities between similar institutions at different times: that is too crudely chronological, as these nineteenth-century studies indicate. It is more interesting to analyse different interpretations of a basic social form by different ages, to see what this reveals about a society at each historical moment.[31]

Susan Reynolds in her recent influential study of *Kingdoms and Communities in Western Europe* sees characteristics associated with gilds as features of many medieval institutions. She treats the gilds as one of a range of manifestations of collective activity in medieval society, including the parish, rural and urban communities, provinces, lordships and realms.[32] She argues for a reappraisal of horizontal bonds, of late neglected in favour of those which emphasised hierarchy. It was this tradition of collective activity, not confined to the history of corporate bodies, which underlay many fundamental developments in western European society between the ninth and the thirteenth centuries.[33] It is within this context that gilds of all types must be understood, rather than as self-contained entities, or the quaint repositories of ancient custom. They are just part of the kaleidescope pattern of overlapping jurisdictions: royal, seignorial, episcopal, burghal, manorial, parochial and communal which characterised medieval life, both in the town and in the countryside.

The publishing milieu into which nineteenth-century authors introduced their volumes consisted, at a national level, of series such as the Rolls Series, Public Record Office publications, the Early English Text Society, and the Camden Society. These existed for the publication of indices, calendars and records, such as those contained in Toulmin Smith, Gross and Westlake, to make the scientific evidence for the events of the past available to the reading public. At a regional level, the same thirst for knowledge was catered

30 G. Le Bras, 'Les Confréries Chrétiennes: Problèmes and Propositions', *Revue Historique du Droit Français et Etranger*, series 4 xix–xx, Paris 1940–1, 310–63, esp. 362; see also G. le Bras, *Études de Sociologie Religieuse*, 2 vols, Paris 1955–6, ii, 418–62, a reprint of this article with a Preface.

31 O.G. Oexle, 'Conjuratio et Ghilde dans l'Antiquité et dans le Haute Moyen Age: Remarques sur la Continuité des formes de la Vie Sociale', Francia x, 1982, 1–19, 2 'Il est permis de dire que dans l'histoire médiévale la ghilde est un indicateur de tous les courants importants aussi bien économiques et sociaux qu'intellectuels et religieux, et qu'en même temps, a l'intérieur même de ces courants, elle représente un facteur déterminant'; W.R. Jones, 'English Religious Brotherhoods and Medieval Lay Piety: The Inquiry of 1388–9', *The Historian* xxxvi, 1974, 646–59, esp. 655.

32 Reynolds, *Kingdoms and Communities*, 3; religious, household and kinship, mercantile and craft groups are beyond the scope of her study due to lack of space; P. Michaud Quantin, *Universitas: Expression du Mouvement Communautaire dans le Moyen Age Latin*, Paris 1970.

33 Reynolds, *Kingdoms and Communities*, esp. Introduction 1–11.

for by the publications of local archaeological and historical societies.[34] These circulated to their subscribers papers read at their meetings, results of archaeological digs and historical researches and, once again, transcripts of documents of local and national interest. They had their heyday from the mid-nineteenth to the early twentieth century, although many still continue to this day, but with a smaller and more specialised readership. It was on these publications, along with local antiquarian works, that the early gild scholars were able to draw for examples to support their general conclusions. These general works in turn inspired further interest in their subject. Local record society proceedings contain most of the research on English gilds undertaken during the first half of the twentieth century,[35] and indeed much of that generated by a revival of interest in gilds in England over the last ten years.[36] Their contributors have continued to work within the English empirical tradition of historical writing, and within the framework of analysis provided by the early gild scholars.[37] However, due to the survey of local data and the large number of gild documents printed, these volumes are still useful today.

It may be said that the dominant strand of English gild historiography as represented by Toulmin Smith and others is secular, viewing the gilds in relation to trade, towns and local government. These are lines of enquiry derived from economic, political and constitutional history. By contrast the sentimental apology for gilds as religious institutions represented by Westlake's work derived from traditions of ecclesiastical and social history. These two approaches are also apparent in the French historiography. There are two important articles written in the 1940s which, while emerging from the two

34 Those relevant to the Cambridgeshire area are: *Proc. Camb. Antiq. Soc.*, Cambridge 1851–date; *Publns Camb. Antiq. Soc.*, Cambridge 1851–date; *East Anglian N. & Q.* i–iv, Lowestoft 1858–71; v–xvii, Ipswich 1885–1910; *Cambs. & Hunts. Arch. Soc.* i–vii, 1901–52.

35 General works of this period on Cambridgeshire gilds are: T.D. Atkinson, 'On the Gilds of Cambridgeshire', *Proc. Camb. Antiq. Soc.* ix, 1894–8, 385–90; W.M. Palmer, 'Village Gilds of Cambridgeshire', *Cambs. & Hunts. Arch. Soc.* i, 1902, 330–402; also separately printed, Ely 1904; *Cambridge Gild Records*, ed. M. Bateson, *Publns Camb. Antiq. Soc.* xxxix, Cambridge 1903.

36 See for example: *History of Chesterfield*, ed. P. Riden and J. Blair, Records of the Borough of Chesterfield v, Chesterfield Borough Council 1980; *Parish Fraternity Register: Fraternity of the Holy Trinity and Saints Fabian and Sebastian in the Parish of St Botolph Without Aldersgate*, ed. P. Basing, London Record Society xviii, London 1982; A.G. Rosser, 'The Town and Gild of Lichfield in the late Middle Ages', *Transactions of the South Staffordshire Archaeological and Historical Society* xxvii, 1985–6, 39–47; 'The Gild of St Mary and St John the Baptist, Lichfield: Ordinances of the late Fourteenth Century', ed. A.G. Rosser, *Staffordshire Record Society Collections for a History of Staffordshire*, 4th series xiii, 1988, 19–26.

37 J.A. Sparvel-Bayly and H.W. King, 'Records Relating to the Gild or Fraternity of Jesus in Prittlewell', *Transactions of Essex Archaeological Society*, new series ii, 1884, 153–64, 155 'The Gild of Prittlewell was one which comes under the denomination of Religious (or Social) Gilds'; see below for categorisation of gilds into different types by the early gild scholars.

traditions, nevertheless transcend this binary divide. As Charles Gross pointed out, religious elements were a part of the corporate life of all types of gilds. Their mixture of religious and secular activities defies their simple classification as essentially either secular or religious.[38]

In 1941 Gabriel le Bras, an ecclesiastical historian and authority on Canon Law, surveyed 'Les Confréries Chrétiennes: Problèmes et Propositions'. Like Westlake, he concentrated on those gilds or fraternities which could be perceived as primarily religious institutions. He employed the tools of sociology to propose new lines of research on the various roles which *confréries* or *charités* had played in French society from the first to the eighteenth century. He addressed this problem of their identity as neither fully secular nor fully religious in the context of legal history: they were institutions which were intermediate between the jurisdictions of the state and the church. A further contribution Le Bras made was to apply the concept of the supernatural to the gilds. Shared religious experience sanctioned group identity and sanctified all shared activities. The distinction which we acknowledge today between the religious and the secular did not exist: in medieval society, the immanent infused the everyday.[39]

Le Bras was responding to the accumulation of published material over the preceding decades, which it was now possible to synthesise, as was Coornaert in his article 'Les Ghildes Médiévales (Ve – XIVe Siècles). Définition – Évolution'.[40] Coornaert was working within the general framework of previous economic historians, but nevertheless emphasised the importance of both religious ritual and social activity in the formation of group identity. Coornaert applied the logic which his predecessors had purported to use, to make an incisive critique of historians who abandoned scientific reason to seek a common root for the diverse institutions which bear the name gild. He describes their history as 'la longue et confuse lignée des ghildes'.[41] He cut through much of the mythology and confusion in the earlier historiography to create a starting point for further researches.

One issue which had greatly preoccupied nineteenth-century historians was the evidence for the origin of such groups contained in the etymology of the word gild. As many as seven different theories of their beginnings are identified by William Kahl, another revisionist historian, in his 1963 introduction to the fourth edition of Unwin's book. They were said to have originated variously in Germany, Scandinavia or Italy, and to have emerged from other social forms, the tribe, the village, sacrificial gatherings, associations of

38 Gross, *The Gild Merchant*, i, 177.

39 See John Bossy, Review Article: 'Holiness and Society', *P&P* lxxv, 1977, 119–37, 134. Bossy states that the central issue in the Reformation was 'immanence versus transcendence'.

40 E. Coornaert, 'Les Ghildes Médiévales (Ve – XIVe Siècles) Définition – Évolution', *Revue Historique* cxcix, 1948, 22–55, 208–43.

41 Coornaert, 'Les Ghildes Médiévales', 22–23, 40.

Frankish priests, or the family.[42] The variety of etymological roots proposed for the term gild also stressed the obscurity and complex nature of their origins. The term gild and its variants is commonly assumed among English historians, following Toulmin Smith, to have derived from the Saxon *geld*, a tax, and thence a group which exacted payments from its members.[43] According to Brentano, the earliest use of the term was to describe the sacrificial meals of Scandinavia. Furnivall, anxious to assert the English origins of the gilds, footnoted an alternative etymology derived from Gaelic.[44] In the 1940s Coornaert examined the linguistic debates, by which time all etymologists were agreed on the Germanic origins of the word. He questioned the meaning given to it, however. He suggested that the financial bond could not be the fundamental expression of group identity, but rather it was the feast 'une communion alimentaire sacrificielle', which fulfilled this role.[45]

New perspectives were brought to bear on medieval gild scholarship through the studies of the French *Annales* school of historians. Gilds as voluntary associations, leaving records of their aspirations their activities and their corporate identities, were an ideal subject for the study of the *mentalités* of the past, one of the chief hallmarks of this school of history. The vast expansion of social history over the last twenty years or so, and the borrowing of ideas from other disciplines: political theory, sociology, anthropology, and psychology, has been the impetus for an increasingly rich literature on the role of religion in society. Just as social history defined itself against the traditional disciplines of political and constitutional history, the study of elites, their ideologies and institutions: so the new religious history defined itself against traditional ecclesiastical history, that of the clergy, their beliefs and organisational structures. The new subjects of research were the lives of the people and the religion of the laity; 'popular culture' and 'lay piety'.[46]

42 Unwin, *The Gilds and Companies of London*, 4th edn, London 1963, with a new Introduction by W.F. Kahl, xvii–xliv, esp. xxii.

43 Toulmin Smith, xix–xx; A.G. Rosser, 'Communities of Parish and Guild in the Late Middle Ages', in *Parish, Church and People: Local Studies in Lay Religion 1350–1750*, ed. S. Wright, London 1988, 29–55, 35.

44 Toulmin Smith, lvii–lviii, note 1, lxi. This is the subject of the first of the notes with which Brentano prefaced his essay. Evidently this, like religion (note 2), had been a subject of controversy with the editor Furnivall, who had appended a footnote to Brentano's Contents page with the Gaelic etymology, p. lxi. Brentano states in note 1 'Mr Furnivall asks me to make much more emphatic my statement as to England's being the birthplace of gilds'.

45 Coornaert, 'Les Ghildes Médiévales', 29–31, esp. 30.

46 It is not possible here to address these debates in detail but see: J. Van Engen, 'The Christian Middle Ages as an Historiographical Problem', *American Historical Review* xci, 1986, 519–52, for a thoughtful history of the shift in preoccupations among ecclesiastical historians from the last century to the present; R.W. Scribner, 'Review Article: Interpreting Religion in Early Modern Europe', *European Studies Review* xiii, 1983, 89–105, a review of a number of major works on popular culture and religion;

Much of this research has been stimulated by a reassessment of the course of the Reformation, and the emergence of a large body of work on early modern European popular culture.[47] Once the implementation of the Reformation from 'above', the contribution to religious change of enthusiastic minorities with strongly held convictions, and its implementation by political and intellectual elites had been examined, it became necessary to appraise its reception at a local level by those 'below', the 'people', in so far as we have records of their response. This process has led to a blurring of the formerly rigid division between medieval and early modern scholarship, as historians have sought to understand the progress of the Reformation at a popular level through a reassessment of late medieval religion. Here the study of gilds, fraternities, and brotherhoods has been important due to their sponsorship of religious activities. There were many such groups of varying size and importance called by different names in the towns and villages of Europe. These groups were among the most significant and included some of the humblest lay institutions to leave records through which such responses might be gauged.[48]

Recent studies of such western European institutions, which may for convenience here be termed gilds, address a number of themes.[49] It is possible to draw distinctions between their role in southern and northern Europe, and in urban and rural communities, although this in part reflects the pattern of the historiography.

The study of urban institutions has continued to flourish, especially of those which were particularly prominent and whose records therefore tend to be more numerous. For example there has been much work on the *arte* and

The Pursuit of Holiness in Late Medieval and Renaissance Religion, ed. C. Trinkaus and H.A. Oberman, Leyden 1974, see esp. Foreword by C. Trinkaus, ix–xvii, esp. ix–x, and N.Z. Davis, 'Some Tasks and Themes in the Study of Popular Religion', 307–36, for new directions in religious history including the study of lay fraternities; *Religion and the People 800–1700*, ed. J. Obelkevich, Chapel Hill University of North Carolina 1979; *Religion and Society in Early Modern Europe 1500–1800*, ed. K. Von Greyerz, London 1984.

47 P. Burke, *Popular Culture in Early Modern Europe*, London 1978.

48 Among studies in the current revisionist debate in England see: J.J. Scarisbrick, *The Reformation and the English People*, Oxford 1984, esp. ch. 2 where documents such as fraternity records are used to assess the state of lay piety on the eve of the Reformation; *The Church in Pre-Reformation Society*, ed. C.M. Barron and C. Harper-Bill, Woodbridge 1985, esp. C.M. Barron, 'The Parish Fraternities of Medieval London', 13–27; C. Harper-Bill, *The Pre-Reformation Church in England 1400–1530*, London 1989, for a synthesis of current knowledge of late medieval lay piety in England; *Parish, Church and People*, ed. S. Wright, for a collection of work which transcends the late medieval/early modern boundary; esp. Rosser, 'Communities of Parish and Gild'.

49 Little has been written on the gilds of medieval Byzantium, but for an introduction see: P. Horden, 'The Confraternities of Byzantium', *SCH* xxiii, 1985–6, 25–45; E.H. Freshfield, *Roman Law in the Later Roman Empire: Byzantine Guilds Professional and Commercial: Ordinances of Leo VI c.895 From the Book of the Eparch*, Cambridge 1938.

scuole grandi, trade and social groupings which were prominent in the city states of Renaissance and early modern Italy. Such work has continued to reflect the traditional preoccupations with their role in town government and religious life.[50] More modern themes, however, have also been explored: their expression of the structure of society, of corporate and civic identities, and their role in the ritual life of the city.[51] The association of many of these studies with the Renaissance period has led to the examination of their patronage not only of ritual both liturgical and public, but also of drama, music and art.[52] Such themes are also a feature of recent work on northern gilds.[53]

The continuity of Catholicism in southern Europe ensured the survival of lay brotherhoods beyond the Reformation period, although they were subsequently more strictly controlled for the purposes of the Counter-Reformation Catholic Church.[54] By contrast the northern European Reformation made medieval gild records more liable to loss or destruction. Such records were neither fully ecclesiastical, although tainted with 'superstition' through their recording of religious practices such as prayers for the dead, nor were they fully secular and therefore essential for the continuity of secular government. Furthermore, gilds were voluntary associations in an age when central government intervened increasingly in local affairs. In northern Europe the Reformation abolished social groups whose main activities were expressed through the religious rituals of their times, and ended the religious practices of crafts, trade gilds and corporations. In southern Europe the rituals of social, craft and trade groupings continued to be embedded in Catholic culture. The gilds of northern Europe seem to have lacked the devotional intensity of the southern *disciplinati* (flagellant) or *laudesi* (worship) fraternities,

50 B. Pullan, *Rich and Poor in Renaissance Venice: The Social Institutions of a Catholic State to 1620*, Oxford 1971, a magisterial study of the *Scuole Grandi* and other institutions involved in the implementation of state policy towards the poor; J.S. Henderson, *Piety and Charity in Late Medieval Florence*, Oxford 1994; R. Mackenney, *Tradesmen and Traders: the World of the Gilds in Venice and Europe c.1250–1650*, London 1987.

51 R.F.E. Weissman, *Ritual Brotherhood in Renaissance Florence*, New York 1982; R.C. Trexler, *Public Life in Renaissance Florence*, New York 1980.

52 *Renaissance et Réforme*, new series, xiii, no. 1 spring 1989, special edition on Confraternities; *Crossing the Boundaries*, ed. K. Eisenbichler, Kalamazoo 1991, Papers on Italian Confraternities: religious ritual, drama, music, art, death.

53 C. Phythian-Adams, 'Ceremony and the Citizens: the Communal Year at Coventry', in *Crisis and Order in English Towns 1500–1700*, ed. P. Clark and P. Slack, London 1972, 57–85; C. Phythian-Adams, *The Desolation of a City: Coventry and the Urban Crisis of the late Middle Ages*, Cambridge 1979, esp. 118–24; A.F. Johnston, 'The Plays of the Religious Guilds of York: The Creed Play and the Pater Noster Play', *Speculum* l, 1975, 55–90; A.F. Johnston, 'The Guild of Corpus Christi and the Procession of Corpus Christi in York', *Medieval Studies* xxxviii, 1976, 372–403; M. Rubin, 'Corpus Christi Fraternities and Late Medieval Piety', *SCH* xxiii, 1985–6, 97–109; R. Strohm, *Music in Late Medieval Bruges*, Oxford 1985, esp. ch. 4.

54 Le Bras, 'Les Confréries Chrétiennes', 349, 358.

with their regular meetings to participate in penitential processions or special liturgical rites, their emphasis on deepening the spiritual life of participants, and the grand scale of their charitable works. Northern gilds were also less frequently attached to religious houses as 'tertiary' orders.[55] Thus work on northern Europe influenced by the Reformation both in terms of source material and Protestant ideology has tended to concentrate on the gild contribution to secular life.[56] Recently Professor Otto Gerhard Oexle has done much to stimulate modern research on German gilds, integrating all aspects of their activities, religious and secular.[57]

The study of smaller urban brotherhoods whose influence did not extend beyond the confines of their own neighbourhoods, which were not influential in city life, nor an arena for the activities of the leading citizens, is only now beginning to be undertaken.[58] The study of rural gilds too has been less common due to the paucity of documentation. Registers and bede rolls of high quality were not produced as lasting memorials to the brethren in poorer rural areas.[59] Their memorials were more likely to have been ephemeral or forgotten contributions to church and village life. In the absence of records it becomes necessary to rely on indirect evidence.[60] Recent studies locate rural gilds within the context of parish, diocese, county or province.[61] They draw

55 Lay members of an ecclesiastical house, who undertook regular devotions in return for access to the spiritual wealth of the house, but who remained in the world.

56 A.G. Rosser, 'The Essence of Medieval Urban Communities: the Vill of Westminster 1200–1540', *TRHS*, 5th series xxxiv, 1984, 91–112, on the role of the Gild of the Assumption in the Abbey manor of Westminster.

57 O.G. Oexle, 'Gilden als Soziale Gruppen in Der Karolingerzeit', in *Das Handwerk in Vor- und Frühgeschichtlicher Zeit: Teil i, Historische und Rechtshistorische Beiträge und Untersuchungen zur Frühgeschichte der Gild*, ed. H. Jankuhn and others, Göttingen 1981; O.G. Oexle, 'Conjuratio und Gilde im Frühen Mittelalter: Ein Beitrag zum Problem der Sozialgeschichtlichen Kontinuität Zwischen Antike und Mittelalter', *Vorträge Und Forschung* xxix, 1985, 151–214.

58 W. Scharrer, *Laienbruderschaften in der Stadt Bamberg vom Mittelalter bis zum Ende des Alten Reiches – Geschichte, Brauchtum, Kultobjekte*, Bamberg 1990; J. Gerchow, 'Bruderschaften im Spätmittelalterlichen Freiburg im Breisgau', *Freiburger Diözezesan-Archiv* cxiii, 1993, 5–74; 'Trinkstuben, Zünfte und Bruderschaften: Die Freiburger Genossenschaften im Mittelalter,' *Geschichte der Stadt Freiburg im Breisgau*, ed. H. Haumann and H. Schadek, Stuttgart 1995, forthcoming.

59 Compare for example the records of large town gilds of Boston, Lincolnshire and Wisbech, Cambridgeshire (The Register of Corpus Christi Gild, Boston, BL Harleian Ms. 4795; The Account Book of St Mary's Gild, Boston, BL Egerton Ms. 2886; and the Register of Holy Trinity Gild, Wisbech, WCR1) with the account fragments of St Christopher's 'gild' or 'light', March, Cambridgeshire (CCRO, P116/1/4, pp. 131–7) a small gild in a smaller town whose records are an unusual survival.

60 For example visitation records, manorial records, churchwardens' accounts, and wills.

61 The analytical framework set out by Le Bras in *Études de Sociologie Religieuse* has provided the structure for various regional studies such as: J. Toussaert, *Le Sentiment Religieux en Flandres à la Fin du Moyen Age*, Paris 1963; A.N. Galpern, *The Religions of the People in 16th Century Champagne*, Cambridge Massachusetts 1976; J.-P. Gutton,

on the framework of analysis initiated by Le Bras and the *annalistes*, viewing them not as isolated institutions, but as part of the tissue of rural communities, thus moving towards a more integrative form of history. In this context the term 'community' is one which has become tired through over-use in recent medieval and early modern historiography, but nevertheless this has been a useful concept as may be illustrated by the number of works which employ it.[62]

As the chronological approach has been the basis for English gild studies, it is necessary to address it briefly here. Statutes exist for five gilds dating from the late tenth to the early eleventh century,[63] although there are some sparse references enshrined in legal codes and charters which point to the existence of institutions identified as gilds, with administrative and judicial responsibilities at an earlier period.[64] These include the *cnichten* gilds composed probably of moderately wealthy landowners and their followers in the areas of London, Canterbury, Winchester and Cambridge.[65] The regulations known as the *Judicia Civitatis Londoniae* (924–39) have been seen as the statutes of a *frith* or peace gild, whose members formed a militia to police an area around London, with particular vigilance for cattle thieves.[66] As with the question of gild origins, mythologies were created by the early gild historians to link these materials together. These sources are, in fact, too fragmentary to create any pattern.[67] One of the most important of these myths was that which

'Confraternities, Curés and Communities in Rural Areas of the Diocese of Lyons under the Ancient Regime', in *Religion and Society in Early Modern Europe*, ed. Von Greyerz; L. Remling, *Bruderschaften in Franken: Kirchen- und Sozialgeschichtliche Untersuchungen zum Spätmittelalterlichen und Frühneuzeitlichen Bruderschaftswesen*, Wurzburg 1986; J. Mattingley, 'The Medieval Parish Guilds of Cornwall', *Journal of the Royal Institution of Cornwall*, new series x, 1989, 290–329.

62 See for example: *Lordship and Community in Medieval Europe*, ed. F.L. Cheyette, original edn 1968, New York 1975, esp. P. Duparc, 'Confraternities of the Holy Spirit and Village Communities in the Middle Ages', 341–56; M. Spufford, *Contrasting Communities: English Villages in Sixteenth and Seventeenth Century Cambridgeshire*, Cambridge 1974, reprinted 1979; M.K. McIntosh, *Autonomy and Community: the Royal Manor of Havering 1300–1500*, Cambridge 1986; M. Rubin, *Charity and Community in Medieval Cambridge*, Cambridge 1987.

63 See note 21.

64 *EHD* i, ed. Whitelock, 'The Laws of Ine (688–94)', 398–407; 'The Laws of Alfred (c.885–99)', 407–16; 'The Ordinance of the Bishops and Reeves of the London District ("Judicia Civitatis Londoniae", VI Athelstan, 924–39)', 423–7; *EHD* ii, ed. D.C. Douglas and G.W. Greenaway, 1042–1189, 2nd edn, London 1981, *Leges Henrici Primi* (1100–35), 491–5; Coornaert, 'Les Ghildes Médiévales', 211; Kahl, Introduction to Unwin, *The Gilds and Companies of London*, 4th edn, xxiii.

65 N. Fryde, 'Gilds in England before the Black Death', *Vorträge Und Forschung* xxix, 1985, 215–29, 219.

66 *EHD* i, ed. Whitelock, 423–7.

67 For a critique of previous theories see: Gross, *The Gild Merchant*, vol. i, Appendix A, 'The Literature of English Gilds', 167–73; Appendix B, 'Anglo-Saxon Gilds', 174–91; Kahl, introduction to Unwin, *The Gilds and Companies of London*, 4th edn, xvii–xliv.

emphasised their English origins. Gilds did, of course, exist in Europe at the same time. There are references to gilds in Merovingian and Carolingian Gaul. Coornaert discussed the Anglo-Saxon gilds in the context of their continental contemporaries, and recently Professor Oexle has made a detailed analysis of the role of gilds in Carolingian society.[68] This research suggests that gilds were already an established social form throughout Europe by the tenth century. Le Bras distinguished three waves of gild activity which reflect to a large extent the surviving documentation: few gilds before 1000; some between the eleventh and twelfth century; and many from the fourteenth century onwards.[69]

In England it is not until the cluster of tenth- and eleventh-century statutes that much detail exists as to the nature of these groups. The statutes of the gilds of Exeter (early 900s), Bedwyn (late 900s), Cambridge (late 900s), Abbotsbury (early 1000s), and Woodbury (late 1000s) contain elements which are common to later medieval statutes. The brethren swore an oath which entailed certain obligations: commemoration of the dead; collective worship; charity to the living; mutual support and good behaviour towards their fellows; and the enforcement of these obligations through a system of penalties. The difficulty, as with any legal evidence, is that it is not the letter of the law but its interpretation which provides more historical information. Despite similarities between these early statutes and their later medieval counterparts, they were the products of very different societies. Unfortunately there are no additional gild documents from the earlier period, as there are later, to show how these codes were used in practice. Gervase Rosser has speculated that the early gilds, three of which were located in the diocese of Exeter, along with the rural gilds for which there is evidence in the bede roll of the Kalendar Gild of Exeter, may have been instrumental in the transition from minster to parish as the basic unit of church organisation in the tenth and eleventh centuries.[70] Although there are similarities between the pre-Conquest gilds and the so-called parish gilds of the fourteenth to sixteenth centuries, their relationship cannot be presumed to be other than complex. For example, the pursuit of the blood-feud on behalf of fellow brethren prescribed by the statutes of the Cambridge gild suggests a very different social context in the earlier period.[71]

68 Coornaert, 'Les Ghildes Médiévales', Section III, 'Les Ghildes Franques et Carolingien'; IV, 'Les Ghildes Anglo-Saxon'; V, 'Les Ghildes Frisonnes et Scandinaves'; Oexle, 'Conjuratio et Ghilde'.

69 Le Bras, 'Les Confréries Chrétiennes', 332.

70 A.G. Rosser, 'The Anglo-Saxon Gilds', in *Minsters and Parish Churches: The Local Church in Transition 950–1200*, ed. J. Blair, Oxford 1988, 31–33; N. Orme, 'The Kalendar Brethren of the City of Exeter', *Report and Transactions of the Devonshire Association for the Advancement of Science, Literature and Art* cix, 1977, 153–69; J. Gerchow, *Die Gedenküberlieferung der Angelsachsen mit einem Katalog der Libri Vitae und Necrologien*, Berlin, New York 1988, 78, fn. 504, and review in *Research on British History in the Federal Republic of Germany 1983–8*, ed. F. Rexroth, London 1990, 25–26.

71 *EHD* i, ed. Whitelock, 557.

Reynolds stresses that the rural gilds of the Anglo-Saxon period were of less importance than the London Frith Gild.[72] This points to the next type of gild to have attracted attention in the secondary literature. These were the bodies of burgesses and merchants organising the structure of trade and self-government in the emerging towns of the tenth to twelfth centuries. Much work has focused on the development of the borough; the granting by the King or lesser lord, to a group of freemen through a borough charter of the rights to collect taxes, to hold and control a market and to elect officers.[73] 'Voluntary' associations as represented by the gild merchant and the borough were contrasted with those imposed by seigneurial authority. The contribution of the gilds to the development of the borough was addressed most fully by Charles Gross, and more recently by Professor Geoffrey Martin.[74]

Gross believed that merchant gilds did not exist before the Conquest but were introduced when union with Normandy increased trade after 1066.[75] However, there is clear evidence of their continuity with pre-Conquest institutions in many towns.[76] The relatively early centralisation and increasing power of the Anglo-Norman monarchy eroded the autonomy of town government where it conflicted with royal prerogative. It was not until after the reign of Henry II that changes in the structure of the borough took place, which resulted in the development of the borough court at the expense of the gild merchant.[77]

Nineteenth-century historians believed that the gild merchant declined, not only because it had given its life-blood to the borough, but also because of the rise of the craft gilds. These, however, are already recorded in the earliest surviving pipe-roll of 1130.[78] Gross attributed to Brentano the theory, later taken up by Unwin and others, that emergence of the craft gilds as regular features of town life in the later thirteenth and fourteenth centuries, overthrew the oligarchic power of the merchant elite in a 'democratic' victory.[79] Eileen Power, writing in 1920, described two contemporary approaches to the history of the craft gilds, those of the romantic socialists led by William

72 Reynolds, *Kingdoms and Communities*, 68.

73 Gross, *The Gild Merchant*, i, 6; H. Pirenne, *Economic and Social History of Medieval Europe*, translated by I.E. Clegg, London 1936, esp. ch. II, 'The Towns'. This work was particularly influential on the continent. In England the main authorities were: Maitland, *Township and Borough*; C. Stephenson, *Borough and Town: A Study of Urban Origins in England*, Cambridge Massachusetts 1935; J. Tait, *The Medieval English Borough: Studies on its Origins and Constitutional History*, Manchester 1936; S. Reynolds, *An Introduction to the History of English Medieval Towns*, Oxford 1977.

74 Gross, *The Gild Merchant*; G.H. Martin, 'The English Borough'.

75 Gross, *The Gild Merchant*, i, 2.

76 Fryde, 'Gilds in England', 217–19.

77 Martin, 'The English Borough', 127; Fryde, 'Gilds in England', 218.

78 Fryde, 'Gilds in England', 219.

79 Gross, *The Gild Merchant*, i, 109; Unwin, *The Gilds and Companies of London*, 74–89; Kramer, *The English Craft Gilds*.

Morris, and the gild socialists led by G.D.H. Cole, both propagating this myth of early democracy.[80] According to Gross, it was the opposite which was in fact true. Less wealthy craftsmen were squeezed out of municipal government and of necessity formed their own groups, while power became concentrated in the hands of a few.[81]

Recently Heather Swanson has painted a more complex picture of the relationship of the crafts with municipal authority in the later Middle Ages.[82] Swanson argues that they were instruments of the town council with little independent power,[83] and have traditionally been allocated too much importance, for example in their supposed contribution to the demise of the towns in the fifteenth and sixteenth centuries through closed shop practices. Instead the crafts symbolised an ideal of hierarchical and patriarchal authority reaffirmed in an atmosphere of economic decline. Their importance to members lay chiefly in their fraternity or religious and social aspects, and the shared expense of funding civic ritual such as Corpus Christi processions.

The type of gilds known as religious or social gilds, which appear more numerous from the fourteenth century on, were first specifically addressed by Westlake in his study of what he termed the 'parish' gilds. All gilds consecrated their activities to the patronage of a saint: in all gilds the religious and social aspects were just as important as the economic and political, although this is not stressed adequately in the previous historiography.[84] The crafts and trade associations consisted of a gild and a fraternity, a parallel institution involving the same members and existing for religious and social purposes, which Reinhardt Strohm terms the 'shadow' of the gild.[85] Likewise, even those gilds which had apparently no specific governmental role were just as involved in the organisation of community life. Smaller towns and villages were not structured with the same complexity as the large towns, nor did they contain enough craftsmen to warrant separate groups. Nevertheless, in late medieval England many small communities did contain one or more gilds or fraternities, controlled by their ruling oligarchies no less than those of larger towns.[86]

One of the recurrent themes in the history of the gilds is the tension between autonomy and lordly control. The reason so much is known about them from the earliest times until their eventual demise is through documentation

80 Eileen Power, 'English Craft Gilds in the Middle Ages', *History* iv, 1919–20, 211–14.

81 Gross, *The Gild Merchant*, i, 110.

82 H. Swanson, 'The Illusion of Economic Structure: Craft Gilds in Late Medieval Towns', *P&P* cxxi, 1988, 29–48; Trexler, *Public Life*, 15, argues that the major *scuole* used minor trade associations to dominate and control political life in the city.

83 This picture is supported by B. Champion, 'The Gilds of Medieval Beverley' in *The Medieval Town in Britain*, ed. P. Riden, Cardiff 1980, 51–66.

84 Coornaert, 'Les Ghildes Médiévales', 217, 231.

85 R. Strohm, 'The Use of Music by Flemish Confraternities' (unpublished Seminar Paper, Institute of Historical Research, London 16 Nov. 1990).

86 See below, ch. 6.

resulting from royal and episcopal attempts to define and curtail their power. In the sixth century there was episcopal legislation against groups of priests. From the eighth century there were attempts to purify lay fraternities of 'pagan' elements such as feasts with their inevitable accompaniment of drunkenness and violence, and to bring them further under church control. Between 779 and 885 the Carolingian emperors issued a series of interdicts against sworn associations.[87] Official pronouncements in twelfth- and thirteenth-century France, Germany and the Netherlands continued to prohibit gilds as a source of public disorder and political subversion.[88] In England from the twelfth century there were regular enquiries into the financial and judicial infringements of illegal gilds on the royal prerogative.[89]

The oath, which gave priority to horizontal rather than vertical loyalties, evoked the greatest fear among the authorities, and those fears were not always without cause. The Florentine government initiated a campaign against confraternities in 1377, while the state was at war with the papacy, fearing that the confraternities might undermine the war effort for their own purposes. The campaign against them continued amidst suspicion of confraternity involvement in tax evasion and corrupt elections.[90] The French government moved against fraternities throughout the fourteenth century.[91] In England, fear that fraternities might provide a cover for general lawlessness,[92] or for collective action against the restrictions of serfdom, common since the thirteenth century, and culminating in the Revolt of 1381,[93] led Richard II, at the petition of the commons in Parliament, to initiate an enquiry into their activities in 1388. The gilds had always been conservative in religious terms. Their spread was fostered by the Church to combat heresy in the twelfth century, and again as a tool of the Catholic Counter-Reformation in the sixteenth century.[94] It was this very orthodoxy which made them potentially subversive and led to their abolition in Protestant England in 1547, and in revolutionary France in 1792.

The royal survey of 1388–9 is the most comprehensive body of information on medieval English gilds, until the records of their dissolution in the sixteenth century. Unfortunately the returns made by the craft gilds in response to a separate writ issued at the same time, rarely survive. Following the ascendancy in 1387–8 of the Apellants, Richard II needed the support of the lesser nobility and the gentry to renew the credibility of his personal government.

87 Coornaert, 'Les Ghildes Médiévales', 33–35; Le Bras, 'Les Confréries Chrétiennes', 315; Oexle, 'Conjuratio et Ghilde', 3–12.

88 Coornaert, 'Les Ghildes Médiévales, 213–14.

89 Fryde, 'Gilds in England', 218, 223–6, 229.

90 Weissman, *Ritual Brotherhood*, 164–6.

91 Le Bras, 'Les Confréries Chrétiennes', 360.

92 R.H. Hilton, *The English Peasantry in the Later Middle Ages*, Oxford 1975, 91–94.

93 R.H. Hilton, 'Peasant Movements in England before 1381', *EcHR*, 2nd series ii, 1949, 117–36.

94 Le Bras, 'Les Confréries Chrétiennes', 326.

He was thus prepared to agree to measures in the Cambridge Parliament of 1388 which were important to the Commons, including the confirmation of labour legislation and the survey of the gilds.[95] The writ was issued in November 1388 to be proclaimed by the sheriff of each county. It required the masters and wardens of all gilds and fraternities to make returns concerning their 'oaths, gatherings, feasts and meetings', the authority by which they held their liberties and practised their customs, and the value of lands, tenements, rents and other possessions and how these were held.[96] That the enquiry was also motivated by a desire to assess their taxable potential is suggested by the interest in their property, and the fact that all gilds and fraternities along with other corporate bodies were brought within the scope of mortmain legislation in 1391.[97] The returns generally took the form of copies of the statutes or ordinances by which the fraternities were governed.[98] On these it is possible to base a definition of the institutions with which this study is concerned, the gilds of later medieval Cambridgeshire.

These were groups of men and women joining together for communal purposes, and bound to each other by common ties of loyalty. Their common identity was expressed through symbolic and ritual activity. The gilds were formed under the patronage of a particular saint, for example the Virgin Mary was especially popular, or in devotion to religious symbols, such as Corpus Christi or the Holy Cross. As a body, they met at least once a year to celebrate the patronal festival with a mass, and perhaps a feast. Members attended the funerals of all departed brethren, and ceremonies for the commemoration of their dead and their benefactors. On such occasions there were processions, lights and torches, and perhaps livery was worn to affirm their sense of belonging. Attendance was compulsory, as was obedience to the gild officers who presided over such occasions. The officers and holders of gild property were chosen from among the wealthier and more senior members of the gild, who were often those in positions of authority in the wider community of the town or parish, thus reflecting within the microcosm of the gild the ordering of society as a whole.

Members acquired certain spiritual benefits from the gilds, and they in their turn were able to contribute to the spiritual life of the communities in which they lived. The religious function which the gilds most frequently undertook was the provision of lights in the parish church, either before the

95 J.A. Tuck, 'The Cambridge Parliament 1388', *EHR* lxxxiv, 1969, 225–43; *The Westminster Chronicle*, ed. L.C. Hector and B. Harvey, Oxford 1982, 482–3.

96 Toulmin Smith, 127–9; PRO, C47/38/1–2.

97 Jones, 'English Religious Brotherhoods', 647–8; S. Raban, *Mortmain Legislation and the English Church 1279–1500*, Cambridge 1982; *Statutes of the Realm* ii, 1377–1509, London 1816, 79–80, Anno 15 Ricardi II AD 1391 Item V.

98 PRO, C47/38–46; Westlake, 137–238, Appendix 'The Gild Certificates of 1389: An Analysis', has been the traditional guide to the returns, but more have been found in the PRO since this was written.

image of their patron saint, or at the high altar on Sundays and feast-days. The greatest contribution which they were able to make, was to hire a perpetual chaplain who would assist with the services and the religious life of the parish, alongside his work for the gild. For most gilds, however, this was beyond their means, and chaplains would have been hired on a temporary basis or for individual services. Through such collective endeavour, gild members were able to participate more fully in the rituals and sacraments of the church. The spiritual benefits of membership extended from this world into the next. Apart from their provision of lights, the gilds were largely concerned with the administration of funeral and commemorative rites for their dead. Members rested in the assurance that their brethren would arrange for prayers and masses to be said both at the time of their death, and as long as the gild lasted.

The gilds were far more than religious organisations. Their functions covered a broad spectrum of both religious and secular activities. They were of profound importance to the social lives of members and to their economic well-being. Business meetings and feasts were a part of the annual patronal festival. Conviviality among gild brethren was not confined to an annual patronal feast. Brewing and baking, drinking and eating together took place on a more regular basis. By the time of their abolition in 1547, in many parishes there was a gildhall equipped with cooking facilities and utensils. Bassingbourne gildhall contained enough plates and dishes to feed over one hundred people in 1546. By 1548 they had all disappeared, perhaps appropriated by gild members.[99] Eating and drinking together was important, as it strengthened the ties of friendship and loyalty which bound them to each other. Such activities also had a more serious economic basis. Brewing and baking may have been undertaken communally because this made good financial sense. The brethren of St James's Gild in the small village of Dullingham ate together several times a week. The alderman was paid 16*d* each quarter for brewing and baking.[100] By contrast the feasts of the great merchant gilds of Cambridge and Wisbech were more ceremonial affairs. These great gilds concentrated their joint economic activities on business and trading ventures. In the countryside lands were accumulated, and stocks of cows. These were hired out to members for the profit of the gild. If members fell on hard times, or became impoverished at the end of their lives, charity was given out of common funds, and their funeral expenses were paid.

The advantages of membership, the spiritual no less than the practical, had to be bought. To belong to a gild implied a certain amount of surplus wealth. Entry fees where they are recorded, ranged between 3*d* and 14*s* in money, and between one and four bushells of barley with one or two pounds

99 Palmer, 368.
100 CUL, MM1 47, Baker Mss. vol. 36, pp. 161–2, The Statutes of St James' Gild, Dullingham 1517.

of wax. There were also annual subscriptions. Those members whose names are recorded were among the wealthier in their towns and villages. Membership was carefully controlled by the officers and brethren who already belonged. The gild formed an interest group within a community. It existed to protect and enhance the status of its members. This it did through ensuring their spiritual and economic well-being. Gild ceremonial, funeral and commemorative rites, and contributions to local religious and public life ensured members' status, in the eyes of the rest of their social world.

2

Geography and Society: Patterns of Gild Activity

Geography

Cambridgeshire, the area covered by this survey, may be divided into two distinct areas according to the topography (see Map 1).[1] These are roughly identical in terms of size. The rolling arable land on the chalk and clay soils of the shire of Cambridge, with its compact villages, gives way to the peatland marshes and waterways of the Isle of Ely. In contrast the vast fenland parishes were characterised by diffused and scattered settlement, with villages and hamlets following the pattern of clay and gravel islands rising from the marsh and the immensely fertile alluvial floodplain along the coast.

The eastern areas of England, of which Cambridgeshire forms a part, were among the wealthiest and most densely populated throughout the medieval period.[2] The intractability of the medieval taxation documents, on which population estimates are based, is such that it is only possible to produce the most general indications of totals and trends.[3] However, this information may

1 *VCH Cambs.* i, ed. L.F. Salzman, London 1938, J.E. Marr and H. Dighton-Thomas, 'Geology', 1–33, esp. 1; 37, fig. 1 reproduced here by kind permission of the general editor; H.C. Darby, 'The Domesday Geography of Cambridgeshire', *Proc. Camb. Antiq. Soc.* xxxvi, 1934–5, 35–57, 37, fig. 1; H.C. Darby, *The Domesday Geography of Eastern England*, Cambridge 1971, ch. vi, 'Cambridgeshire'; H.C. Darby, *The Medieval Fenland*, Cambridge 1940, 2nd edn 1974.

2 M. Spufford, *Contrasting Communities: English Villages in the Sixteenth and Seventeenth Centuries*, Cambridge 1974, part 1, ch. 1, 'The Peopling of a County', 3, 'From before the Conquest to the present day, Cambridgeshire has belonged fully neither to East Anglia nor to the East Midlands'; 18–22 on the strong contrasts between the shire and Isle regions.

3 J.C. Russell, *British Medieval Population*, Albuquerque 1948, esp. ch. x, 'Trends of Gross Population', 235; E. Miller and J. Hatcher, *Medieval England: Rural Society and Economic Change 1086–1348*, London 1978, 28–33; C. Dyer, *Standards of Living in the Later Middle Ages*, Cambridge 1989, 4–6, esp. 4, fig. 1.

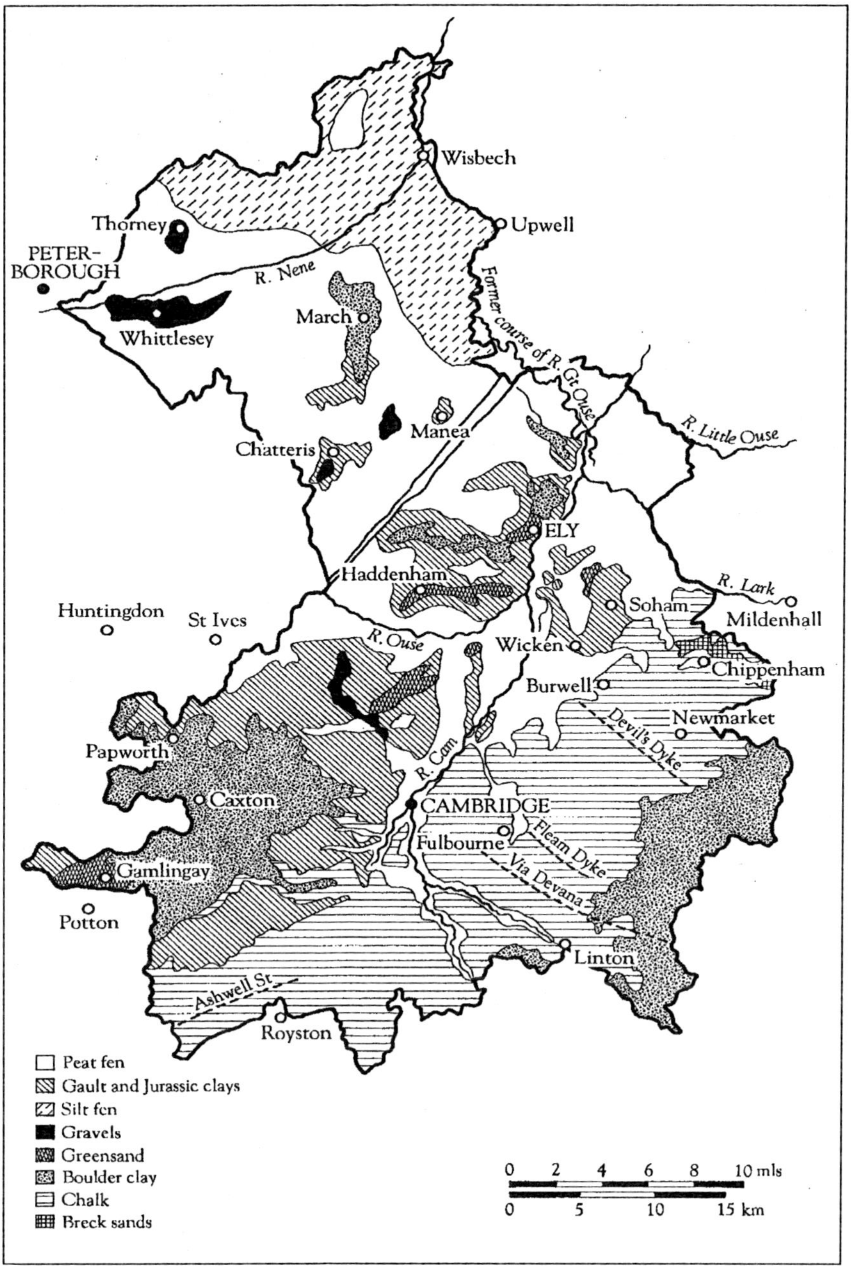

Map 1. Map of Cambridgeshire showing the geological structure which determines the chief soil and vegetation types

be supplemented with information on changes in distribution of wealth over the course of time.[4]

The Domesday Survey of 1086 shows relatively high concentrations of people in the shire, while the fenlands of the Isle of Ely were amongst the most sparsely inhabited areas of England.[5]

The documents of the collection of the 1327 lay subsidy give complete figures for Cambridgeshire.[6] While it may be seen that wealth remained concentrated in the shire, there had been a remarkable development of the silt lands of the Northern Isle in the intervening 250 years.[7] It was this silt belt, together with the north of England devastated by William the Conqueror, and areas of marsh, wood and forest scattered over the rest of the country, that experienced the most substantial economic growth in the period 1086 to 1334.[8] Professor Darby writes: 'During the later Middle Ages, this silt zone . . . seems to have been among the most prosperous parts of England'.[9]

Between the lay subsidies of 1334 and 1525, the peat area of the southern fenland, including the southern part of the Isle of Ely, in its turn experienced economic growth,[10] which continued into the sixteenth and seventeenth centuries.[11] By the fifteenth century, however, the balance of wealth in England as a whole was shifting away from East Anglia as other areas of the country developed.[12]

4 E.J. Buckatzsch, 'The Geographical Distribution of Wealth in England 1086–1843: An Experimental Study of Certain Tax Assessments', *EcHR*, 2nd series iii, 1950–1, 180–202, esp. 186–7, table 1, 197 maps; R.S. Schofield, 'The Geographical Distribution of Wealth in England 1334–1649', *EcHR*, 2nd series xviii, 1965, 483–510, 506 maps; H.C. Darby, R.E. Glasscock, J. Sheail, G.R. Versey, 'The Changing Geographical Distribution of Wealth in England: 1086 – 1334 – 1525', *Journal of Historical Geography* v, 1979, 247–62; J. Sheail, 'The Regional Distribution of Wealth in England as indicated in the 1524/5 Lay Subsidy Returns', Ph.D., London 1968.

5 H.C. Darby, *Domesday England*, Cambridge 1977, ch. 3, 'Population', esp. 90–91, figs 34–35; 93, fig. 36.

6 C.H. Evelyn-White, 'Cambridgeshire and the Isle of Ely, Lay Subsidy for the Year 1327', *East Anglian N. & Q.* new series x–xii, 1903–8, 366 et seq., and separately printed, Introduction 1, esp. 366; W.M. Palmer, 'A List of the Cambridge Subsidy Rolls 1250–1695', *East Anglian N. & Q.*, new series vii–xx, 1897–1904, 362 et seq.; Rev. J.B. Pearson, 'The Assessments of Cambridgeshire 1291–1889', *Proc. Camb. Antiq. Soc.* viii, 1891–4, 283–91, esp. 288–91 table; Rev. J.B. Pearson, 'On the Cambridgeshire Subsidies', *Proc. Camb. Antiq. Soc.* ix, 1894–8, 120–37; *The Lay Subsidy of 1334*, ed. R.E. Glasscock, British Academy Records of Social and Economic History ii, London 1975, xxvii map, 23–28.

7 Darby, *The Medieval Fenland*, ch. iv, 'The Changing Prosperity of the Fenland', 123 fig. 17, 129 fig. 21.

8 Darby and others, 'The Changing Geographical Distribution of Wealth', 261.

9 Darby, *The Medieval Fenland*, 131. Wills made by testators from Wisbech illustrate the late medieval wealth of this region.

10 Darby and others, 'The Changing Geographical Distribution of Wealth', 261.

11 Spufford, *Contrasting Communities*, 18–22.

12 Schofield, 'The Geographical Distribution of Wealth', 483, 506, maps.

As much as geographical factors affected agriculture and settlement patterns, they also necessitated different forms of local administration. The shire was divided into fourteen hundreds, the Isle into only three.[13] The pattern of lordship in the shire was fragmented into small units,[14] the Isle was entirely under the dominion of one lord, the Bishop of Ely.[15] Parishes, like settlements in the shire were small and compact, in the Isle vast and sparsely inhabited. To compensate for the lack of coherence in parish structure, the fens were laced with a network of free chapels, supported by people from neighbouring settlements, and gild activity was more in evidence here.[16]

There is evidence for gild activity in Cambridgeshire from the late 900s, with the survival of the Statutes of the *Thegns'* gild of Cambridge, which was associated with the cult of St Etheldreda at Ely.[17] Thereafter and until the survey of 1388–9 only a scattering of gilds or fraternities may be traced. There may have been others: these few are known only because of their possession of property, through the records of their endowments and foundations. Geographically all these are associated with two of the three most important towns of Cambridgeshire, Ely and Cambridge. Membership of those who were among the most powerful in these communities and beyond, and the social and political networks revealed through the documents show these groups to have been of more than local significance.

The gild survey of 1388–9 generated information on a far wider scale than hitherto available. Despite the many questions raised by this material, for example the uses for which it was intended and the proportion of documents which have been lost over the course of time, it constitutes a unique source on fourteenth-century gilds. That the majority of the returns are from East Anglia, then the wealthiest part of the country, suggests that their pattern of survival does reflect the original response to the survey. The documents themselves are formulaic in structure. As well as caution, which these groups exercised when committing their activities to writing, bureaucratic intervention by local scribes and chancery clerks imposed a homogeneity on individual

13 Evelyn-White, 'Lay Subsidy for the Year 1327'.

14 Spufford, *Contrasting Communities*, 28–36.

15 D.M. Owen, *Ely Records: A Handlist of the Records of the Bishop and Archdeacon of Ely*, Cambridge 1971, ch. 6, 'The Temporalities'; E. Miller, *The Abbey and Bishopric of Ely: The Social History of an Ecclesiastical Estate from the Tenth Century to the Early Fourteenth Century*, Cambridge 1951, esp. maps facing 76 and 220.

16 D.M. Owen, *Church and Society in Medieval Lincolnshire*, Lincoln 1971, 10–19. In Lincolnshire, chapels were set up as reclamation of the fens progressed in the 11th and 12th centuries, for example in South Holland, the area adjoining the fens of North Cambridgeshire. As Professor Darby has shown, the fenlands form a coherent geographical and social region, and so this pattern of chapel foundation is undoubtedly repeated in the fen regions of Cambridgeshire and Norfolk. Until 1109 when Ely Diocese was founded, covering an area almost exactly conterminous with the county of Cambridgeshire (Owen, *Ely Records*, vii), this region was part of Lincoln Diocese.

17 *Diplomatarium Anglicum Aevi Saxonici*, ed. B. Thorpe, London 1865, 610–13.

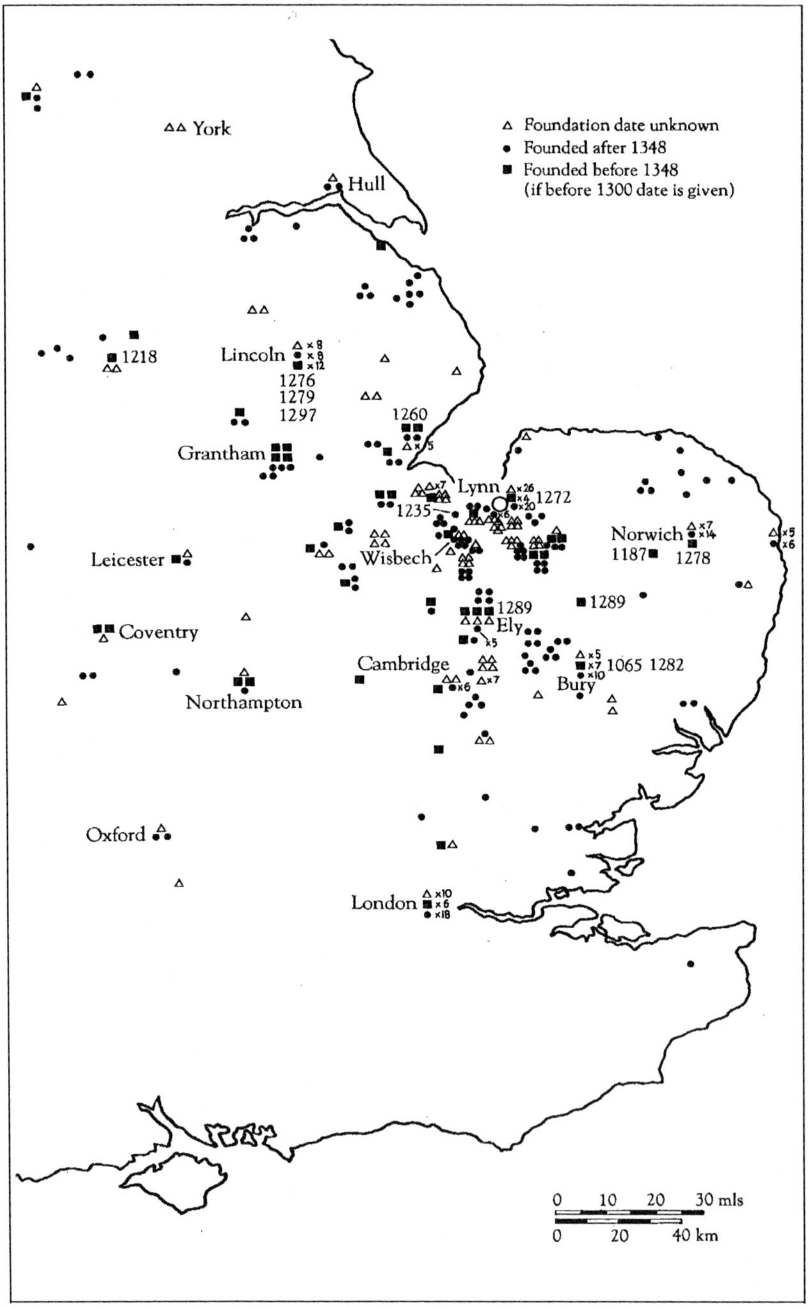

Map 2. The geographical distribution of the returns to the survey of religious or social gilds of 1388–9, listed in Westlake's appendix

organisations, an impression compounded by the calendar contained in Westlake's book.[18] Westlake and his assistant Miss Lillian Redstone calendared 471 documents mainly in Latin, with a few in French and English, which provided an account of 521 gilds. Although other returns have subsequently come to light,[19] Westlake's appendix has been the starting point for most subsequent work, so for convenience its figures will be used here. When plotted on a map, it may be seen that the greatest concentration of gilds is in the alluvial silt-lands around the coast of the Wash, from which they fan out over the rest of the fenlands, and thence into the rest of the country with decreasing density (see Map 2).[20] There are returns for 165 gilds from Norfolk, 51 of these from Lynn alone, 124 from Lincolnshire, 60 from Cambridgeshire, 39 from Suffolk, 13 from Yorkshire, 8 each from Derbyshire, Northamptonshire and Essex, a scattering from 15 other counties to the south and west, and 42 from the metropolis, London, including some craft returns. It is interesting to note that a higher proportion of the East Anglian returns, from the richest part of the county, came from smaller towns and villages than elsewhere. Returns from other parts of the country tend to have been sent by gilds of the greater urban centres of late medieval England, or significant towns of the next rank.[21]

It is possible to examine the Cambridgeshire material in the context of the fourteenth-century taxation documents, to provide more information on patterns of gild activity in 1389. Of the 60 Cambridgeshire gilds for which 1389 returns survive, 29 (48%) are from the shire; 31 (52%) are from the Isle, 20 (33%) located on the islands of the peat fens, and 11 (18%) in the silt-lands (see Map 1).[22]

Unfortunately, the poll tax returns for 1377, 1379 and 1381, which might have provided population figures, are incomplete. Although there is some information for all fourteen hundreds of the shire, there is none for two out of the three hundreds which comprise the Isle. There are no returns for the most important towns, Cambridge in the shire, Ely in the peat-lands and

18 J. Gerchow, 'Memoria als Norm: Aspekte Engilscher Gildestatuten des 14 Jahrhunderts', in *Memoria in der Gesellschaft des Mittelalters*, ed. D. Geuenich and O.G. Oexle, Göttingen 1994. Westlake, Preface vi, Appendix 137–238; included twelve craft gilds which have not been added to the figures in this chapter.

19 PRO, C47/46/462, return of Trinity Gild, Caldecote, Cambridgeshire, was drawn to my attention by Margaret Condon of the PRO too late to be included in this study. It is only three lines long, so contains little information.

20 I am grateful to John McCann, formerly of Essex County Council Historic Buildings Division, for permission to reproduce Fig. 2, a map of the gilds listed in Westlake's Appendix plotted geographically; Darby, *The Medieval Fenland*, xiii–v, figs a, b, c; 5, fig. 2.

21 Such towns include York, Coventry, Lincoln, Lynn, Great Yarmouth and Norwich; and then Grantham, Boston, Cambridge, Ely, Bury St Edmunds, Hull, Chesterfield, Beverley, Leicester, Northampton, Canterbury, Lancaster, Lichfield, Stratford, Warwick, Oxford, Ludlow, Tewkesbury, Shrewsbury, Malmesbury and Bath.

22 Miller, *The Abbey and Bishopric of Ely*, map facing 220.

Wisbech in the silt-lands. Bearing in mind these limitations, and thus the very limited usefulness of these figures, 83% of tax payers in the extant records of the 1377 poll tax lived in the shire, and 17% in the Isle.[23] A more accurate picture of relative wealth distribution, but prior to the Black Death, may be derived from the lay subsidy returns of 1327.[24] At that date 82% of tax payers paying 80% of the tax lived in the shire, and 18% of the tax payers paying 20% of the tax in the Isle.[25] In 1389, 9 (7%) of the 136 towns, villages and hamlets in the shire, and 9 (27%) of the 33 in the Isle contained gilds.[26] The higher proportion of gilds in the Isle of Ely, which all the indicators show was still, as a unit, much more sparsely inhabited and less wealthy, than the shire, is striking. It suggests that the gilds played a different, perhaps more substantial role in the scattered communities out in the fens. Indeed, all nine communities in the Isle, for which evidence for gild activity survives from 1389, were either settlements split between more than one parish, or with outlying hamlets. This is not characteristic of settlements in the shire.

When the 1389 evidence for Cambridgeshire is taken as a whole, 25 (42%) gilds were to be found in an urban context, with 8 in the town of Cambridge in the shire, a borough since 1201, and university town;[27] 11 in Ely in the peat-lands, the seat of the diocese;[28] and 6 in Wisbech in the silt-lands which, although in economic decline from the late thirteenth century when the Great Ouse had changed its course due to the silting of the Wisbech estuary,[29] retained a castle and was a jurisdictional and administrative centre for the surrounding townships and manors of its lord, the Bishop of Ely.[30]

Aside from those gilds located in the larger urban centres in 1389, 35 (58%) were to be found in smaller rural communities. It is possible to estimate the size of community necessary to support a gild or gilds. Poll tax

23 C. Fenwick, 'The English Poll Taxes of 1377, 1379 and 1381: A critical examination of the Returns', Ph.D., London 1983, 281–92; M.W. Beresford, *The Lay Subsidies, Parts 1 and 2, 1290–1334 and after 1334: The Poll Taxes of 1377, 1379 and 1381*, Phillimore Handbooks, no. 2, Bridge Place, near Canterbury 1963.

24 J. Hatcher, *Plague Population and the English Economy 1348–1530*, London 1977, for a concise review of this subject.

25 Glasscock, *The Lay Subsidy of 1334*, p. xxvii map; 23–28.

26 Evelyn-White, 'Lay Subsidy for the Year 1327'. These figures are based on the number of communities assessed for the 1327 lay subsidy. Those with more than one parish, e.g. Cambridge, have been counted once only. Where outlying hamlets were included within a town in 1327, the same approach is followed here. Communities which would be defined today as villages, are referred to in contemporary documents as towns or vills.

27 Gross, *The Gild Merchant*, 2 vols, Oxford 1890, reissued 1927, ii, 357–8; *VCH Cambs.* iii, *The City and University of Cambridge*, ed. J.P.C. Roach, London 1959.

28 *VCH Cambs.* iv, *The Liberty and City of Ely*, ed. R.B. Pugh, London 1953.

29 Darby, *The Medieval Fenland*, ch. 3, 'Communications', esp. 96–99.

30 *VCH Cambs.* iv; F.J. Gardiner, *A History of Wisbech and Neighbourhood*, Wisbech 1898, 232–71.

figures survive for ten out of the fifteen smaller towns and villages which made gild returns in 1389. None of these contained less than 100 tax payers. Gilds were found in four communities with 100–200 tax payers: Pampisford, Stowe Cum Quye and Swaffham Bulbeck in the shire, and Stretham in the Isle; in two communities with 200–300 tax payers: Haslingfield and Sawston in the shire; in two communities with 300–400 tax payers: Bottisham and Chesterton in the shire; and finally in Chatteris and Dodington in the Isle with 450 and 750 tax payers respectively in these two vast parishes.

Table 1. 1377 poll tax returns: community size and gild activity[31]

No. of tax payers per community	No. of Communities	No. of Gilds
100	31 = 26.5%	0
100 – 200	52 = 44.5%	4
200 – 300	17 = 14.5%	2
300 – 400	11 = 9.5%	2
400	6 = 5.0%	2

[No figures survive for the largest towns, Cambridge, Ely and Wisbech, so they are not included in this table.]

When further reasons for their location in these particular communities are sought, for example links with economic activity through their role as market towns, the evidence is once again inconclusive. Markets were held at Cambridge and Wisbech, and various fairs had been granted to the Abbot and the Bishop at Ely, by 1389. However, Whittlesford was the only village to return a gild certificate, which had a manorial market by that date.[32] Thus, although gilds were more likely to be found in larger communities, they were not exclusively associated with places of greater economic activity.

Our knowledge of their location may be due to far more arbitrary factors. A glance at the map shows that most of the Cambridgeshire returns are located in clusters (see Map 3). They came not only from the three large towns, but also from adjacent settlements. There are three returns for gilds in Chesterton, just outside Cambridge; four for Littleport and two for Stretham, villages next to Ely; one each for Elm and Leverington next to Wisbech, and three for Tydd St Giles close by.[33] There are returns from two clusters of rural

31 See Russell, *British Medieval Population*, 119–46, and *Cambridge Economic History of Europe*, ed. M.M. Postan, Cambridge 1966, i, 561–2, for multipliers to estimate community population from the number recorded as paying poll tax.

32 M. Siraut, 'Cambridgeshire Fairs and Markets', unpublished list and map in CCRO, Cambridge Branch.

33 See Appendix for a list of the Cambridgeshire Returns and PRO, C47 numbers. Reference will only be made to the document number if it is discussed in some detail in the text at that point.

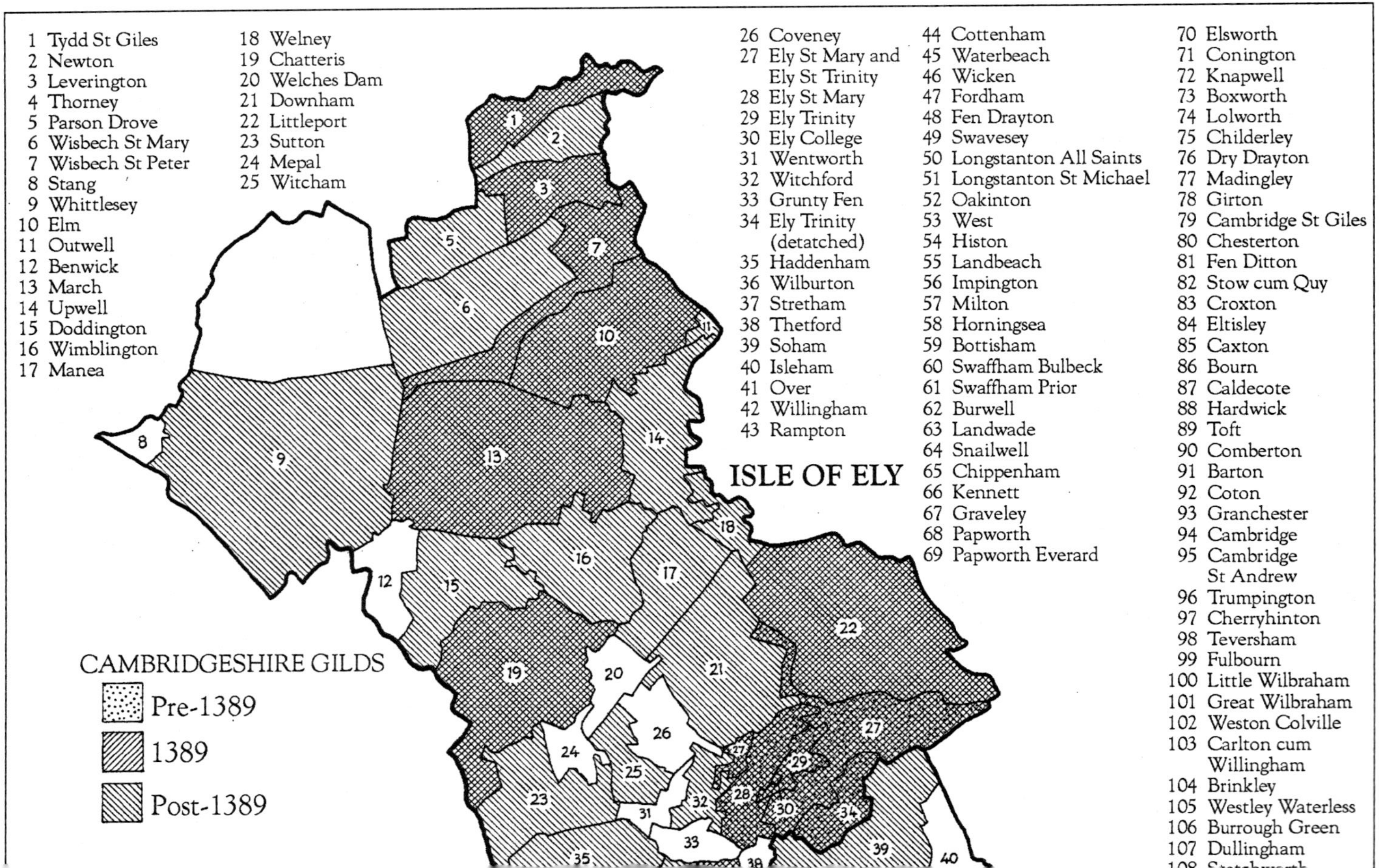

1 Tydd St Giles
2 Newton
3 Leverington
4 Thorney
5 Parson Drove
6 Wisbech St Mary
7 Wisbech St Peter
8 Stang
9 Whittlesey
10 Elm
11 Outwell
12 Benwick
13 March
14 Upwell
15 Doddington
16 Wimblington
17 Manea
18 Welney
19 Chatteris
20 Welches Dam
21 Downham
22 Littleport
23 Sutton
24 Mepal
25 Witcham
26 Coveney
27 Ely St Mary and Ely St Trinity
28 Ely St Mary
29 Ely Trinity
30 Ely College
31 Wentworth
32 Witchford
33 Grunty Fen
34 Ely Trinity (detatched)
35 Haddenham
36 Wilburton
37 Stretham
38 Thetford
39 Soham
40 Isleham
41 Over
42 Willingham
43 Rampton
44 Cottenham
45 Waterbeach
46 Wicken
47 Fordham
48 Fen Drayton
49 Swavesey
50 Longstanton All Saints
51 Longstanton St Michael
52 Oakinton
53 West
54 Histon
55 Landbeach
56 Impington
57 Milton
58 Horningsea
59 Bottisham
60 Swaffham Bulbeck
61 Swaffham Prior
62 Burwell
63 Landwade
64 Snailwell
65 Chippenham
66 Kennett
67 Graveley
68 Papworth
69 Papworth Everard
70 Elsworth
71 Conington
72 Knapwell
73 Boxworth
74 Lolworth
75 Childerley
76 Dry Drayton
77 Madingley
78 Girton
79 Cambridge St Giles
80 Chesterton
81 Fen Ditton
82 Stow cum Quy
83 Croxton
84 Eltisley
85 Caxton
86 Bourn
87 Caldecote
88 Hardwick
89 Toft
90 Comberton
91 Barton
92 Coton
93 Granchester
94 Cambridge
95 Cambridge St Andrew
96 Trumpington
97 Cherryhinton
98 Teversham
99 Fulbourn
100 Little Wilbraham
101 Great Wilbraham
102 Weston Colville
103 Carlton cum Willingham
104 Brinkley
105 Westley Waterless
106 Burrough Green
107 Dullingham
ISLE OF ELY
CAMBRIDGESHIRE GILDS
Pre-1389
1389
Post-1389

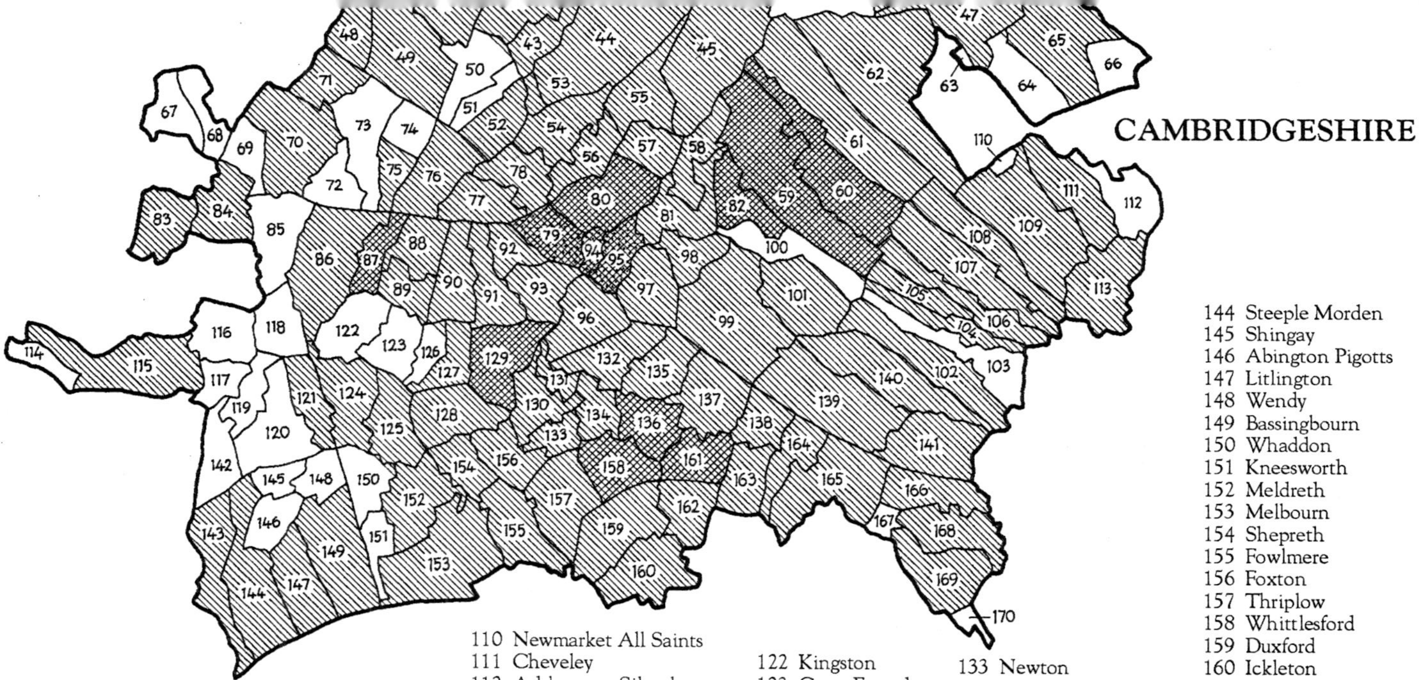

110 Newmarket All Saints
111 Cheveley
112 Ashley cum Silverley
113 Kirtling
114 Tetworth (det)
115 Gamlingay
116 Little Grandens
117 Hatley St George
118 Longstowe
119 East Hatley
120 Croydon-cum-Clopton
121 Arrington
122 Kingston
123 Great Eversden
124 Wimpole
125 Orwell
126 Little Eversden
127 Harlton
128 Barrington
129 Haslingfield
130 Harston
131 Rauxton
132 Great Shelford
133 Newton
134 Little Shelford
135 Stapleford
136 Sawston
137 Babraham
138 Little Abington
139 Balsham
140 West Wratting
141 West Wickham
142 Tadlow
143 Guilden Morden
144 Steeple Morden
145 Shingay
146 Abington Pigotts
147 Litlington
148 Wendy
149 Bassingbourn
150 Whaddon
151 Kneesworth
152 Meldreth
153 Melbourn
154 Shepreth
155 Fowlmere
156 Foxton
157 Thriplow
158 Whittlesford
159 Duxford
160 Ickleton
161 Pampisford
162 Hixton
163 Great Abington
164 Hildersham
165 Linton
166 Horseheath
167 Bartlow
168 Shudy Camps
169 Castle Camps
170 Helions Bumpstead

Map 3. Map of Cambridgeshire showing the distribution of gilds by parish c.1350–1558

villages, both in the shire. Brief returns written in French exist for one gild each in Pampisford and Whittlesford, and three for Sawston, all of which are almost identical in wording.[34] Seven gilds or fraternities in Bottisham claimed to have identical statutes: elaborate statutes for the first gild, that of the Holy Trinity, were written out in full; the others, recorded on the same parchment left only their names and a few idiosyncratic details. The same statutes appear again as regulations for the Holy Cross Gild in the neighbouring village of Swaffham Bulbeck: it too had three other gilds recorded on the same parchment, also purporting to observe the same regulations. Stowe Cum Quye, a third neighbouring village, had one gild, but it had different statutes. Ely provides another example of several gilds recorded on the same parchment: three from Holy Trinity Church and two from St Peter's.

Three isolated settlements produced returns for which some tentative explanations may be advanced. At Chatteris in the Isle, for which two separate returns survive in French, there was a Benedictine nunnery.[35] At March, also in the Isle, the fraternity of St Wendreda was associated with her shrine.[36] At Haslingfield in the shire Lord Robert de Scales had purchased a mortmain licence so that the gild of the Assumption of the Virgin could administer his chantry there.[37]

Westlake suggests a degree of collusion over what information should be returned to the King, to explain the similarity of statutes from the same towns.[38] Some gilds, ten in Cambridgeshire, employed clerks to write documents for them.[39] Jan Gerchow has shown that many gilds sent representatives to the Royal Chancery, to convey their statutes either orally or in writing.[40] If one messenger acted for several gilds, this would explain the clustering and duplication of detail. Despite various hypotheses, for example, that responses to the writ might have come from the vicinities where it was proclaimed, or that these gilds may have had a high profile due to property or connections, it

34 Palmer, 359–60, transcribes and translates the Pampisford return. He asserts that those for Sawston and Whittlesford 'are almost exactly like this'. Returns for Pampisford and Sawston were lost in the PRO at the time of my survey, so I was unable to compare all three.

35 D. Haigh, *The Religious Houses of Cambridgeshire*, Cambridge 1988, 17–18.

36 PRO, C47/38/27.

37 See ch. 6 for detailed discussion of this point.

38 Westlake, 37; W.R. Jones, 'English Religious Brotherhoods and Medieval Lay Piety: The Enquiry of 1388–9', *The Historian* xxxvi, 1974, 646–59, esp. 649–50, follows Westlake on this point; J. Blair, 'Religious Gilds as Landowners in the Thirteenth and Fourteenth Centuries: the Example of Chesterfield', in *The Medieval Town in Britain*, ed. P. Riden, Cardiff 1980, 35–49. All Chesterfield gilds submit calendars of deeds, although these are not to be trusted, as may be seen when compared with other extant material.

39 Gilds in Cambridge, Ely, Stretham, Wisbech and Leverington.

40 J. Gerchow, 'Memoria als Norm: Aspekte Englischer Gildenstatuten des 14 Jahrhunderts', in *Memoria in der Gesellschaft des Mittelalters*, ed. D. Gueunich and O.G. Oexle, Göttingen 1994

is still not possible to explain fully why sixty gilds or fraternities should come from only 18 out of 172 towns and villages in Cambridgeshire in 1389. This illustrates the difficulty of using medieval survey material when knowledge of both the method of collection and the criteria for response are lost.

In Cambridgeshire between c.1350 and 1558, 350 gilds or fraternities have been traced. These were located in 125 of the 172 towns and villages of Cambridgeshire, or 73% of these settlements (see Map 3) In the fourteenth century, as already noted, 52% were located in the shire and 48% in the Isle. In the fifteenth century, 54% were located in the shire and 46% in the Isle. In the period 1500 to 1547, 81% were located in the shire and 28% in the Isle. Overall, 67% of the gilds were to be found in the shire and 33% in the Isle. By that time there had been gild activity in nearly every town and village in Cambridgeshire in the preceding two hundred years.[41] It seems appropriate here to discuss chronological patterns of gild foundation, and the factors which influenced this over the course of time.

Chronology

Of the 350 Cambridgeshire gilds identified by this present study, 6 (2%) are first referred to in documentary sources between c.1000 and 1300; 63 (18%) during the fourteenth century; 113 (32%) during the fifteenth century; and 152 (43%) between 1500 and 1547 (see Map 3).[42]

The earliest surviving evidence for gild activity is the statutes of the *Thegns'* Gild of Cambridge, dating from the late 900s. Its members were drawn from among those in the region who held power both locally and nationally, joined together in devotion to St Etheldreda.[43] Etheldreda, who lived between 630 and 699, was the daughter of King Anna of the East Angles.[44] She founded a double monastery at Ely,[45] on the site of which stands the cathedral and mother-house of the diocese created in 1109.[46] The saint had considerable power both temporal[47] and spiritual, undiminished in the later Middle Ages when her shrine was still an important place of pilgrimage

41 These figures refer to the dates at which gilds are first documented, for example in wills, rather than their foundation. However, this gives some indication of the pattern of gild activity.

42 A further 16 (5%) gilds are referred to in secondary sources, which give no date.

43 *EHD*, i, ed. D. Whitelock, 2nd edn, London 1979, 603.

44 *Dictionary of National Biography*, ed. L. Stephen and S. Lee, vi, reprinted Oxford 1921–2, 883–5; D. Attwater, *The Penguin Dictionary of Saints*, 2nd edn Harmondsworth 1983, 118.

45 Monasteries with men and women on the same site were common in early medieval Europe.

46 Owen, *Ely Records*, vii.

47 Miller, *The Abbey and Bishopric of Ely*, esp. ch. ii, 'Origins'.

and her cult flourished in the fenlands.[48] The gild brethren were to make an offering to St Etheldreda when any of their members died.[49]

In the early twelfth century the Abbot of Ramsay granted the cemetery of St George and adjacent lands in Cambridge to the fraternity of the Holy Sepulchre to build a church in honour of God and the Holy Sepulchre.[50] In the thirteenth century a gild of St Etheldreda was associated with the same church, and a chantry of St Mary founded by Mayor William Trillet and served by priests from St John's hospital nearby.[51] A gild of St Edward and St Thomas the Martyr in St Edward's Church, Cambridge, is known from its application for confirmation and a licence for two chaplains made in 1291.[52] There was also a gild of St Mary associated with the church of Great St Mary, Cambridge. The minutes of this gild, beginning in 1298, are preserved in Corpus Christi College. Its members and those of Corpus Christi Gild, burgesses of Cambridge and their aristocratic confederates, came together in 1349 to found the college, a sumptuous memorial to their worldly rank, and a chantry college of priests dedicated to piety and learning and the commemoration of their souls.[53]

The existence of these fraternities is recorded because of their wealth. They follow the pattern of medieval lay piety: in the early Middle Ages, focused on the relics and cult of the Saints, and monasteries which grew up around these; later, associated with parish churches as the locus of religious ritual, the re-enactment of salvation through the drama of the Eucharist and supplication to the saints; and then with hospitals, chantries and colleges, institutions so typical of the later Middle Ages.

The 1389 certificates are the main source of evidence for gilds in the fourteenth century. Information on 59 of the 63 Cambridgeshire gilds recorded in that century comes exclusively from these documents. The 1389 evidence has been used by English historians to argue for an increase in gild activity as a result of the Black Death.[54] However, when examined in detail, the gild statutes and other sources are ambivalent on this point. Westlake advances some economic arguments: that poverty and famine inhibited the foundation of gilds in the early fourteenth century; that many gilds and their records probably perished at the time of the Black Death; and that afterwards, due to the increased wealth of certain sectors of the laity, they were eager to augment parish finances, which had suffered at the time of the crisis, through setting

48 See ch. 3 below.

49 Thorpe, *Diplomatarium Anglicum*, 611.

50 J.E. Foster, 'On Charters granted by Ramsay Abbey to the fraternity of the Holy Sepulchre', *Proc. Camb. Antiq. Soc.* ix, 1894–8, 367–70. The charters are dated c.1114–30; *VCH Cambs*. iii, 124; Bateson, xii.

51 *VCH Cambs*. iii, 124.

52 *VCH Cambs*. iii, 128, 134.

53 Bateson, xii–xxvii.

54 Westlake, ch. 3, esp. 26–30.

up gilds.[55] The real thrust of his book, however, was that many gilds were founded in response to the need to ensure the rituals of salvation in the face of sudden death.[56] This is difficult to substantiate from the 1389 documents. Indeed, for Cambridgeshire, only one certificate mentions the plague as a reason for foundation and 20 (40% of those gilds which give foundation dates) were founded between 1370 and 1389.[57]

When the English evidence is examined in a continental context, it may be seen that it conforms to a broader pattern. Jacques Chiffoleau in his study of the area around Avignon in southern France has discerned two phases of confraternity foundation in the later Middle Ages: the first between 1280 and 1370, when they were becoming more widespread, and the second between 1370 and 1500 when increasing documentation suggests not only greater numbers, but also a wider social significance. This was also the case with the *Contado Florentin*.[58]

Catherine Vincent in her study of the *Confréries* of Normandy also found a vast increase in the fifteenth century with the peak period of registration by the dioceses between the 1430s and 1550s.[59] Vincent discounts the possibility of a single explanatory factor such as the Black Death in their later medieval increase and Chiffoleau states that the relationship between the two phenomena is complex and must be explored with caution.[60]

In England evidence for increased numbers of foundations comes from the later thirteenth and early fourteenth centuries. After the mortmain legislation of 1279 such institutions, particularly those in the towns, are recorded in the Calendar of Patent Rolls when licensed to hold lands for the payment of chaplains or other purposes.[61] Such licences are found frequently from the reign of Edward II on.[62]

Alan Kreider shows that the number of mortmain licences granted for perpetual chantries including those organised by the wealthier gilds peaked

55 Westlake, 28–29; Dyer, *Standards of Living*, 182–3, describes peasant contributions to the 'ceremonial funds' of parish church or religious brotherhood.

56 Westlake, ch. i, 9–10; J. Huizinga, *The Waning of the Middle Ages*, London 1924, Harmondsworth 1955. This book, first published in English in 1924, gives a vivid portrait of an age obsessed with death (esp. ch. xi, 'The Vision of Death') and the autumnal atmosphere of decay as the Middle Ages gave way to the modern age. Such ideas were current until the recent revisionist emphasis on the continuities between the two periods.

57 PRO, C47/38/36; Westlake, 32.

58 J. Chiffoleau, *La Comptabilité de l'Au-delà: Les Hommes, La Mort et la Religion 1320–1480*, Rome 1980, 266–87, esp. 268–70 and graphique no. xix.

59 C. Vincent, *Dès Charités Bien Ordonnées: Les Confréries Normandes de la fin du Treizième Siècle au debut du Seizème Siècle*, Paris 1988, ch. 2, 52–54, 54 graphique no. 2.

60 Vincent, *Dès Charités Bien Ordonnées*, 64–69; Chiffoleau, *La Comptabilité de l'Au-delà*, 273–4.

61 Westlake, 24.

62 PRO, *Calendar of the Patent Rolls, Edward II 1317–21*, London 1903, and successive volumes.

between 1300 and 1350.[63] He too attributes this to anxieties about death, but derived from the climate of over-population, famine and epidemic disease in the half-century prior to the Black Death.[64] Bequests to fraternities in wills enrolled in the Hustings Court of London begin to appear in the 1340s.[65]

Of the 509 religious or social gilds listed by Westlake, 3% were founded before 1300; 11% between 1300 and 1348; 22% between 1348 and 1370; and 28% after 1370. Unfortunately though, 35% did not give founding dates. Some of these had been 'recently founded', or had existed 'time without memory'; others simply gave no indication.[66] This calls into question the pattern of foundation dates derived from the 1388–9 Survey.

Furthermore, for the Cambridgeshire returns, 14 (23%) of all founding dates, were only approximate, or the return suggested that there had already been gild activity prior to that date. The gilds described themselves as *incepta* or *inchoata* (begun), or *fundata* (founded). From the context *fundata* is not merely an equivalent term but can have the added meaning of the formalising of an institution or its confirmation on an official basis.[67] Certainly *fundata* has this force where three Cambridge gilds were concerned. They were definitely in existence prior to their official foundation before the Bishop of Ely in the 1380s.[68] One of them, Holy Trinity Gild, Holy Trinity Church, had acquired an indulgence from the Bishop in 1378 six years prior to the foundation date it gave. In such cases foundation before the Bishop seems much like the incorporation of a borough: an already existing and prosperous entity receiving seigneurial confirmation.

Although there may have been gild activity in one place over a long period of time, it may not have been continuous. There are references to gilds of St Mary associated with Great St Mary's Church, Cambridge, from the later thirteenth to the mid-sixteenth centuries which historians have tended to conflate. They were probably a number of separate institutions.[69]

63 A. Kreider, *English Chantries: the Road to Dissolution*, Harvard 1979, 72.

64 Kreider, *English Chantries*, 86. Although it must be noted that famine and the diseases of poverty were more likely to kill those who could not have afforded gild membership.

65 C.M. Barron, 'Parish Fraternities of late Medieval London' in *The Church in Pre-Reformation Society*, ed. C.M. Barron and C. Harper-Bill, Woodbridge 1985, 13–27.

66 These figures are based on Westlake's Appendix, excluding the returns from twelve craft gilds of the City of London.

67 Westlake, 25, gilds often used the date of a Royal charter or licence as their foundation date.

68 PRO, C47/38/5, 9, 10 indulgence.

69 Bateson sees it as an institution separate from the Gild Merchant granted by John in 1201, which probably became active in the 1290s when the church of St Mary burnt down; Rev. J.P. Rushe, 'The Origin of St Mary's Gild and its Connection with Corpus Christi College', *Proc. Camb. Antiq. Soc.* xvi, 1912, 20–52, follows Bateson on this point, but speculates that the gild was part of an international network of confraternities of the Carmelite order; Bateson, p. xviii. It is uncertain whether this gild died out when Corpus Christi College was founded. There were two gilds of St Mary associated with Great St Mary's Church in 1389, one dedicated to the Annunciation and the

The comparatively short life-span of many gilds is illustrated by the 1389 returns. Many state that they were founded to repair church buildings or to revive former devotions. Perhaps these had lapsed due to the plague, but equally, local disasters, or merely mundane factors may have had this effect. The falling into neglect of religious buildings and devotions was a common occurrence in this period, as was their revival by later individuals or groups of pious men and women.[70] The fraternity of the Assumption of the Virgin at Leverington was founded in 1386

> in honour of the Assumption, to renovate a picture of the Blessed Mary, and to renovate and sustain the chapel there in honour of Mary, in which the gild brethren intend to maintain a chaplain.[71]

At Littleport all the property of the gilds of St Mary and St John the Baptist had been destroyed by a sudden fire.[72] The brethren of St Wendreda's Gild made provision that if the gild failed through plague or any other disaster, its goods were to be donated to the fabric of the chapel at March.[73] There are no further references to any of these gilds apart from St Wendreda's, March: they were fragile institutions and there is no sense here that the corporate entity would survive its members, unlike the wealthy merchant fraternities in Cambridge and Wisbech, confident enough to purchase indulgences, or endow chaplains.

Of the 350 Cambridgeshire gilds, 160 (46%) are known to have been active only at one specific date. Before and after this chance emergence into documentation nothing further is known. One hundred and seven (31%) are known to have existed for under 50 years; 35 (10%) for between 50 and 100 years; 37 (11%) for between 100 and 200 years. A further 8 (2%) are known to have existed only through documentation relating to their abolition, so it is not possible to know how long they had survived. These figures confirm the relatively short life-span of the gilds, with the largest number in existence for under fifty years, and only a small proportion on any long-standing basis. It is useful here to look at the survival rate of gilds for which there are 1389 returns. Seventeen (28%) were still in existence in the sixteenth century, 32% of urban and 26% of rural fraternities. This is not entirely representative of the sample as a whole, for which 82% of urban and 94% of rural fraternities were

other to the Purification: PRO C47/38/4, 9; J.F. Williams, 'A Medieval Squabble', *Proc. Camb. Antiq. Soc.* liv, 1960, 109–11 conflates the Purification Gild with the thirteenth-century institution and believes that it remained in existence until 1547. Certainly there are two obligations describing money owed to the Purification Gild in 1535: CCRO, x. 28.

70 W. Christian, *Apparitions in late Medieval and Renaissance Spain 1399–1523*, Princeton 1981.

71 PRO, C47/38/25.

72 PRO, C47/38/26(3), (4).

73 PRO, C47/38/27.

mentioned once or are known to have existed for under fifty years.[74] It is probable that a high proportion of those which replied to the 1388–9 Survey were wealthy and well-established. Their endowments rendered them vulnerable to the authorities and were also recorded in the valuation and sale of religious properties from the 1540s on. This would account for the higher figure of survivals in the 1389 sample. The smaller poorer gilds came and went more readily.

Wills provide most evidence for general trends in gild foundation in the fifteenth and sixteenth centuries. The increase in the number of gilds recorded (2% before 1300, 18% 1300–1400, 32% 1400–1500, 43% 1500–46) is in part a reflection of the increase in the number of wills made over this period.[75] Of course there are problems with using wills as a source. It was unusual to make a will, although it became more common during the course of the sixteenth century. It is impossible therefore to know of the existence of many gilds, whose members either did not make wills or did not mention them in their wills.[76] Often only one chance reference is found. This pinpoints a gild's existence at a given moment of time, but does not supply a foundation date nor any indication of how long it was active. It is only when a group of wills contains bequests to the same gild, with some degree of detail on different facets of its activities, that the wills may be used to build up a

74 Urban areas are defined as the towns of Cambridge, Ely and Wisbech. Urban gilds make up 19% of the sample of 350.

75 Chiffoleau, *La Comptabilité de l'Au-delà*, 266–87; the detailed chronology of gild foundation which Chiffoleau is able to expound for an earlier period is only possible because of the large number of wills which survive from c.1320 for the Avignon region.

A sample of approximately 2,000 (1,909) wills has been analysed in detail for this project. Cambridge University Library (CUL) is the repository for the Ely Diocesan Archives (EDA). The wills lodged here which were consulted were proved in the Episcopal Consistory Court of Ely (ECC), Original Wills 1485, 1503–58 (953 wills); Episcopal Consistory Court of Ely, Registered Copy Wills, Microfilm no. HK2791, Liber A, 1449–59 (263 wills); Archdeaconry Court of Ely (ACE), Original Wills 1513–58 (373 wills); Archdeaconry Court of Ely, Registered Copy Wills, Microfilm no. VLP427, 1513–22 (29 wills). Cambridge University Library also holds the wills proved under the Peculiar Jurisdiction of the Court of the Vice-Chancellor of the University (VCC), Original Wills 1521–58 (38 wills). King's College Cambridge holds the wills proved by the Peculiar Court of King's College, Registered Copy Wills, Ledger Book 1, 1449–1558 (39 wills). The Public Record Office (PRO) holds the wills proved by the Prerogative Court of Canterbury (PCC Prob. 11) for testators with either moveable goods worth £5 or more, £10 in London, or lands held in more than one diocese. PCC Registered Copy Wills, 1383–1558 (214 wills) have been analysed from 23 towns and villages, from which 1389 returns or other substantial evidence for certain gilds or fraternities survive. The folium reference of registered wills has been given. Original wills are indexed alphabetically, so the number given in brackets consists of the box, bundle and number within the bundle of the will cited. The majority of the wills were made by members of yeomen and husbandmen families of the later 15th and 16th centuries.

76 C. Burgess, 'For the Increase of Divine Service: Chantries and the Parish in Late Medieval Bristol', *JEH* xxxvi, 1985, 46–65, esp. 46–47.

clearer profile. For example, a group of sixteenth-century wills from Gamlingay, a market town in the south-west of the county near the Bedfordshire border, shows the esteem with which the Brotherhood priest Sir Robert Parson was held and his close working relationship with the vicar. These wills show money, lands and goods, even a third share in a boat, left to the gild; and they show the gilds involvement in administering the obits of departed members, the building of a church-house and the repair of the highways.[77]

Parish records also provide a large amount of information on local fraternities in the fifteenth and sixteenth centuries. As with wills, many more of these records exist from the mid-fifteenth century on, although lay administration of the parish church and related affairs was of long-standing custom.[78] Churchwardens' accounts for the parishes of Saints Peter and Paul, Bassingbourne, and Holy Trinity, Cambridge, contain references to gilds in these contrasting rural and urban parishes in the shire.[79] Preserved among the records of Holy Trinity parish is a small notebook containing St Katherine's Gild accounts. These may be cross-referenced with the churchwardens' accounts to develop a broader understanding of the role of the gild and its officers in the parish.[80] A nineteenth-century parish register for St Wendreda's, March, containing accounts of St Christopher's Gild, and the churchwardens' accounts for St Leonard's, Leverington, likewise illustrate the role of the gilds in the parishes of the Isle.[81]

Other major sources for the gilds or fraternities are national government records, this time from the sixteenth century. Just as the survey of 1388–9 had made enquiries into the finances of each gild, so the lay subsidy of 1542 did the same. The subsidy rolls for Whittlesey in the Isle of Ely, for example, reveal ten gilds in the church of St Mary and two in the church of St Andrew for which no other records exist. The only information given is the names of

77 These nine wills range in date from 1505 to 1546 and are proved in PCC, ECC, and ACE courts.

78 W.E. Tate, *The Parish Chest*, Cambridge 1951, see esp. 83–107 for churchwardens' accounts; J.C. Cox, *Church Wardens' Accounts from the Fourteenth Century to the close of the Seventeenth Century*, London 1913.

79 CCRO, P11/5/1–2, Churchwardens' Accounts, Parish of Bassingbourne, Church of Saints Peter and Paul 1490–1540; CCRO, P22/5/1, Churchwardens' Accounts, Parish of Holy Trinity Cambridge 1504–58.

80 CCRO, P22/5/15, Accounts of St Katherine's Gild, Holy Trinity Church, Cambridge 1514–37.

81 CCRO, P116/1/4 Register of the church of St Wendreda the Virgin, March which includes a 19th-century copy of the Accounts of St Christopher's light or gild 1472–1525, pp. 131–7; WFM, Microfilm 8, Item 1, Leverington Church Accounts 1497–1600; *The Transcript of the Churchwardens' Accounts of the Parish of Tilney All Saints Norfolk 1443–1589*, ed. A.D. Stallard, London 1922, gives additional information on the Isle region, as it adjoins Cambridgeshire parishes; *Churchwardens' Accounts of St Mary the Great Cambridge 1504–1635*, ed. J.E. Foster, *Publns Camb. Antiq. Soc.* xxxv, Cambridge 1935, is the only other pre-Reformation Churchwardens' account for Cambridgeshire.

the gilds, and the amount each paid in taxation. They paid between 10*s* and 30*s* each.[82]

Unfortunately only four of the 1546–8 chantry certificates are extant for Cambridgeshire, only one of which, from Horseheath, is for a fraternity.[83] These documents survive for neighbouring counties such as Lincolnshire, Suffolk and Essex, and provide comparative information on gilds or fraternities and related institutions, chantries, obits, lights and free chapels.[84] Other government documents concerned with the dismantling of medieval Catholicism are able to fill this gap to some extent. These include the 1552 parish inventories of church goods;[85] records of pensions assigned to the priests of gilds and chantries;[86] ministers' accounts and patent rolls for the reign of Edward VI, recording the sales of lands and guildhalls;[87] and records of the Exchequer Special Commissioners' enquiries into concealed lands and goods previously used for superstitious purposes, which continued into Elizabeth's reign and beyond.[88]

The records of the dis-establishment of the Catholic faith under Edward VI and Elizabeth I, and the sale of lands, tenements and goods which had been given for religious purposes by the faithful were written primarily from a financial point of view. They were unlikely to describe the items which were sold in terminology which was itself superstitious. It is impossible therefore to know to which lights, chantries, gilds or obits, lands sold by the crown had belonged. The sale of a gildhall in a particular place informs us that there was gild activity there in 1547, but if there had been several gilds, not which ones were still active at that date. It seems that most of these properties not sold in 1547 passed into the hands of the parish or township for collective use, so that recollection of former ownership may have become blurred, at least by Elizabeth's reign. To betray their existence to the commissioners would have been to lose communal assets. In Whittlesford the gildhall became part of the town stock, and was successfully retained until the hunt for concealed lands had ceased. It was eventually sold by the Parochial Church Council in 1966.[89] Obviously the existence of some gilds was successfully concealed.

82 *VCH Cambs*. iv, 133; Palmer, 355.

83 PRO, DL38/5. The surviving Cambridgeshire chantry certificates: one each from Cambridge, Duxford, Horseheath and Upwell.

84 For comparative printed material see L.P. Wenham, 'The Chantries, Guilds, Obits and Lights of Richmond Yorkshire', *York Archaeological Journal* xxxviii, 1952–5, 96–111; *Kent Obit and Lamp Rents*, ed. A. Hussey, Ashford 1936.

85 'Cambridgeshire Church Goods', *East Anglian N. & Q.*, ed. J.J. Muskett, vi–x, 1895–1904, 145 et seq., esp. ix, 311–14.

86 E. Ventris, 'Notes upon Chantries and free Chapels', *Proc. Camb. Antiq. Soc*. i, 1859, 201–40.

87 Palmer, esp. 355, 386–402.

88 C. Kitching, 'The Quest for Concealed lands in the reign of Elizabeth I', *TRHS*, 5th series xxiv, 1974, 63–74.

89 *VCH Cambs*. iv, 272.

Many others may have slipped away without government knowledge, because they had no land or property worth assessing. Despite the inadequacy of these records for present purposes, they show extensive gild activity in 1547.

The pattern of gild activity which is apparent is largely dictated by the historical sources through which we are able to perceive it. The survey of 1388–9 and continental evidence from the same period do lend support to the theory of an increase in the number of gilds or fraternities from the later fourteenth century, although there seems to have been a previous wave of foundations, less well-documented, during the century before. In England, on the evidence of wills, lay enthusiasm for fraternity membership showed no sign of abating on the eve of the dissolution:[90] in Catholic Europe it was encouraged by the counter-Reformation church.[91]

The date of the 1388–9 Survey itself influenced the information obtained. If it were not for this, very little would be known about those organisations prior to 1450 when wills became more numerous. It is not until the sixteenth century that it is possible to verify impressions by the use of a number of sources. As Alan Kreider pointed out in his study of chantries, the greater the distance between their foundation dates and the surveys of 1546 and 1548, the less likely the chantries were to have survived.[92] Thus, with the gilds, the documents of 1389 and those of the dissolution of Catholicism from the 1540s on show the most intense phases of their activity to have been the later fourteenth and early sixteenth centuries, the periods which directly preceded these two surveys.

Society

The increase in the number of fraternities, particularly in the two centuries following the outbreak of the Black Death, has been established as a European trend. It is necessary to examine some of the reasons for this, the hypotheses put forward by historians, the evidence of fraternity documents themselves, and the wider social context of the time.

Since the desire to bond together in groups is a phenomenon to be observed in all cultures, and one which manifested itself in many forms in medieval European society, the explanation for the proliferation of gilds or fraternities in the later Middle Ages is complex. The simple assertion that their numbers grew as a response to the Black Death, which satisfied the early

90 Ninety-eight gilds (28% of the sample) were founded between 1520 and the dissolution. Given the religious disturbances of the latter part of this time, this figure is particularly significant.

91 Chiffoleau, *La Comptabilité de l'Au-delà*, 274, interestingly says that although earlier fraternities had been associated with heresy, the second wave from the 14th century on were controlled by the church.

92 Kreider, *English Chantries*, 89.

gild historians such as Westlake, is no longer enough.[93] Le Bras calls them *families artificielles*,[94] a useful definition, and one which has broad application. It has been suggested that the increase in the number of the fraternities goes back beyond the later Middle Ages and in fact has its origins in the twelfth and thirteenth centuries,[95] which would place it within the context of a period of intense economic development and increased disposable wealth. Indeed, Chiffoleau attributes the elaboration of funeral and commemorative rituals, for which fraternities provided a framework, to the development of towns: the move away from tight-knit rural communities, family and homeland, to a more alienated urban environment.[96]

Zvi Razi detects the same process occurring in rural England from the late thirteenth century, with the gradual breakdown of the manorial system. The development of a peasant land-market and the mobility of family members away from their manor of origin, meant that they were no longer able to rely on the family for economic or charitable assistance or for burial as had been customary. There was a proliferation of fraternities or gilds in the areas where such changes had occurred much earlier, such as Redgrave in Suffolk, in contrast with Halesowen, in the champion heartlands of the west midlands, where fraternity formation only begins in the fifteenth century.[97] This may provide an explanation for the foundation of larger numbers of gilds in the Isle of Ely especially along the alluvial flood plains around the Wash at an early date, in comparison with foundations in the shire, which only accelerated to a comparable density in the sixteenth century.[98]

Gervase Rosser notes that the crystallisation of the parochial system in England from about 1300 created a need for a more fluid form of association to affirm belonging to other communities.[99] Certainly, fraternities fulfilled

93 Vincent, *Dès Charités Bien Ordonnées*, 64–69.

94 Le Bras, 'Les Confréries Chrétiennes: Problèmes et Propositions', *Revue Historique Du Droit Français et Etranger*, series 4 xix–xx, 1940–1, 310–63, esp. 310, 'families artificielles dont tout les membres sont unis par une fraternité volontaire, les confréries ont pour object de satisfaire dans un cadre étroit les plus poignants besoins du corps et de l'âme'.

95 W.R. Jones, 'English Religious Brotherhoods', *The Historian* xxxvi, 1974, 646–59, esp. 646.

96 Chiffoleau, *La Comptabilité de l'Au-delà*, Preface by J. Le Goff, ix; Bateson, 14–25: the bede roll of St Mary's gild, Cambridge, served this purpose.

97 Z. Razi, 'The Myth of the Immoveable Peasant Family' (unpublished paper given at the Institute of Historical Research, London, May 1989). I am also grateful to Dr Razi for discussion of this point; G.C. Homans, *English Villagers of the Thirteenth Century*, Cambridge, Massachusetts, 1941, see Book I, esp. section II, for a description of the champion region.

98 Other factors, of course, influence regional diversity. Marjorie McIntosh has found virtually no gild activity in the manorial records of Kent and Sussex in the post-plague period. I am grateful to her for this observation.

99 A.G. Rosser, 'Communities of Parish and Guild in the Late Middle Ages', in *Parish, Church and People*, Local Studies in Lay Religion 1350–1750, ed. S. Wright, London 1988, 29–55, esp. 33.

this function in the cities of late medieval Italy, where they cut across the boundaries of parish, neighbourhood and class.[100] In England from the fourteenth century on many changes were taking place in the structure of local government. Examples of this may be seen in the development of the office of the Justices of the Peace,[101] the experiments in taxation of the 1370s onwards,[102] the introduction of the Use and feoffees as methods of land tenure,[103] and the extension of mortmain legislation to cover corporate bodies. It is against this background that the rise in the number of fraternities, another facet of local organisation, must be viewed. Westlake attributes their demise in the sixteenth century to their increasing involvement in secular affairs, as they moved steadily away from their original spiritual purity.[104] Certainly there is little evidence for anything other than religious activity in the 1389 returns, but these were carefully drafted to allay government suspicion. However, when other documents are available to augment this information, it is clear that they did play a role in the government of their communities even at that date.[105]

On an economic level, it was from the 1380s that recovery began to be felt after the Black Death, heralding what has been called the 'Golden Age' of the English peasantry.[106] Lacking the earlier cohesion of the manorial structure, certain sectors of the peasantry became richer, amassing larger holdings, although other sectors became dispossessed of their land, relying increasingly on wage labour for income. Among the wealthier peasants greater surplus wealth increased the amounts which they were able to contribute to what has been termed the 'ceremonial fund': money held by churchwardens and gild officials to be used for celebrations, festivals and processions which brought colour and diversity to the day to day lives of local communities.[107]

It seems appropriate here to examine what may be discovered about the men and women who entered into the fellowship of the gilds. There is little direct information on the occupations, status, wealth, sex or age of the members; the factors which influenced the joining of a fraternity; and

100 R. Weissman, *Ritual Brotherhood in Renaissance Florence*, New York 1982, esp. 40–41.

101 *EHD* iv, ed. A.R. Myers, London 1970, 533–43.

102 Fenwick, 'The English Poll Taxes', 19. In her introduction she points out that the experiments began with the 1371 parish tax and ended with the income and land taxes of the early 15th century.

103 M.H. Keen, *England in the Later Middle Ages: A Political History*, London 1973, 150–3; J.M.W. Bean, *The Decline of English Feudalism 1215–1540*, Manchester 1968, ch. iii, esp. 79, 'the practice of enfeoffing had permeated the lowest ranks of the Peasantry' by 1504.

104 Westlake, 74; J. Scarisbrick, *The Reformation and the English People*, Oxford 1984, 32, follows Westlake on this point.

105 See ch. 6.

106 Dyer, *Standards of Living*, 2.

107 Dyer, *Standards of Living*, 182, borrows this term from E.R. Wolf, *Peasants*, Englewood Cliffs, New Jersey 1966.

whether these changed over the course of time. Gild statutes and accounts tend to mention by name only founders, benefactors, officers or stockholders, who would have been those of higher social rank within the gild. Bede rolls provide additional names but, unless these can be correlated with other documents, nothing further is known of these people. Wills identify the social rank of others who belonged. In 1389 the statutes of two gilds indicated that bequests were made by their members, St John the Baptist, Wisbech, and The Annunciation, Great St Mary's, Cambridge.[108] Will-making was practised at that date only among town elites like these gildsmen, or among the gentry and nobility. By the sixteenth century it had spread to yeomen, husbandmen and other moderately wealthy tenant-farmers. It is unlikely that membership ever descended below this level.

The size of fees and fines expected of brethren give an indication of their disposable wealth and therefore of their social status. According to the statutes, entry fines were required by 20 (33%) Cambridgeshire gilds in 1389, and by the four other Cambridgeshire gilds whose statutes survive, dating from the fifteenth and sixteenth centuries.[109] Sums ranged from 13*s* 4*d* plus 6*d* for the alderman and 3*d* for the dean to join Holy Trinity Gild, Holy Trinity Church, Cambridge, to 3*d* in total to join St Peter's Gild, Holy Trinity Church, Ely.[110] Payments in money were made in the towns of Cambridge, Ely and Wisbech, and also in Chesterton and Chatteris. Payments in kind or sometimes partly in kind and partly in cash were made in other rural settlements. These ranged from four bushels of barley and 2 pounds of wax at Bottisham, to one bushel of barley and 1 pound of wax to join the Nativity Gild at Stretham.[111] On provision of sufficient surety, some gilds allowed new members to pay over a period of time.

It is clear from the statutes that regular contributions towards the upkeep of lights, chaplaincies and for general purposes were a requirement of membership, although not all statutes mention specific fees. Members of Cambridge fraternities paid large sums in regular instalments or quarterage four times a year. The highest annual subscription specified was 6*s* to the Holy Sepulchre

108 PRO, C47/38/39, 4.

109 In addition to the 1389 Statutes, there are three sets of 15th-century statutes and one set of 16th-century statutes extant for Cambridgeshire. The three from 15th-century Cambridge are virtually identical documents preserved in various antiquarian copies. Toulmin Smith, 272–82, prints those of St Clement's Gild, St Clement's Church, Cambridge. Those to which I have referred are: BL Add. Ms. 5846, fos 5–13, statutes of St Clement's Gild, St Clement's Church, Cambridge, 1431; CUL, MM1 36, Baker Mss. vol. 25, item 10, pp. 361–6, statutes of the Gild of Saints Peter and Paul, Church of Saints Peter and Paul, Cambridge, 1448; CUL, MM1 36, Baker Mss. vol. 25, item 10, pp. 367–71, statutes of All Saints' Gild, All Saints' Church, Cambridge, 1473. Statutes also exist for the 16th-century rural Gild of St James' Dullingham, CUL, MM1 47, Baker Mss. vol. 36, item 16, pp. 161–2, 1517.

110 PRO, C47/38/10, 23(1).

111 PRO, C47/38/3(1), 33(4).

Gild, Chatteris, and the lowest 2*d* to the Resurrection Gild, Chesterton.[112] Once again some contributions were made in grain or wax.

Offerings at mass on the patronal festival or alms at funerals were also required by 28 (47%) 1389 statutes, and by the four fifteenth- and sixteenth-century ones. In some cases the alderman made a symbolic offering of a penny on behalf of the gild, elsewhere all brethren had to give a farthing or a half-penny.

Not only were such payments compulsory, but their non-payment was punished by a system of fines, as were failure to attend meetings and funerals and breach of ordinances. Eighteen (30%) of the 1389 statutes and all three fifteenth-century statutes specified a system of penalties. These penalties were exclusively financial, apart from expulsion in the most serious cases. Forfeits ranged from 13*s* 4*d* for bringing St Peter's Gild, Wisbech, into disrepute,[113] to a widespread charge of 1*d* for failure to attend meetings or make offerings at church; and from 5 pounds of wax for disobedience to the master of the Annunciation Gild, St Botolph's Church, Cambridge, to ½ a pound of wax for disturbing the meetings of St Peter's Gild, Holy Trinity Church, Ely.[114]

Although information on wages and prices for the Middle Ages is open to considerable debate, when laid beside that on fees and fines, it indicates which social groups would have had the possibility of belonging to gilds or fraternities. Christopher Dyer, in his study of standards of living in the later Middle Ages, calculated the annual surplus from peasants' holdings in Bishops Cleve, Gloucestershire from a survey of 1299.[115] The yardlander with a surplus equivalent to one or two pounds of money a year would easily have afforded membership of a rural fraternity; the half-yardlanders who comprised the majority of peasant landholders with no surplus or perhaps two bushels of grain would have found this hard, and it would have been totally out of reach of the small-holders. With the improved economic circumstances of the fifteenth and early sixteenth centuries, membership would have come within reach of a greater number of the increasingly wealthy middle ranks of the peasantry, which accounts for the greater number of gilds.

When the levels of wages are set against the prices of payments in kind, it gives some idea of their real value. Thorold Rogers suggested that the most representative wage-data for agricultural workers was threshing assessed as piece-work, and for craft workers, carpentry assessed by day rate.[116] In the 1380s average wages for threshing in the south and east of England ranged

112 PRO, C47/38/12(b), 13.

113 PRO, C47/38/41.

114 PRO, C47/38/8, 23(1); see ch. 6 for discussion of gild discipline.

115 Dyer, *Standards of Living*, ch. 5, esp. 110–18. This is regional data but does have broader implications.

116 J.E. Thorold Rogers, *A History of Agriculture and Prices in England*, 7 vols, Oxford 1866–1902, i, 268, 275.

between 3*d* and 10*d* per day.[117] For carpentry the average was 5*d* per day.[118] The price of barley in the 1380s was just over 4½*d* a bushel,[119] and locally on the Huntingdonshire manor of Slepe, 4½*d* a bushel in 1381 and 6*d* in 1390.[120] Wax was just under 6*d* a pound although much would have been home-produced.[121] These statistics suggest that membership of the rural gilds was limited to the wealthy peasantry, and that in the towns the less prestigious fraternities were open to craftsmen and artisans, while the most expensive gilds of Cambridge and Wisbech were exclusive to far wealthier men.

Most gilds were open to men and women. Medieval society was one in which tasks and activities were more gender segregated than today,[122] and where the influence of women in economic and public life was limited. The religious or social gilds were one form of institution in which women appear to have been accepted as members as readily as men,[123] although, within them, their participation was confined to certain activities. The 1389 returns describe their members as *confratres*, *fratres* or *sorores*. *Confratres* seems to have been a neuter term, best translated as brethren, *fratres* and *sorores*, of course, brothers and sisters. Thirty eight (63%) of the 1389 statutes from Cambridgeshire specifically mention women members, as do the four from the fifteenth and sixteenth centuries. Other gilds probably had women members. Of the testators who mention gilds in their wills, 10% were women, 9% priests, and 81% laymen. This is roughly comparable to the percentage of these groups in the overall sample.[124] When the 1389 statutes are analysed closely the occurrence of the term *soror* shows that some areas of gild life were open to women and others were not. Although women gained the same spiritual benefits as men, participation in the devotional life of the gild and commemoration when they were dead, they did not hold office,[125] nor were

117 Thorold Rogers, *A History of Agriculture and Prices*, i, table I, 303; W. Beveridge, 'Westminster Wages in the Manorial Era', *EcHR*, 2nd series viii, 1955–6, 118–35; 121, table 1.

118 Thorold Rogers, *A History of Agriculture and Prices*, i, table IV, 322; Beveridge, 'Westminster Wages', 27, table 3; H. Phelps-Brown and S. Hopkins, *A Perspective of Wages and Prices*, London 1981, Essay 1, 'Seven Centuries of Building Wages', 11, table 1; Dyer, *Standards of Living*, 247.

119 Thorold Rogers, *A History of Agriculture and Prices*, i, 234, table 1.

120 J.A. Raftis, *The Estates of Ramsay Abbey*, Toronto 1957, 214, table XLVII.

121 Thorold Rogers, *A History of Agriculture and Prices*, i, 446.

122 M. Aston, 'Segregation in Church', *SCH* xxvii, 1990, 237–94.

123 Toulmin Smith, xxx; Scarisbrick, *The Reformation and the English People*, ch. 2, 24, is unjustifiably enthusiastic on this point; M. Flynn, *Sacred Charity: Confraternities and Social Welfare in Spain 1400–1700*, London 1989, 33–34. Women could be members but did not hold governing positions, nor, frequently, voting rights, unless they formed their own groups.

124 See note 76 above. Out of approximately 2,000 wills, 15% were made by women, 7% by priests, and 78% by laymen; J. Mattingley, 'The Medieval Parish Gilds of Cornwall', *Journal of the Royal Institution of Cornwall*, new series x, 1989, 290–329, esp. 296, 2–10% of members were women.

125 Barron, 'The Parish Fraternities of Medieval London', 31–32.

they generally consulted as part of the collective decision-making process. However, they did in certain circumstances hold stock and appear as foundresses and benefactresses, often linked with their husbands, for these purposes.

In all the urban statutes of 1389 the term *soror* is confined to the passages detailing funerals, commemorative rites and prayers for the dead. In the statutes of the great Cambridge gilds, the term *uxor fratris* (wife of a brother) is used more frequently than *soror*. These organisations may have been rather like the gentlemen's or working men's clubs which still exist today: male clannish affairs with ladies in attendance only on high days or holidays, at feasts and funerals. The Annunciation Gild, Great St Mary's, excluded women whose husbands were not members; the Purification Gild in the same church did not bury impoverished widows of former members; and to belong to the Holy Trinity Gild, Holy Trinity Church, single women had to pay the same fee as a husband and wife.[126]

In the statutes from rural fraternities the term *soror* is used more widely, which suggests that women may have played a broader role in rural gild life. On occasions there is evidence that they were involved when decisions were made 'with the assent of the whole brotherhood',[127] as with the gild of the Resurrection, Chesterton, where the brothers and the sisters fixed the entry fine.[128] In the accounts of the light and fraternity of St Christopher, March, there is evidence of a woman holding stock. Alice Spenser had certain quantities of hemp for the wick of the light in 1480 and 1481, and 2*s* 4*d* in 1481.[129] In 1472 she had been named as one of the founders, along with her husband John Spenser, a shipwright. It is most likely that she was holding stock on her husband's behalf, either that which was in his hands when he died, or as he had not held stock in previous years, as a widowed head of household taking her turn. This may also be seen in the churchwardens' accounts of Holy Trinity, Cambridge. Harry Cressewell, churchwarden, and also stock-holder of St Katherine's Gild in the same parish died part-way through his year of office 1509–10.[130] Fortunately the 20*s* he held for St Katherine's Gild were paid by George Ffoyster who had stood surety,[131] but

126 PRO, C47/38/11; Bateson, 127; PRO, C47/38/9; PRO, C47/38/4, 'et si aliqua mulier non maritata in eadem fraternitate fuerit admissa tunc in eadem forma solvat sicut frater et uxor eius solvant prout superius declaratum est'.

127 A phrase used frequently in the 1389 returns.

128 PRO, C47/38/13, 'ordinati sunt per fratres et sorores predictos quod quilibet intrans gildam predictam, in primo introitu sue ad minus solvet quinque solidas'.

129 CCRO, P116/1/4, pp. 131–7, 19th century transcript, fos 11, 21, 22.

130 CCRO, P22/5/1, Churchwardens' Accounts, Holy Trinity Church, Cambridge, 1504–58. He was obviously prominent in local affairs. He had been churchwarden a number of times: (1505–6, fo 12v; ?1506–7, fo 17r; 1508–9, fo 21r). He rented part of the great barn, a church property in Wall's Lane for 7*s*: (fos 11r, 20r, 25r) and his wife paid 6*s* 8*d* for his burial inside the church (fo 25r).

131 CCRO, P22/5/15, St Katherine's Gild Accounts, Holy Trinity Church, Cambridge, 1514–37, fo 2r.

his widow Johanna was left with the responsibility to repay 66*s* 5*d* which had been in his hands as churchwarden.[132] In the reduced economic circumstances of widowhood she was able to repay this at the rate of only a few shillings a year. Meanwhile she is recorded in the accounts receiving payments for washing surplices and brewing ale.[133] She was also one of the two women guardians of Our Lady light in 1516–18, as she had been at other times before her husband died.[134] This position was occupied by the wives of men prominent in parish affairs, and also, it seems, their widows. In 1522 23*s* 4*d* still remained unpaid, when 'John Balenger late husband to Johanna Cressewell' paid 7*s* 4*d* at the annual account and promised to pay the remaining 16*s* in instalments at Michaelmas and Easter of the next two years.[135] The details afforded by this personal misfortune show that although it was the man who held office, he did so as the head of an economic unit, the household, and only at the stage in the life-cycle when he had attained this status: office-holding was not open to single men.[136]

As well as being strongly gender segregated, this society was one which made sharp distinctions between groups and activities appropriate at different stages in the life-cycle.[137] Just as the wives took turns as guardians of Our Lady light in Holy Trinity, Cambridge, so in the rural parish of Bassingbourne, a wives' group is occasionally recorded collecting money at Hocktide and making donations to the church.[138] A single men's group 'lately begun' held stock for the rood loft light.[139] The Resurrection Gild, Chesterton, had originally been founded by the young men and women of the town in 1336, but had evolved into a gild over the course of time.[140]

There is better evidence for such groups in the West Country. In Croscomb in Devon, there were groups for young men, maidens, wives, and men of various occupations.[141] In Cornwall, groups of young men and maidens were associated with May Day entertainments and the festivities of youth, like the youth abbeys and kingdoms Natalie Zemon Davis describes for France.[142] The

132 CCRO, P22/5/1, fo 43v, she had to enter into an obligation for this.

133 CCRO, P22/5/1, fo 43r (ale); fo 53v.

134 CCRO, P22/5/1, 1505–6, fo 14r; 1508–9, fo 22v; 1516–18, fo 52r. There were four lights in the church: Sepulchre, Rood, St Erasmus and Our Lady. The light wardens were elected at the same time as the churchwardens.

135 CCRO, P22/5/1, fo 67r.

136 See ch. 6 for further discussion of office-holding.

137 M. Aston, 'Segregation in Church', 239.

138 CCRO, P11/5/1–2, Bassingbourne Churchwardens' Accounts 1498–1540, vol. 2, fos 20v, 69v; C. Phythian-Adams, *Local History and Folklore: A New Framework*, Standing Conference for Local History, London 1975.

139 CCRO, P11/5/1–2, vol. 2, fos 8v, 29v, 32v.

140 PRO, C47/38/13. See ch. 3 for a detailed discussion of this interesting certificate.

141 Westlake, 61.

142 J. Mattingley, 'The Medieval Parish Gilds of Cornwall', 302; N.Z. Davis, *Society and Culture in Early Modern France: 8 Essays*, Essay 4, 'The Reasons of Misrule', 104–23.

Assumption Gild of St Mary's Church, Ely, did not provide a full trental of masses for those dying under the age of sixteen: this was the privilege of adulthood. The gilds or fraternities were not only the preserve of the well-to-do but, more specifically, for the adults among them: those who were younger or poorer had their own groups. Joanna Mattingley suggests that within each parish there was a hierarchy of such groups, with the gilds or fraternities at the top and below them, lights before the saints, the plough light, the wives' groups, which conferred limited benefits on those never wealthy enough to attain gild status.[143]

Women featured more prominently as founders and benefactors of the gilds than as officers or stock-holders; but women's influence here was limited to those of higher wealth or social status. Women were mentioned as founders of ten gilds in 1389 and of St Christopher's Gild or light at March in 1472. Few were named: the documents record only that a man and his wife were founders. Out of twenty-seven named, only three were single women: Margeria Scheremann and Helwysia Kempster, whose surnames suggest craft occupations, both foundresses of St Katherine's Gild, St Andrew's Church, Cambridge; and Agnes, foundress of St Christopher's Gild, March, who had joined with her brother William Southwold, senior, and Margaret his wife.[144] It was common for people to join as couples, but this last example illustrates the evidence for other family ties among members.

The bede roll and other records of St Mary and Corpus Christi Gilds, Cambridge, show that husbands and wives, brothers and sisters, parents and children joined together; not only those who were living, but also those who were already dead. Former spouses, parents and possibly adult children who had pre-deceased their parents were enrolled into fraternity.[145] Thus the fellowship of the gild stretched from the world of the living into the world of the dead, united by prayer and the hope of salvation.[146]

As benefactresses to the gilds, women are generally recorded as widows. In order to be commemorated for their donations, they had to leave quite substantial sums. In fifteenth-century Cambridge 40s 'for the furtherance of our gild' was the price of an anniversary mass.[147] Out of fourteen anniversaries recorded in the statutes of St Clement's Gild, only three were for women, Isabelle Cappe, Alice Hethe and Jonet Togode; only three of the fourteen commemorated the spouse of the deceased; the rest were for individuals, as the surviving spouse might remarry.[148] The gild of Saints Peter and Paul

143 J. Mattingley, 'The Medieval Parish Gilds of Cornwall', 304, 307, windows in St Neot's church were paid for by the different groups within the parish.

144 PRO, C47/38/6, 11; CCRO, P116/1/4, pp. 131–7, fo 6.

145 Bateson, 14–25.

146 J. Bossy, *Christianity in the West 1400–1700*, Oxford 1985, 28–29.

147 BL Add. Ms. 5846, fos 1–13; CUL, MM1 36, Baker Mss. vol. 25, pp. 361–6; CUL, MM1 36, Baker Mss. vol. 25, pp. 165, 170.

148 BL Add. Ms. 5846, pp. 9–13.

recorded eleven masses: ten for men and one for a man and his wife.[149] Annes Smythe was the only woman benefactor. She left a table-cloth and a brass pot, probably worth only a few shillings.[150] On the evidence of wills this was the sort of bequest more usually within women's economic reach. Thus women's position in the gilds was linked primarily to their social status: this determined their economic circumstances as wives and widows and set the pattern for their participation in, and benefaction to, the fraternities.

149 CUL, MM1 36, Baker Mss. vol. 25, pp. 366–7.
150 CUL, MM1 36, Baker Mss. vol. 25, p. 367.

3

Gild Life and Religious Practice

Medieval Piety and the Reformation Debate

Before the recent wave of revisionist debate in Reformation studies, the consensus of opinion on late medieval piety was epitomised by Johan Huizinga in *The Waning of the Middle Ages*, first published in 1924.[1] Manifestations of religious devotion possessed an over-ripe quality; they had overreached themselves in superstitious excess and the mindless replication of ritual.[2] A clear change of direction towards a more rational faith was inevitable.[3] This interpretation was consistent with Enlightenment thought and certain later strands of writing on comparative faith, which made a distinction between magic or superstition, and religion or belief.[4] In the British context the theory of late medieval decay was particularly persuasive due to the important political role in society of the post-Reformation Anglican church. It was when consensus in the Anglican church itself began to break down, for example, with the nineteenth-century Oxford Movement, that hitherto suppressed discourses, such as that of the vitality and richness of late medieval Catholic life, began to be explored.[5] With the dramatic decline of organised religion in late twentieth-century western life, paradoxically historians have been able to view religion as a far broader social and cultural phenomenon than before.[6]

The difficulties derived from the historiographical division between the

1 J. Huizinga, *The Waning of the Middle Ages*, London 1924, Harmondsworth 1955.

2 J. Chiffoleau, *La Comptabilité de l'Au-delà: Les Hommes, La Mort et la Religion 1320–1480*, Rome 1980, part II.

3 A.G. Dickens, *The English Reformation*, London 1964, represents the supreme scholarly achievement of this line of argument.

4 J. Estlin-Carpenter, *Comparative Religion*, Home University Library of Modern Knowledge, no date, but post-1912, is an example; J. Bossy, 'Some Elementary Forms of Durkheim', *P&P* xcv, 1982, 3–18, esp. 7.

5 C. Haigh, 'The Recent Historiography of the English Reformation' in *The English Reformation Revised*, ed. C. Haigh, Cambridge 1987, 19–33. See also the conclusion to this volume, 209–15; D. MacCulloch, 'The Myth of the English Reformation', *Journal of British Studies* xxx, 1991, 1–19.

6 C. Trinkaus and H.A. Oberman, *The Pursuit of Holiness in Late Medieval and Renaissance Religion*, Leyden 1974.

'late medieval' and 'early modern' era prevent the immense changes of these times from being viewed as a whole. It must also be recognised that, in British historiography, studies of late medieval piety derive their conceptual framework from the traditional 'Protestant' interpretation of the Reformation. Oxford Movement writings on the medieval Catholic church were polemics against criticisms made by Reformation Protestants and Anglican apologists after them.[7] The traditional interpretation of the Reformation has continued to shape recent revisionist debate. Writers such as Professor Scarisbrick, Christopher Harper-Bill and most recently Eamon Duffy have advanced scholarly refutations of widely-held views on the medieval church.[8] However, like those whose writings they refute, Scarisbrick and Duffy also construct 'normative' versions of the mood among the people of late medieval England. Duffy particularly argues for the promotion of social harmony and individual spiritual fulfilment by late medieval Catholic practice.[9] This is valuable as he re-integrates the hitherto fragmentary understanding of medieval religion into the coherent system it once was. Nevertheless this leaves two distinct versions of English Reformation history which in no way link together. In one, with the certainty of hindsight, the Reformation was inevitable; in the other it was imposed on a reluctant populace for various political reasons.[10] In reality, these two views represent opposite ends of a spectrum of religious belief and practice current in early Tudor society. It is in the centre between these two extremes, in the inconsistencies and uncertainties of the views of those on the middle ground, that a deeper understanding of the course of the Reformation in England is to be found.

One of the central problems of examining the impact of the Reformation on the majority of the population, those who were not vocal about their religious stance, is the difficulty of determining beliefs held by individuals. It is hard enough to comprehend our own relationship to belief structures, even harder to evaluate the inconsistencies between the standards by which our contemporaries profess to act, and their actions. The faith of the majority of individuals in the past, refracted through documents such as wills, remains opaque. They are merely the record of the professions which people were content to make public, not of their inner doubts or dissension. Institutions

7 F.A. Gasquet, *Parish Life in Medieval England*, London 1906; Westlake.

8 J.J. Scarisbrick, *The Reformation and the English People*, Oxford 1984; C. Harper-Bill, *The Pre-Reformation Church in England 1400–1530*, London 1989; E. Duffy, *The Stripping of the Altars: Traditional Religion in England c.1400–1580*, Yale 1992, 3.

9 Duffy, *The Stripping of the Altars*, 4, 121–3 argues in favour of corporate experience in late medieval religion against the 'privatisation' of devotion put forward by C. Richmond, 'Religion and the Fifteenth Century English Gentleman', in *The Church, Politics and Patronage in the Fifteenthth Century*, ed. R.B. Dobson, Gloucester 1984, 193–208.

10 C. Haigh, *Reformation and Resistance in Tudor Lancashire*, Cambridge 1975; C. Haigh, 'The Continuity of Catholicism in the English Reformation', and 'Conclusion', in *The English Reformation Revised*, 176–208, 209–15; C. Haigh, *English Reformations: Religion, Politics and Society under the Tudors*, Oxford 1993.

such as gilds or the parish, important providers of devotional practices, displayed collective not individual faith.

It is necessary here to define the terminology used to describe the expression of religious beliefs around the time of the Reformation. Prior to the Reformation period, there had been orthodox religious practice and heretical practice. The inner understanding of the people was taken to manifest itself in their acts of worship or of speech.[11] However, the challenge of heterodoxy had not yet confronted what will henceforth be called traditional medieval Catholicism.[12] Neither on the eve of the Reformation nor in England for the subsequent three generations or so, is it possible to speak of confessional faiths.[13] Heterodoxy, or clearly defined distinctions in religious belief and practice held by different sects, was yet to emerge from the decades of turmoil prior to the 1580s. It is only after this that it is possible to speak of confessional Catholicism as opposed to traditional medieval Catholicism; or of confessional Protestantism of varying brands.

Those individuals or groups whose faith has been most studied during the early years of the Reformation, both humanists and Protestant reformers, were in the vanguard of the movement for religious change and renewal. Those occupying the middle ground, the majority of the population, have been condemned by their more enthusiastic contemporaries, and by later historians, as apathetic, 'the lukewarm'.[14] Here it is necessary to introduce an alternative definition of their religious motivation: pragmatism.[15] A particular strand of late medieval thought from Langland through to Erasmus and later reformers of the sixteenth century condemned the giving of material wealth in the hope of spiritual reward as credulity or cynicism.[16] This was epitomised by such practices as the purchase of indulgences, commemorative masses, or the giving of religious ornaments and objects to the church. However, this condemnation obscures the medieval notion that the spiritual was infused in the material, the religious in mundane social acts.[17] The medieval concept of

11 G. Leff, *Heresy in the Middle Ages. The Relation of Heterodoxy to Dissent c.1250–1450*, 2 vols, Manchester 1967.

12 J. Bossy, *The English Catholic Community 1570–1850*, London 1975, paperback 1979, 4, speaks of the posthumous history of 'medieval' or 'pre-Reformation' Christendom in England; Duffy, *The Stripping of the Altars*, 3, uses the phrase 'traditional religion'.

13 Bossy, *The English Catholic Community*; P. Collinson, *The Birthpangs of Protestant England: Religious and Cultural Change in the Sixteenth and Seventeenth Centuries*, London 1988, xi, argues that Protestant England was born only in the 1570s.

14 Revelation, 3, v 14–22.

15 Duffy, *The Stripping of the Altars*, 483, 502.

16 W. Langland, *Piers the Ploughman*, translated by J.F. Goodridge, Harmondsworth 1975, 36–37; D. Erasmus, *Pilgrimages to St Mary of Walsingham and St Thomas of Canterbury*, ed. J. Gough Nichols, London 1849; T. More, *A Dyalogue of Syr Thomas More Knyght, wherein be treated dyvers maters as of the veneration and worship of ymages and relyques, praying to the saintys, and goyng on pylgrymage with many other thyngys touchyng the pestylent sect of Luther and Tynedale*, Johannes Rastell, London 1529.

17 Bossy, 'Holiness and Society', *P&P* lxxv, 1977, 119–37.

charity included pious gifts to God through his church, no less than those to the community through mending highways and bridges or giving to the poor. Furthermore the careful stewardship of one's material resources and their use for God's purposes was passed down into Protestant teaching. It was according to such principles that churchwardens and gild officials administered the material wealth given for religious purposes by the laity, and disposed of such assets swiftly, once confiscation by the Crown became a strong possibility.[18]

The Laity and The Late Medieval Church

Both traditional ecclesiastical history and recent social history have emphasised the distinction between the estate of the clergy and the estate of the laity, between elite and popular religion. Popular religion has tended to be identified, too simplistically, with parish life.[19] Nevertheless, it is true to say that from the time of the early church to the Reformation period and beyond, both clerical and secular elites had sought to impose constraints, political, financial, intellectual, doctrinal and moral, on the mass of the laity, at the expense of a more superstitious, amoral and localised religion.[20] Over the course of the later Middle Ages there was a shift of emphasis from withdrawal from the world to lead a religious life, to the pursuit of religious fulfilment while living a life in the world. There was a corresponding shift of control over religious practice from monastery and clergy to the laity.[21] It is in this

18 R. Whiting, *The Blind Devotion of the People: Popular Religion and the English Reformation*, Cambridge 1989, ch. 9; Duffy, *The Stripping of the Altars*, ch. 14; WCR1, pp. 109–10, the inventory of the plate sold in London at the dissolution of the Trinity Gild and records of the money's swift re-deployment: on sending troops to Norfolk to assist the King in putting down the rebellion there, and various other municipal projects, repair of banks and waterways, the church and market-cross, and paving the market-place with ragstone; CCRO, P22/5/1, Holy Trinity Churchwardens' Accounts, Cambridge, fos 113v–14r, an inventory of church ornaments made in 1548; fo 115, is torn out – perhaps it recorded their sale. Entries begin again on fo 116v in 1556 and are sporadic until the volume ends on fo 126 in 1558; CCRO, P11/5/1–2, Bassingbourne Churchwardens' Accounts end in 1540. This lack of entries for the period c.1540–60 is typical of Churchwardens' Accounts of this time.

19 A.N. Galpern, *The Religions of the People in Sixteenth Century Champagne*, Cambridge, Massachusetts, 1976; Haigh, *Reformation and Resistance*, ch. 9.

20 P. Vrijhof and J. Waardenburg, *Official and Popular Religion: Analysis of a theme for Religious Studies*, The Hague 1979.

21 J.R.H. Moorman, *Church Life in England in the Thirteenth Century*, Oxford 1945; W.A. Pantin, *The English Church in the Fourteenth Century*, Cambridge 1955; R.N. Swanson, *Church and Society in Late Medieval England*, Oxford 1989. These books focus largely on ecclesiastical structure, the following on religious practice: J. Toussaert, *Le Sentiment Religieux En Flandre A La Fin du Moyen Age*, Paris 1963; P. Adam, *La Vie Paroissale en France au XIV Siècle*, Paris 1964; D.M. Owen, *Church and Society in Medieval Lincolnshire*, Lincoln 1971; N. Tanner, *The Church in Late Medieval Norwich 1370–1532*, Toronto 1984.

long-term context that the Reformation must be viewed. However, this must not ignore the complex interplay between the two estates, nor the often tortuous paths of ideas which lead ultimately to change.

It is unclear, for example, whether the laity's responsibility for the provision of liturgical ornaments, books and vestments, and repair of parish churches, was enforced by the ecclesiastical hierarchy, or had developed out of their own desire to make gifts to God and his saints. Nevertheless, this obligation was shifted from priests to people by the fourth Lateran Council in 1215. Thereafter as part of Canon or Church Law it was ratified throughout Europe in diocesan legislation.[22] Dr Emma Mason argues that, while church upkeep placed an increased burden on the parishioners, paradoxically it increased their consultation in religious matters. During the course of the thirteenth century, references to the office of churchwarden and to an increasing number of fraternities suggest the development of strategies for organising these responsibilities.[23]

The aristocracy continued to seek commemoration through lavish gifts to the Church. By the end of the thirteenth century the advowsons of between a third and a half of all English parish churches had been given to monasteries. This process continued until the eve of their dissolution.[24] The appropriation of such revenues by the monasteries, and the substitution of a poorly-paid chaplain or vicar for the rector, placed an additional burden on the laity: that of making decent provision for the sacraments and rituals of the church in their parishes. This is one of the keys to understanding the growing numbers of chantries and gilds in the later Middle Ages. It was an act of piety, indeed of spiritual necessity where local arrangements were particularly inadequate, to make provision for the increase of divine service.[25]

Toulmin Smith's marginalisation of the gilds' role in religious life and Westlake's emphasis on their commemorative function have obscured the importance of their contribution to the English medieval church.[26] The writ which initiated the survey of 1388–9 asked 'as to the manner and form and authority of the foundation, beginning and continuance and governance of

22 *Councils and Synods: with other Documents Relating to the English Church*, ed. F.M. Powicke and C.R. Cheney, Oxford 1964, Part II, 1205–1313; *Vetus Liber Archidiaconi Eliensis*, ed. Rev. C.L. Feltoe, *Publns Camb. Antiq. Soc.* xlviii, Cambridge 1917; C. Platt, *The Parish Churches of Medieval England*, London 1981, ch. 2.

23 E. Mason, 'The Role of the English Parishioner 1100–1500', *JEH* xxvii, 1976, 17–29. She does not mention fraternities in this context.

24 Moorman, *Church Life in England*, 24, 42, says half were appropriated; Harper-Bill, *The Pre-Reformation Church*, 45, says over one-third.

25 Moorman, *Church Life in England*, ch. 2, chapels, chantries and collegiate churches grew in number in the 13th century; C. Burgess, 'For the Increase of Divine Service: Chantries in the Parish in Late Medieval Bristol', *JEH* xxxvi, 1985, 46–65, esp. 59–60 stresses the contribution of chantry priests to the parish church and its worship.

26 Toulmin Smith, xxviii–xxix; Westlake, esp. 9–10.

the gilds and brotherhoods aforesaid'.[27] All but 13 (78%) Cambridgeshire certificates included a summary of their reasons for foundation or continuing purposes. Thirty-two (53%) expressed their devotion to the saint or that aspect of the Trinity to which they were dedicated, as their prime motivation for existence. Fifteen (25%) said they provided lights; 12 (20%) wanted to increase religious devotion or divine worship; 8 (13%) existed for the glory of God; and 11 (18%) to repair church fabric and contents. Other motivations were general deeds of charity (8), assistance for the souls of the dead (7), the maintenance of a chaplain (6), the election of officers (5), the revival of former devotions (3), and the relief of the poor (2). Paul Adam identified the fraternities as the vehicle for revitalising French parish life, after a low point had been reached in the thirteenth and early fourteenth centuries.[28] As their contribution to parish life makes clear, the English gilds of the two centuries before the Reformation were essentially conservative institutions, composed of the *homines prudentes* of their day.[29] They are to be located at the centre of the spectrum of religious enthusiasm, between the two extremes of mystical devotional fervour and heretical Lollard and later Protestant belief. Theirs was the safe middle ground of a religion of good works which obscures any evidence of individual faith.

There are a number of aspects of late medieval devotion which it is difficult to distinguish one from another in the documents. These are lights, images, altars, chapels and gilds. This is at first disconcerting, but in fact reflects contemporary confusion between these things.[30] Lights were kept burning before the images of saints in a church. Sometimes there was an altar before the image, upon which the lights burned. Occasionally the image was housed in a chapel of its own, either a side-chapel in a parish church, a separate structure standing in the churchyard, or a free-chapel some distance away. A light needed maintaining, as did an altar with its various furnishings, altar cloths, vestments and ritual objects, and the fabric of a chapel had to be kept in good repair. The parish gilds and similar but smaller organisations known as lights, provided the administrative framework for these devotions.[31]

There are chance references to gilds and lights in churchwardens' accounts where the parish functioned as an 'umbrella institution' to these smaller bodies which existed in parallel. Their officers, named *custos* or warden like

27 Toulmin Smith, 127–8.

28 Adam, *La Vie Paroissale*, Introduction by G. Le Bras, 1–2; Conclusion, 315–17.

29 B.A. Hanawalt and B. McRee, 'The Guilds of "Homo Prudens" in Late Medieval England', *Continuity and Change* vii, 1992, 163–79, esp. 169–71.

30 Palmer, ch. 4; Owen, *Church and Society*, ch. 8; Scarisbrick, *The Reformation*, 24–27; J. Mattingley, 'The Medieval Parish Gilds of Cornwall', *Journal of the Royal Institution of Cornwall*, new series x, 1989, 290–329.

31 See ch. 6 for details of their administration and the relation of these groups to the parish; C.M. Barron and J. Roscoe, 'The Medieval Parish of St Andrew Holborn: Light Wardens' Accounts 1477–8', in *London Topographical Record*, ed. A.L. Saunders, xxix, 1980, 55–59.

parish officers,[32] also gave annual accounts to their members during their terms of office, of which written notes recorded the original public act. They, too, like churchwardens used donations and bequests of land, animals, grain and wax for the upkeep of the various devotions for which they were responsible.

The benefaction of wealthy medieval patrons is emphasised to the present day. Their monuments adorn the interiors of churches and their substantial contributions are commemorated in guide books. The church of Saints Peter and Paul, Bassingbourne, received a Mass Book from Parson Goldeborne, the fourteenth parson, and several gifts, including devotional books and silverware from local gentry, Robert and Katherine Bolnest.[33] However, it must not be forgotten that such endeavours were part of a pattern of collective benefaction. Alongside these entries in the 1498 inventory of Bassingbourne's parish goods were recorded the gifts of a *cowcher* or antiphoner, and a processionary both 'of the gift of the whole parish'.[34] There are two lists at the back of the same accounts, dated 1497 and 1499, when money was raised for repairs to the church bells and for a new bell. Donations, probably levied as a parish rate on households, ranged from 40*s* paid by Master Richard Lynn, gentleman, to 4*d*.[35] Wealthy benefactors often put forward large sums to initiate a project. Money from smaller gifts and bequests and parish fund-raising efforts were then accumulated by churchwardens until work was able to begin. In 1540, Thomas Cause of Haslingfield left the large sum of £6 13*s* 4*d* to the church 'on condition that the township go forward with the repairs of the said church within the space of six years'.[36] Gilds, lights and other groups within the community, the wives, single men and the like, also donated substantial sums of money to collective enterprises. Holy Trinity Church, Cambridge, undertook the expensive process of erecting an image of St George. Alongside other benefactors, the gild of St George gave £1 8*s* 2½*d* from gild money, out of a sum totalling £6 12*s* ½*d* in 1506–7.[37]

The information in the 1389 returns presents the gilds or fraternities primarily in isolation rather than placing them within the context of the parish. However, some details of gild contributions to parish life are included. The eleven gilds of Bottisham and Swaffham Bulbeck were founded out of the devotion of the parishioners 'ex devocione parochianorum'.[38] Six fraternities assisted with the repair of their church roofs, and each year at Stowe Cum Quye, the warden of St John the Baptist's Gild donated the residue after the accounts had been settled, to the fabric and works of the church, 'ad

32 W.E. Tate, *The Parish Chest*, Cambridge 1951, 83 discussion of this name.
33 CCRO, P11/5/1–2, vol. 1, fos 1v, 2r.
34 CCRO, P11/5/1–5, vol. 1, fo 2r.
35 CCRO, P11/5/1–2, vol. 2, fos 76v, 77r; Tate, *The Parish Chest*, 92–93 church rates.
36 ECC (1/5/2), 1540 will of Thomas Cause.
37 CCRO, P22/5/1, fo 17r.
38 PRO, C47/38/3(1–7); 33(1–4).

fabricium et opus ecclesie predicte fideliter per custodem distribuatur'.[39] The gild of the Resurrection, Chesterton, had given money for particular projects:

> The Alderman, brothers and sisters had given, out of the goods of the gild collected for God . . . £10 for building a new [Easter] sepulchre, £11 for building a bell tower, and £18 to help buy two bells for the church.[40]

The 1389 Return for St John the Baptist's Fraternity, Wisbech, indicates the similarities between the administration of specific devotions by gild wardens and the more general responsibilities of the churchwardens. A list of expenses appended to the statutes reads like an extract from a set of churchwardens' accounts. Since 1384 when the gild was founded, a total of £86 6*s* had been spent on the upkeep of a chapel attached to the church of Saints Peter and Paul; on building work, the purchase and repair of ornaments, images, vestments, maintenance of lights, and the salary of a priest.[41] On the first page of the register of the gild of the Holy Trinity, the most important gild in Wisbech, written in 1379, are recorded expenses for the repositioning of a 'parclose' or wooden screen partitioning off a private chapel within the body of the church.[42] There are also expenses for the making of an image and a tabernacle.

The two sets of Wisbech gild expenses coincide with the culmination of a phase of extensive re-building work in the later fourteenth century. This left the church of Saints Peter and Paul with a double nave, one of only two in the country. Walker and Craddock, two local historians, wrote in 1849: 'An unpolished taste prevails over every part of the building, which seems as if it had been put together by unskilled workmen out of the second-hand fragments of various churches.'[43] This unfortunate structure can only be explained by the various contributions of wealthy gilds, who undertook to enlarge the overall building so that their private enclosures within it could be more substantial. In 1389 there are records of six gilds or fraternities associated with this church, and a further four are subsequently known to have existed. The Holy Trinity Gild is associated with the room above the church porch, built around this time. This was probably the dwelling-place of the gild priests, and where they later held the grammar school administered by the gild. It also built a large chapel onto the south side of the chancel in about 1500, probably to house the mass of Our Lady, a new devotion sponsored by

39 PRO, C47/38/30.
40 PRO, C47/38/13.
41 PRO, C47/38/39.
42 WCR1, p. 1; the Sprynge Parclose at Lavenham, Suffolk, is one of the finest existing examples: for a picture see Duffy, *The Stripping of the Altars*, plate 52.
43 Quoted in Canon A. Nicholas, *St Peter and St Paul, Wisbech*, Wisbech 1988, 2; *VCH Cambs*. iv, 247–50; N. Pevsner, *The Buildings of England: Cambridgeshire*, Harmondsworth 1970, 494–7.

the gild.[44] The fifteenth-century wave of church building, generally with more harmonious results, to which we owe so much of our architectural heritage, must be linked with the desire of gilds, lights, crafts, families, chantries and other groups of laity to have their own altars within their parish churches.[45] They were, in a sense, renting a part of the church in return for contributions towards repair, for example of the roof above their particular space. Elsewhere, as the will of Thomas Jecson, 'capellanus ac custos Capelle Sancte Trinitatis in Walsoken iuxta Stathedich',[46] illustrates, certain gilds undertook entire administrative responsibility for outlying chapels. A gild dedicated to the Trinity administered this particular chapel in the fens between Cambridgeshire and Norfolk.

There is a similarity between wills and the gild certificates of 1389 as source material: they are snapshots taken by those in authority, and as such do not provide a chronological perspective. However, one Cambridgeshire certificate is unusual in that it gives evidence of change over time. The Resurrection Fraternity, Chesterton, was said to have been founded in 1336, although its customs dated back to a time without memory, 'a tempore quo non extat memoria'.[47] When it was first begun 'in prima fundacione' by the young men and women of the town it was a fairly simple organisation, collecting grain to fund its purposes, each member giving what they liked. The plague did not curtail gild activities, rather it enhanced them. Around the time of the first pestilence, 'circa primam pestilenciam', eighteen acres of land came into its possession, held in 1389 by fine and court roll. The gild had until recently brewed ale, presumably for fund-raising, but did so no more because the equipment was too worn out to be mended. After the passage of time, 'postea vero processu tempore', the gild seems to have become established on a more formal basis with a substantial entry fee of 5*s* In the sixteenth century, known as the 'Great Gild', it played a prominent role in the life of the town.[48] The 1389 statutes recite fairly standard functions including a solemn procession and mass in honour of the Resurrection; lights in the church at feast days and at the funerals of brethren; the hiring of a chaplain from time to time, and the annual election of officers. Like the company dedicated to St Christopher at March, which was described variously in its accounts as either a light or a gild,[49] the Resurrection Fraternity at Chesterton modified its functions over the course of time, illustrating the

44 PRO, Prob 11/15/5, fos 40r and v, 1505 will of William Gaytsend. He left 73 acres of land to fund a priest to sing Our Lady mass in Our Lady Chapel, to be administered by the Trinity Gild; Prob 11/20/8, fos 55v, 56r and v, 1520 will of Robert Smythe. He left 79½ acres to the Holy Trinity Gild to support the same devotion.

45 Platt, *The Parish Churches*, 116.

46 PRO, Prob 11/6/20, fos 148r, v, 1475 will of Thomas Jecson; see ch. 6 for details of the relationship between gilds and chapels.

47 PRO, C47/38/13.

48 PRO, Prob 11/22/8, fo 64v, 1526 will of John Gardyner of Chesterton.

49 CCRO, P116/1/4, pp. 131–7.

fluidity between gild, light and young person's group within the parish context. The certificate of the Resurrection Gild is immensely rich in detail. Its metamorphosis reflects the increased economic opportunities open to the upper strata of the late medieval English peasantry, and their increased contributions through the gilds and other groups to parish religious life.

The Laity and Devotional Practice

The provision of images, paintings and liturgical ornaments are indivisible from drama, processions and liturgical ritual. They are all part of the story the community tells about itself, the embodiment of memory in collective life.[50] Individuals and communities were part of emotional and economic networks which stretched beyond parish boundaries. Annis Laci left 20*s* to the church of St Andrew, Barnwell, where she was to be buried next to her husband; 10*s* to the church where she was born; and 5*s* to St Andrew's Church, Cambridge.[51] John Skyphon of Ely left 6*s* 8*d* to the gild of St George at Lynn in Norfolk.[52] The church at Bassingbourne, the market town for the surrounding area, hosted a play of St George in 1513 in which all the neighbouring villages participated.[53] Thus the relationships of individuals and groups were affirmed through devotional practice.

The physical environment too was sacralised by crosses and chapels along route-ways. Unlike the compact villages of the shire of Cambridge, the vast fenland parishes of the Isle were characterised by sparse and isolated settlement. The fens themselves were laced with a network of free chapels, many located, like St John of Doddyke, on dykes and causeways and associated with their upkeep.[54] Just as the dykes and causeways made it possible to traverse the treacherous fenlands, so the spiritual succour of these reference-points may have comforted both the real and supernatural fears of travellers.

50 N.Z. Davis, 'The Sacred and the Body Social in Sixteenth Century Lyons', *P&P* xc, 1981, 40–70; M. James, 'Ritual, Drama and Social Body in the Late Medieval English Town', *P&P* xcviii, 1983, 3–29; G. McMurray-Gibson, *The Theater of Devotion: East Anglian Drama and Society in the Late Middle Ages*, Chicago 1989.

51 VCC (1/1/30), 1557 will of Annis Laci.

52 ECC HK2791/A/36, fo 14r, 1456 will of John Skyphon.

53 CCRO, P11/5/1–2, vol. 2, fo 30v.

54 See ch. 6 for details of administration of chapels. The chapel of St John of Doddyke was located in the fens between Tydd St Giles, Newton and Leverington. It received bequests from people in all these communities: ECC HK2791/A/82, 1452 will of John Drewe of Newton; ECC HK2791/A/98, 1454 will of Beatrix Edmunde of Leverington; ECC HK2791/A/143, 1454 will of Margareta Derby of Tydde; ECC HK2791/A/188, 1457 will of John Derby of Newton; W.A. Christian, *Local Religion in Sixteenth Century Spain*, Princeton 1981, 91; V. and E. Turner, *Image and Pilgrimage in Christian Culture: Anthropological Perspectives*, New York 1978.

The Cult of the Saints

Etheldreda, a local saint, extended her protection over this area from her shrine in Ely Cathedral. There her body was visited by pilgrims and her shrine attracted benefaction such as the gold rings with precious stones left to her by Margaret Coppefelde and Alicia Messanger.[55] Although it was not a common name there are records of some girls being named after her.[56] Other evidence of the extent of her cult is the dedication of churches to her, at Histon and Linton in the shire, as well as Ely Cathedral and Thetford and Mundham churches in Norfolk.[57] Etheldreda was the subject of veneration by the Gild of *Thegns* in the tenth century; a gild at Holy Sepulchre Church, Cambridge, begun in the thirteenth century; a gild at Holy Trinity Church, Ely, recorded in 1389 but originally founded in 1289; and a gild at St Mary's Church, Ely, mentioned in the will of William Palfreyman in 1490.[58] There were probably more which went unrecorded. Lights too burned in her honour in the fenlands; at the churches and cathedral of Ely; St Andrew's Church, Whittlesey; the churches of Saints Peter and Paul, Wisbech; St Leonard's, Leverington; and one of the two churches of Terrington in Norfolk.[59]

To understand lay people's experience of the cult of the saints, it is necessary to accept their belief in the supernatural. William Christian in his important book, *Local Religion in Sixteenth Century Spain*, argues against the sceptical approach, initiated by the Humanists and Reformers, to the 'magical' or 'superstititious' nature of local religion.[60] Eamon Duffy's concern to refute

55 ECC HK2791/A/107, fo 38r, 1454 will of Margaret Coppefelde; ECC HK2791/A/205, fos 58r and v, 1457 will of Alicia Messanger.

56 Bateson, 27, Thomas de Badburgham and his wife Etheldreda entered the fraternity of Corpus Christi, Cambridge, in 1350; ECC HK2791/A/208, fos 59r and v, 1458 will of Richard Pulfryman: his daughter was called Etheldreda.

57 Palmer, 393 Histon St Etheldreda, cites the 1519 will of Thomas Raynes; ECC (1/2/13), 1521 will of Kateryn Ward, Linton St Audrey (a derivation of Etheldreda); F. Arnold-Forster, *Studies in Church Dedications, or England's Patron Saints*, 3 vols, London 1899, ii, 368–9 Thetford and Mundham dedications.

58 Thorpe, *Diplomatarium Anglicum Aevi Saxonici*, London 1865, 605–17; *EHD* i, ed. D. Whitelock, 2nd edn, London 1979, 603, gild of *Thegns*; *VCH Cambs*. iii, 124, 13th-century gild of St Etheldreda; PRO, C47/38/23(2), Ely Holy Trinity Church Gild of St Etheldreda; PRO, Prob 11/9/18 fos 140r and v, 1490 will of William Palfrayman.

59 PRO, C47/38/23(2), Holy Trinity Church, St Etheldreda's Gild; *VCH Cambs*. iv, 146, 1335 lamps to St Peter and Etheldreda in the cathedral; ECC HK2791/A/115, fo 39v, 1454 will of Margareta Reynalde who left 2*d* to the light of St Etheldreda, St Andrew's Church, Whittelsea; ECC HK2791/A/75, fos 23r–24v, 1452 will of Walter Rokeland left 4*d* to St Etheldreda's lamp in the church of Saints Peter and Paul, Wisbech; ECC HK2791/A/98, fo 35v, 1454 will of Beatrix, wife of Robert Edmunde, who left 2*d* to St Etheldreda's light, St Leonard's Church, Leverington; ECC HK2791/A/96, fos 34r–35r, 1454 will of Alicia Masse, wife of John Masse, alderman of Holy Trinity Gild, Wisbech, who left 6*d* to St Etheldreda's light at Terrington.

60 Christian, *Local Religion*, Introduction, esp. 4; Whiting, *The Blind Devotion of the People*, ch. 4.

the charge of 'superstitition' and to argue instead for the 'reasonableness' of late medieval Catholicism, and his emphasis through his use of sources on a late and literate piety, places too little stress on people's awe at the supernatural, and the subterranean and irrational elements incorporated within medieval christianity. These elements were at the core of its vitality and are well-described by Keith Thomas, after they had been outlawed from the early modern church.[61]

The saints to which men and women were attached by namesake, personal devotion and group cult, were their patrons in the supernatural realm, and they the clients.[62] Many testators bequeathed their souls to Almighty God, the Blessed Virgin Mary and the Holy Company of Heaven. The Virgin was the Queen and the Holy Company of Heaven were the feudal courtiers of the Celestial Being, who, with persistent supplication, would press the suits of their vassals. William Christian identifies three main phases of devotion in Castile.[63] Prior to the eleventh century, the veneration of saints was almost entirely associated with the relics of local holy men and women. This may be seen in Cambridgeshire in early gild dedications to St Etheldreda and to St Edward the Saxon boy-king and martyr.[64] The cult of East Anglian Saxon saints continued until the Reformation, a reminder of loyalty to the Saxon cause which had lingered locally after the Norman conquest, when the Isle of Ely had been a stronghold of Saxon resistance. The cult of St Etheldreda was still strong and in the sixteenth century gilds existed, dedicated to her two sisters St Sexburga and St Withburga and to St Ethelnoth, a pre-Conquest archbishop of Canterbury.[65] St Wendreda, foundress of a nunnery at March, lay in a sumptuous chapel there, to which her body had been translated by the gild dedicated to her. However, her cult does not seem to have extended beyond the location of her corpse.[66] There are no further references to the cult of St Pandwyonia, a royal virgin, after her body had been translated to the church at Eltisley in 1344. The church was later dedicated to Saints

61 Duffy, *The Stripping of the Altars*, 277 argues against Thomas; K. Thomas, *Religion and the Decline of Magic: Studies in Popular Beliefs in Sixteenth Century England*, London 1971.

62 R.F.E. Weissman, *Ritual Brotherhood in Renaissance Florence*, New York 1982, 47.

63 Christian, *Local Religion*, 20–21; M. Flynn, *Sacred Charity: Confraternities and Social Welfare in Spain 1400–1700*, London 1989, 27–30 confirms this picture.

64 *VCH Cambs*. iii, 128, 134; Arnold-Forster, *Studies in Church Dedications* ii, 335–8 St Edward.

65 *VCH Cambs*. iv, 86 mentions gilds to St Sexburga and St Withburga in 1516–17; Palmer, 395, cites the 1520 will of Alice Hethe which mentions the gild of St Wyburgh at Melbourne; Arnold-Forster, *Studies in Church Dedications* ii, ch. xl, esp. 363–71, 'The East Anglian Saints'; Palmer, 388, 1528 cites the will of John Sygar which mentions the gild of St Ethelnoth at Cottenham All Saint's Church.

66 PRO, C47/38/27; PRO, Prob 11/25/1, fos 202r and v, 1498 will of Richard Sapcote of March, left a close to his wife, and then after her death to the gild of St Wenefrida (sic); Arnold-Forster, *Studies in Church Dedications* ii, 371, 421–3.

Pandwyonia and John the Baptist.[67] This illustrates the second phase of devotion in which the veneration of local saints was supplemented, and often superseded by veneration of 'universal' saints, particularly the Virgin Mary. This process was assisted by the introduction of images which, alongside relics, began to be venerated in the eleventh and twelfth centuries.

A third phase created new relationships between communities and saints with specific intercessory powers, such as Saints Clement and Erasmus, patrons of ships and sailors, popular in this area of busy waterways.[68] Such relations were confirmed by the dedication of chapels and gilds and by collective celebration of new feast days. Often the original inspiration for a cult had been forgotten, or the saint had failed to provide the expected protection, and thus the dedication of the parish church was changed to honour the new patron.[69] This occurred for example at Littleport. In 1389 its church was dedicated to St Andrew. By the sixteenth century its patron was St George to whom a gild had already been dedicated in 1389.[70] In addition to the saints, gilds and fraternities were also dedicated to the Trinity and aspects of Christ's life and passion.

The pattern of gild dedication gives some indication of the popularity of particular devotions over the course of time. Six fraternities are known to have existed in Cambridgeshire prior to 1300. Three were dedicated to St Etheldreda; one to St Edward, king and martyr, and St Thomas, archbishop and martyr, presumably the latter representing a later devotion undertaken by the same gild; one to the Virgin Mary; and one to the Holy Sepulchre.[71] Thereafter the period between c.1300 and 1547 is generally one of homogeneity. Out of the overall number of 350 Cambridgeshire gilds or fraternities, 69 (20%) were dedicated to the cycle of feasts of the Virgin Mary; 55 (16%) to feasts associated with the events of Christ's passion culminating with Corpus Christi. Here the earliest of eight gilds dedicated to Jesus, representing

67 *VCH Cambs.* v, 57–58; Arnold-Forster, *Studies in Church Dedications* ii, 163.

68 BL, Add Mss. 5846, pp. 5–13, 1431 statutes of St Clement's Gild, St Clement's Church, Cambridge; ECC HK2791/A/56, fos 18r and v, c.1450s will of Clara Renlyn of Emneth left 20*d* to St Clement's Gild, Outwell, Norfolk; *VCH Cambs.* iii, 125, in 1504 there was a gild of St Clement, Holy Trinity Church, Cambridge; ECC HK2791/A/146, fo 45r, 1454 will of Walter Kokere, left 2*d* to the light of St Erasmus in Wisbech, church of Saints Peter and Paul; ECC HK2791/A/163, fo 48v, 1457 will of John Stegge left 1*d* to St Erasmus' light at Elm, All Saints' Church; ECC HK2791/A/181, fo 53r and v, 1457 will of William Adam left 2*d* to the same.

69 CCRO, P22/5/1, St Erasmus' light is mentioned throughout Holy Trinity, Cambridge Churchwardens' Accounts; W.A. Christian, *Apparitions in Late Medieval and Renaissance Spain 1399–1523*, Princeton 1981.

70 PRO, C47/38/26(1–4), dedicated to St Andrew the Apostle; *VCH Cambs.* iv, 100 dedicated to St George.

71 *VCH Cambs.* ii, 287, St Mary's Gild, Holy Sepulchre Church, Cambridge; iii, 124, Holy Sepulchre Gild, Holy Sepulchre Church, Cambridge; iii, 128, 134 gild of St Edward the King and St Thomas the Martyr at the church of St Edward, King and Martyr, Cambridge.

the new devotion to the Holy Name was founded only in 1512.[72] Thirty-four (10%) were dedicated to the Trinity; 33 (9%) to St Katherine; 31 (6%) to St John (17 to St John the Baptist, 14 unspecified); 25 (7%) to All Saints; and 15 (4%) to St Peter. The popularity of these devotions was spread evenly throughout the time period. The greatly increased number of wills available from 1450 reveals a far wider range of saints venerated, although 46 (13%) were venerated by between one and four fraternities only.[73] Among those whose veneration seems to have become more popular in the fifteenth century was St Anne, the Virgin Mary's mother, patron of 10 (3%) gilds.

Altogether ten martyr saints, six men and four women, were patrons of 84 (24%) gilds.[74] Their shocking tortures may have brought some comfort to men and women experiencing similarly horrific death beds. Their lurid images adorning churches probably had more to do with fear of bodily mutilation and corruption, which in a society without the sophisticated medical care of the late twentieth century often began long before death. Hermit saints were popular in the inhospitable terrain of the fens, where a number of hermits made their dwellings and may have initiated such devotions. St Giles was patron of three gilds: at Tydd St Giles Church; All Saints' Church, Elm; and St Giles's Church, Cambridge;[75] St Leonard of one gild in St Leonard's Church, Downham, and also patron of the church at Leverington;[76] St Anthony was venerated by one gild at Elm.[77]

Cambridge as a centre of learning might have been expected to host new devotions, or more obscure or academic saints. This was not the case, however, as fraternities were primarily lay institutions and cultural diffusion occurred through many channels.

72 Palmer, 391; *VCH Cambs*. viii, 108, the Brotherhood of Jesus was being founded at Guilden Morden in 1512; R.W. Pfaff, *New Liturgical Feasts in Later Medieval England*, Oxford 1970.

73 Flynn, *Sacred Charity*, 30 confirms this pattern.

74 Saints John the Baptist, Thomas of Canterbury, Clement, Lawrence, Stephen, Edward, Katherine, Margaret, Ursula, Agnes.

75 PRO, C47/38/35, gild of St Giles, St Giles's Church, Tydd; Palmer, 389, St Giles's Gild, All Saints' Church, Elm, 1456; W.M. Palmer, 'Fifteenth Century Visitation Records of the Deanery of Wisbech', *Proc. Camb. Antiq. Soc*. xxxix, 1938–9, 69–75, esp. 73, in 1463 John Dodenet owed St Giles Gild, Elm, 6*d*; ECC HK2791/A/246, fos 68v–69r, 1459 will of Adam Stephenson left 2*s* to St Giles's Gild, Elm; *VCH Cambs*. iii, 135, St Giles's Gild, St Giles's Church, Cambridge; ECC (2/2/24), 1544 will of Edward Tompson, burgess and storeman, possibly refers to St Giles's Gild, St Giles Church, Cambridge.

76 *VCH Cambs*. iv, 93, 100, gild of St Mary and St Leonard, Downham; Palmer, 389, this seems to have been the most important gild in Downham, documented through a number of wills 1455–1525; ECC HK2791/A/38, fo 14v, 1455 will of Simon Jacobs, left 12*d* to the gild; PRO, Prob 11/22/1, fo 3r, 1525 will of Thomas Dunstabell of Ely, left a caser and a cow; J.J. Muskett, 'Cambridgeshire Church Goods', *East Anglian N. & Q*. new series ix, 1901–2, 312, lists 26*s* 8*d* worth of goods, assessed by the Edwardian Commissioners; *VCH Cambs*. iv, 195, Leverington Church dedication to St Leonard.

77 Palmer, 389, St Anthony's Gild, Elm.

The cults of the saints and other significant devotions were linked to cosmology by the cycle of the seasons. The two dominant cycles, the feasts of the solar year leading up to Christ's birth, and the movable feasts of the lunar year culminating in Christ's death and resurrection at Easter, were supplemented by the two cycles of the feasts of the Virgin Mary, and of the obligatory saints' days.[78] As the evidence of the Cambridgeshire sample illustrates, many gilds were founded as financial and administrative structures to augment parish ceremonial at the high feasts. Charles Phythian-Adams divides the year into two halves, the ritual half from December to midsummer containing the major feasts of the solar and lunar cycles, and the secular half from midsummer to December.[79] Then, in a good year, surpluses from the harvest enabled men and women to relax a little and to celebrate the benefaction of their patrons. Cambridgeshire gilds were dedicated to a total of forty-two patrons or feasts. Aside from those of Christ or the Virgin, twenty-nine feast days of the thirty-two patron saints fell into this second half of the year. They were mostly clustered around the feast of St John the Baptist at the solstice on 24 June, in July and August, and in another cluster around All Saints'-tide in November.

The celebration of the patronal festival was an occasion for thanksgiving and for appeasement and supplication of the deity and the saints: also for collective ritual, both religious and secular, affirming corporate identity. The gild of the Nativity of the Blessed Virgin at Stretham was typical in the way it honoured its patronal festival.[80]

> All the Brothers and Sisters of the Fraternity are to gather in the church on the feast of the Nativity of the Blessed Mary; and the Priest is to celebrate a certain solemn Mass to God for them; and the Warden of the Fraternity is to offer 1*d*. for the living and the dead to the same Chaplain, and each Brother and sister, a farthing: And if any member is in town in good health, and does not come to the church, he shall give to the maintenance of the light, one pound of wax.

Non-attendance was punished by fines by 8 (13%) gilds whose Statutes are extant from 1389, and by the three whose Statutes are extant from the fifteenth century. Additional features included vespers on the evening before the feast day; the canonical hours; matins; requiem mass; and vespers on the day itself. The company processed to the church in their best clothing, the richer gilds in livery;[81] held annual meetings for the election of officers and

78 Toussaert, *Le Sentiment Religieuse En Flandre*, part 2, ch. 3, 'Les Devotions Collectives' describes these various liturgical cycles; H. Hörger, 'Organisational Forms of Popular Piety in Rural Old Bavaria, Sixteenth to Nineteenth Centuries', in *Religion and Society in Early Modern Europe 1500–1800*, ed. C. Von Greyerz, London 1984, 212–22.

79 C. Phythian-Adams, *Local History and Folklore: A New Framework*, London 1975, 20–24.

80 PRO, C47/38/32.

81 PRO, C47/38/6, 7, 10, 11, Cambridge Gild Statutes mentioning livery; C47/38/39, 40,

the presentation of accounts; and in the good years, enjoyed the conviviality of feasting and drinking together.

The dedication of gilds is only one indicator of the popularity of the saints in the later Middle Ages. Out of sixty-six chantries documented by this survey, 27 (42%) were known to have borne a dedication to a saint.[82] Sixteen were dedicated to the Virgin Mary for her supreme intercessory power; four to the Trinity; two to St Nicholas, and one each to St Andrew, St Catherine, St Martin and St Stephen. The latter few were probably so named because of a special relationship between the founder and the saint. There seems also to have been a 'second rank' of saints whose powers were too specific to have been considered suitable for church, gild or chantry dedication. This included St Appolonia, virgin and martyr, guardian against toothache, for whom lights burned in the church of Saints Peter and Paul, Wisbech and St Leonard's Church, Leverington.[83]

Religious Imagery

Gilds and lights were a means by which lay men and women were able to adorn the interiors of their churches and chapels. The overall effect is hard to judge as it has been progressively erased over the course of time: first by the cessation of the ritual purposes for which the interiors were intended; by progressive waves of Protestant iconoclasm in the sixteenth and seventeenth centuries, manifested in the whitewashing of wall paintings and the sale and destruction of images; and also by alterations in architectural style and taste which later functions and fashions required. Patterns of imagery may be reconstructed from inventories compiled by churchwardens. These exist for the period prior to the Reformation for only a tiny proportion of parishes, but wills, too, through intended bequests to images, altars and lights, describe the interiors of other churches.

Bassingbourne churchwardens' accounts supply a composite picture of the inside of the church of Saints Peter and Paul over the period c.1498–1530. There was a canopy above the sacrament on the high altar and painted sanctuary curtains; a Lady Chapel with an image and an Easter Sepulchre;[84] altars to the Virgin Mary, St John and other unspecified saints; lights to St

42, Wisbech Gilds mentioning livery, the latter two wore gild caps; WCR1, The Register of Holy Trinity Gild, Wisbech mentions cloth purchased to make livery; 15th-century Cambridge Statutes order Brethren to attend in their best clothing.

82 See ch. 4 for further details on Chantries.

83 ECC HK2791/A/202, fo 57v, 1458 will of Emma, wife of William Belman, St Apollonia of Wisbech; ECC HK2791/A/98, fo 35v, 1454 will of Beatrix, wife of Robert Edmunde, St Appolline of Leverington.

84 J.C. Cox and A. Harvey, *English Church Furniture*, London 1907, 74–78 Easter Sepulchres.

Mary, St Nicholas, at the rood, the chancel and at the Easter sepulchre; carved images of the High Crucifix, the Salvation of Our Lady and Holy Sunday, St Mary, St John, St Christopher, and St George and the king and queen; images of St James, St Margaret, St Katherine and St Mary and St John the Evangelist on the rood loft, all with tabernacles, or canopies; and the apostles painted on cloth over the rood screen. In addition there were other items used on special occasions together with vestments and altar-hangings of various colours and embroidered symbols. In 1643 William Dowsing, a puritan in charge of removing the surviving remains of popery in East Anglia, found it necessary to destroy eight superstitious pictures in the chancel, forty in the church, one brass inscription requesting prayers for the dead, and a cross and the sceptre, which still remained.[85]

On the evidence of fifteen wills from the 1450s, Elm church at this time was indeed the church of All Saints. The large medieval building had room for a chapel of St Giles; altars to St Mary, St Katherine and the Holy Cross; an image of St Mary; and lights, presumably before images or pictures of St Mary, Our Lady of Pity, St Anne, St Katherine, St Anthony, St John the Baptist, St Thomas the martyr, St Giles, St Christopher, All Saints, St Erasmus, St Michael, St James and possibly St Swithin, and before the Holy Cross and the High Crucifix. This was presumably only a proportion of the furnishings of the church, with which gilds of St Mary and All Saints and a gildhall were also associated. The neighbouring churches of Emneth, Leverington, Newton and Tydd St Giles, on this wealthy silt shore of the fens, were similarly adorned. Wisbech as the main town of the region experienced even more lavish benefaction. The acquisition of an image of St George at Bassingbourne in 1520 illustrates the level of investment necessary. Payments for painting, making clothes, a king and queen and other embellishments to the tableau continued until 1527.[86] Meanwhile in 1503–7 an image of St George, possibly associated with the gild of that name, was set up in Holy Trinity Church, Cambridge. In 1514–15 a hearse was purchased, in 1515–16 a canopy and in 1520 a pair of organs: four substantial projects in ten years, supported by the greater wealth of this urban parish.[87]

In 1389, 22 (37%) Cambridgeshire gilds or fraternities for whom returns survive, mentioned images of the saints, crosses and a holy sepulchre, which they had provided. The fraternity of St John the Baptist, Wisbech, also honoured the Trinity, the Virgin Mary, the Apostles Peter and Paul, and All Saints. It funded lights on these feast days and had spent over £10 on images of St John, St Katherine and a crucifix.[88] Fourteen (23%) gilds mentioned

85 J.G. Cheshire, 'William Dowsing's Destructions in Cambridgeshire', *Cambs. & Hunts. Arch. Soc.* iii, 1914, 77–91, 87.

86 CCRO, P11/5/1–2, vol. 2, fos 48r–60v; Arnold-Forster, *Studies in Church Dedications* ii, 464–74, esp. 470 the story of St George.

87 CCRO, P22/5/1, vol. 2, fos 17r, 46r, 48r–49r, 61r–62r.

88 PRO, C47/38/39.

altars, either used solely for their devotions, or shared with other users. Twelve (20%) gilds were associated with chapels, the Assumption Gild, Leverington, having been founded to renovate a picture and a chapel of the Virgin there.[89]

Medieval churches then, were filled with brightly coloured images of the Trinity and the saints. They stood amidst the rich silks and velvets of curtains, canopies, and altar-cloths; their tabernacles were gilded to reflect the lights from lamps, candles and torches. Walls and windows too were painted with religious scenes and symbols. Today we might find the standards of workmanship crude and the overall effect garish, in all but the wealthiest churches. Like classical temples now, we see the medieval parish churches naked, with the paint flaked off and the interior furnishings taken away. To seek a modern parallel, it is necessary to compare them with Orthodox churches, or the temples of various Eastern religions.

The Role of Light in Religion

Light, one of the most powerful of all religious symbols, played a fundamental role in medieval worship. Many different strands of both devotional and social activity constituted a gild: the most important of these was the provision of lights.[90] In 1389, 47 (78%) fraternities provided lights before the images of their patrons to burn perpetually, at feast days, at the elevation of the mass, or at the funerals of brethren. In many statutes this function was the first to be described after the introductory words of the document. The living flame both expressed and inspired devotion through its contribution to worship and emphasis on key moments in the liturgy. It represented the donors in supplication before Christ, the Virgin Mary and the saints,[91] both during their lives and at the hour of their deaths. St Katherine's Fraternity, Chesterton, sustained 'a torch and thirteen votive candles on the altar of St Katherine to burn each feast day'. The Assumption Gild, Leverington 'found five candles or torches to be lit on Sundays and festivals at the elevation of the Body of Christ, and two candles or torches to be lit daily at the antiphon *Salve Regina*'. The aldermen of St Peter's and of Holy Trinity Gilds, Wisbech

> should cause the dean to light all the great candles or torches while prayers were said in the Hall before all the brethren of the gild; and there the chaplain should pray for the souls of the brethren of the gild and all the faithful departed.

89 PRO, C47/38/25.

90 B.A. Hanawalt, 'Keepers of the Light: Late Medieval English Parish Gilds', *Journal of Medieval and Renaissance Studies* xiv, 1984, 21–37.

91 Duffy, *The Stripping of the Altars*, 96.

In Cambridge, the four 40 pound tapers of the Annunciation Gild, Great St Mary's Church, escorted the bodies of their dead to the church for their exequies.[92]

The fact that many subscriptions and penalties laid down in the 1389 and fifteenth-century gild statutes were computed in pounds of wax indicates the need to maintain the supply. The churchwardens' accounts of Holy Trinity Church, Cambridge, illustrate the 'increase', or profit, which lights made for the church by lending out their stock, and those of Bassingbourne list large purchases of wax at Cambridge's Stourbridge Fair. The consumption of wax and other commodities illustrates the role of the church in the local economy.[93]

In her will of 1527 Margaret Everard left between 1½*d* and 2½*d* to the lights of Our Lady, St Anne, the Trinity and St Thomas in Tydd St Giles's Church. In 1528 John London of Burrough bequeathed wax from his bee-hives to burn before the Trinity.[94] Gifts of a few pennies or a quantity of wax involved many thousands of men and women at this basic and modestly affordable level of religious activity. Increasing attacks on the cult of the Saints throughout the 1520s and the ban on lights before their images by the injunctions of 1538 struck at the roots of medieval Catholicism, where it was most broadly based.[95] In Cambridgeshire wills, bequests to Sepulchre lights, rood loft lights and lights before the Blessed Sacrament continued until 1547. Sepulchre lights alone returned in 1556. Holy Trinity churchwardens' accounts for 1556–7 show the church making equivalent income from offerings at quarter-days: the whole devotional economy had changed.[96]

The Role of Sound in Religion

Reinhard Strohm brings the sound of a late medieval city wonderfully to life in his description of *Music in late Medieval Bruges*.[97] Just as church interiors cannot be visualised without reference to their decorations and lights, so it is also necessary to imagine the sounds which filled them; throngs of people; homilies of priests; and the music and voices of liturgy. In East Anglia, as in Bruges, the gilds and fraternities made their contribution. Polyphony or part-singing of the liturgy, referred to as singing 'by note' or 'pricksong', was becoming popular. This reached its artistic peak on the eve of the Reformation. In 1389 two gilds, one in Cambridge and one in Wisbech, had mass

92 PRO, C47/38/14, 25, 41, 43, 44.

93 CCRO, P22/5/1, e.g. fo 100r, 1528–9; P11/5/1–2, vol. 2, e.g. fo 37r, 1514; WCR1, pp. 38, 39; Owen, *Church and Society*, 116–19.

94 ECC (1/2/30), 1527 will of Margaret Everard; ECC (1/3/2), 1528 will of John London.

95 Duffy, *The Stripping of the Altars*, ch. 11, esp. 407.

96 CCRO, P22/5/1, fo 117v.

97 Strohm, *Music in Late Medieval Bruges*, Oxford 1985, esp. ch. 1, Townscape-Soundscape.

'cum nota' on their feast days.[98] In addition, two gilds at Cambridge and one at Tydd St Giles provided sung masses at the funerals of brethren.[99] This may have been more widespread than specified, but was probably concentrated in larger towns where there was more money and more priests. By the late fifteenth century, St Mary's Gild, Boston, Lincolnshire, had ten chaplains, a choir and other junior staff for this purpose.[100] In Wisbech in the 1520s, the Trinity Gild provided a sung mass of Our Lady, anthems to her, and other divine services in the Lady Chapel, possibly the chapel newly built for the gild at the east end of the church. This service together with the hiring of four brotherhood priests, one a schoolmaster, was made possible by substantial chantry benefaction administered by the gild.[101] The schoolboys under their tutor recited daily prayers for the soul of Robert Smythe, and at his anniversary seven priests, the four paid by the brotherhood, the parish priest, and two in addition; six clerks; thirty children; and forty poor men were to sing the *placebo* and *dirige*, and mass for this donor. In this way the gilds and fraternities channelled the surplus wealth of the laity into increasingly elaborate worship on high days and holidays.

The Centrality of the Eucharist

The emphasis of light and sound falls upon the Eucharist, the central devotional rite of late medieval Catholicism and the embodiment of the cosmic drama of salvation.[102] This was a period when men and women focused on the humanity of Christ through the events of his life in the world. Of the 350 Cambridgeshire gilds, spread evenly throughout the period were 55 (16%) gilds dedicated to aspects of Christ's passion and subsequent events; the Holy Cross; Holy Sepulchre; Resurrection; Assumption; Whitsun; Corpus Christi; and the name of Jesus. In addition 34 (10%) were dedicated to the Trinity. The brothers and sisters of Holy Sepulchre Gild, Chatteris, marked Christ's death

> by entering the tomb of the body of Christ, bearing 30 tapers of wax . . . of two pounds in weight . . . to burn from noon on Good Friday to mattins on Easter day, the time of the Resurrection.[103]

98 PRO, C47/38/7, 41.
99 PRO, C47/38/4, 7, 36.
100 Owen, *Church and Society*, 128–30.
101 PRO, Prob 11/20/8, fos 55v–56v, 1520 will of Robert Smythe; Prob 11/20/24, fos 190v–92r, 1521 will of Thomas Wyth, gentleman; C. Burgess, 'For the Increase of Divine Service', 46–65. The Cambridgeshire examples are a useful supplement to Dr Burgess's article, which highlights the contribution of chantry priests to parish liturgy and work. Gilds, too, played an important part in providing extra voices and workers.
102 M. Rubin, *Corpus Christi: The Eucharist in Late Medieval Culture*, Cambridge 1991.
103 PRO, C47/38/12b.

This not only enhanced worship during passion week, but also served as a 'teaching aid', to make the central events of Easter more vivid to participants. The encouragement through such means of a more personalised faith is also found at Wisbech. There the *corpus christi* or body of Christ was treated much like the body of a departed gild brother or sister by the Corpus Christi Gild. As at the funerals of brethren, the gild provided 'a hearse with three candles to burn upon it, around the body of Christ on the occasion of the feast'.[104] Twenty-six (7%) of the 350 fraternities were dedicated to Corpus Christi, the new feast celebrating the Eucharist, instituted in 1264 by Pope Urban IV. From the statutes which survive, these gilds seem to have played an important role in the organisation of the Corpus Christi festival within their towns and villages, and may have been set up especially for that purpose.[105]

The brethren of the Holy Cross Gild, associated with the chapel of Holy Cross by the Sea at Tydd St Giles, provided candles to be lit at the elevation of the mass.[106] This was the most sacred moment: when the bread and wine truly became the body and blood of Christ. In 1389, ten fraternities, not only those dedicated to Christ's passion, venerated the Eucharist in this way and five others arranged for candles to be lit throughout mass, making one quarter of the 1389 sample overall.

Gilds and Priests

Related to Eucharistic piety was the maintenance of chaplains by fraternities. The company could then enjoy the benefits of the mass, the engine of spiritual power, on a frequent basis. The provision of additional priests for the church in which they worshipped was their highest contribution to the increase of divine service. Fifteen (25%) of the 1389 sample were wealthy enough to make such appointments, ten in perpetuity, and a further five at various times, depending on their finances. Furthermore, all fraternities needed to employ priests on certain occasions, such as for masses celebrated on patronal festivals and at the funerals and commemoration of brethren.

The appropriation of parish endowments to monasteries from the thirteenth century, and the inadequate stipends they offered, resulted in poorly qualified parish priests. The increasing thirst for masses for the living and the dead, polyphony and the introduction of parish choirs, suggest a developing religious sophistication among the laity and led to fraternity sponsorship of additional priests. In rural areas this was increasingly common following the Black Death, due to greater disposable wealth among the upper peasantry.

104 PRO, C47/38/38.
105 M. Rubin, 'Corpus Christi Fraternities and Late Medieval Piety', *SCH* xxxiii, 1986, 97–109, esp. 104.
106 PRO, C47/38/34.

Their contribution to general parish duties was recognised by the chantry commissioners in their 1540s surveys of parish life.[107] After the dissolutions of the 1530s, the gentry regained the right of presentation to many livings, which had been granted by their distant ancestors to the monasteries. However, this change has tended to obscure the considerable control which lower ranks of laity had exercised collectively over the appointment of priests in the later Middle Ages.[108]

The 'clerical proletariat' of unbeneficed clergy provided a large pool of labour on which to draw.[109] The clerical poll tax of 1379 recorded 295 unbeneficed priests and clerks living in 102 of the 172 towns and villages of Cambridgeshire.[110] The patent rolls licensed the wealthiest fraternities in England's towns to hold endowments of lands for chaplains' salaries.[111] The clerical poll tax evidence makes clear that even in rural areas the laity were supporting chaplains by a variety of means. It is also clear that the gild returns of 1389 omit or conceal the extent of their patronage of priests, perhaps to conceal their wealth. For example, in 1379 a rector, four chaplains and two members of the Bishop of Ely's household were resident at Bottisham, a medium sized village in the shire.[112] The manorial court rolls which survive for 1386–90 recorded one vicar and seven chaplains.[113] Seven gilds made returns in 1389 on the same piece of parchment.[114] Although none mentioned chaplains, priests were certainly involved in these fraternities. Robert Aleyn and Reginald Leverington, both members of the Bishop's household, who held stock for the gild of the Assumption of the Virgin, were identified as priests by the Court Rolls.[115]

Unlike the south, in northern Europe fraternities were not generally associated with houses of friars: thus their relations were with secular rather than regular clergy.[116] The 1389 survey shows that priests performed a variety of

107 A. Kreider, *English Chantries: The Road to Dissolution*, Cambridge, Massachusetts, 1979, 43–54.

108 K.L. Wood-Leigh, *Perpetual Chantries in Britain*, Cambridge 1965, 314.

109 A. McHardy, *The Church in London*, London Record Society, xiii, London 1977, ix–xv; A. McHardy, 'Careers and Disappointments in the Late Medieval Church: some English Evidence', *SCH* xxvi, 1989, 111–30.

110 'A List of the Cambridgeshire Subsidy Rolls 1250–1625, App. XII: The Clerical Poll Tax of 1379', ed. W.M. Palmer, *East Anglian N. & Q.*, new series xiii, 1909–10, 90–224.

111 PRO, *Calendar of the Patent Rolls: Preserved in the Public Record Office, Edward II* vol. iii *1317–21*, London 1903, 494; *Edward III* vol. ii *1330–4*, London 1893, 346; *Edward III* vol. v *1340–3*, London 1900, 534, are some early examples.

112 'A List of the Cambridgeshire Subsidy Rolls', ed. Palmer, Appendix XII, 155, 191, 192, 224.

113 PRO, SC2/155/53, fos 1–5, Bottisham Court Rolls: Honour and General Courts, 10–17; 21–22 Richard II, 1386–99.

114 PRO, C47/38/3(1–7).

115 For details of other documents relating to Bottisham see ch. 6.

116 C. Vincent, *Dès Charités Bien Ordonnées: les Confréries Normandes*, Paris 1988, 93–101.

functions as a result of their education and social standing.[117] Priests were co-founders of four gilds, hoping, perhaps, to stimulate increased religious devotion. The three fraternities at Haslingfield, Leverington and Tydd St Giles, all dedicated to the Assumption of the Virgin Mary, all named two or three founders, one of whom was a chaplain. The founders of Corpus Christi Gild, St Peter's Church, Ely, were 'Robert Aylesham monk, Walter Florance of Carlton chaplain and others'.[118] Priests were active in the administration of gilds: William Hunden, clerk, was warden of the Gild of the Nativity of the Virgin, Swaffham Bulbeck.[119] Priests often acted as feoffees for lands at this time. Adam Reynalds, chaplain, was one of the feoffees for three acres of marshland belonging to Holy Trinity Gild, Wisbech, and together with John Preste and John Hyne, also chaplains, held further lands. The Trinity Gild Register confirms his importance. In 1379 he was one of the four officials who presented the accounts and was paid a salary of £4 *6s 8d* for celebrating mass for the year.[120] In Cambridge Walter Sutton, the public notary, was clerk to St Katherine's Gild, St Benet's Church. He wrote their statutes, also those of Holy Trinity Gild, Holy Trinity Church, and was one of the senior diocesan officials present at the consistory meeting which ratified the Statutes of the Purification Gild, Great St Mary's Church in 1386.[121]

Priests were members of local communities just as much as laity, and gild priests were no exception. Master Robert Ipswell, rector of the chantry college of Blessed Mary by the Sea at Newton, painted a detailed picture in his will of the involvement of a priest in local farming life through tilling his glebe lands. He left certain goods to his successor on condition that he continued to give hospitality to the poor in his manse, and six cows and a portion of his grain for this purpose. His relations with fellow priests are illustrated by a bequest of 40*s* to the priests of the gilds of Norwich and bequests of nobles, or gold coins, and books to various friends.[122]

John Hobard, the priest of the Trinity Gild, Bassingbourne, supplemented his income by writing the churchwardens' accounts, from their inception in 1498 to his final illness in 1517, and by writing a primer and correcting the mass book in 1511.[123] He directed the play of St George that year and was involved in the general life of the parish, collecting money for '*crabbes* [crab-apples] had of the commons at games, and acquiring wood and wax for

117 Martin, 'The English Borough in the Thirteenth Century', *TRHS*, 5th series xiii, 1963, 122–4.

118 PRO, C47/38/24, 25, 36, 21.

119 PRO, C47/38/33(4).

120 PRO, C47/38/43; WCR1, p. 1; p. 32, duties of the gild priest.

121 PRO, C47/38/7, 10, 9.

122 PRO, Prob 11/10/34, fos 255r–56r, 1495–6 will of Master Robert Ipswell of Newton. He seems to have been independently wealthy and may have been better endowed as rector of a chantry college than the average parish priest.

123 CCRO, P11/5/1–2, vols 1–2, fos 1–44, 33r, 33v.

church purposes.[124] At his death, some pages were left blank and his place eventually filled by a new scribe, Sir John Barret whose handwriting was far inferior. From his will of 1518 it seems his life had revolved around Bassingbourne church. He left most of his possessions, thoughtfully, to effect various improvements in the running of the church, and the residue of his estate to buy a new vestment or to be spent on the image of St George. It seems he was a local man, related to the gentry family, the Bolnests. The executors, supervisors and witnesses to his will included the vicar and other local worthies, and he asked to be buried next to his mother in the south porch.[125]

Although the lives of unbeneficed clergy employed on short-term contracts could be precarious financially, an effort was made to ensure that those who fitted into the local community were retained. In 1521 Thomas Wyth, gentleman, of Wisbech, made an endowment to pay the salary of a chaplain and school master for Trinity Gild for twenty years. Thomas Dorre, notary, who was already a chaplain of Our Lady mass in the gild chapel was named to fill the post.[126]

A group of sixteenth-century wills from Gamlingay, a market town in the south-west of the shire, shows the esteem in which the brotherhood priest, Sir Robert Parson, was held by the parishioners and the vicar. Sir Thomas Peckett, the vicar who died in 1542, left him a cow and 'one of my best gowns for the great pains that he has taken with me in times past'.[127] Reformation historians have used lay appointment of priests to suggest a model of conflict and anti-clericalism between the laity and the clerical hierarchy.[128] However, the detailed evidence from Cambridgeshire suggests the opposite: the laity appointed priests, both gild and chantry chaplains, to work in co-operation with parish clergy. The only evidence of tension comes from Cambridge in 1389, when two gilds excluded or limited the participation of priests, but this was probably a symptom of the relationship between the university and the town.[129] Conflict is inevitable as an aspect of human nature and antagonism between laity and clergy was as much about power and local authority as religious sentiment. Anti-clericalism escalated with the worsening economic conditions of the mid-sixteenth century and the uncertainty of religious change at that time.[130] The generally harmonious

124 CCRO, P11/5/1–2, vol. 2, fos 31r, 32r, 40r, 34r, 37r.

125 Palmer, 369–70.

126 PRO, Prob 11/20/24, fos 190v–92r, 1521 will of Thomas Wyth.

127 ACE (2/3/19), 1546 will of John Filborne left Robert Parson a bushell of barley; ACE (2/3/23), 1546 will of Johanne Gold, left a bequest to Robert Parson; ECC (1/7/16), 1542 will of Sir Thomas Peckett, vicar.

128 McIntosh, *Autonomy and Community: The Royal Manor of Havering 1300–1500*, Cambridge 1986, 3, 235–40.

129 PRO, C47/38/4, 10.

130 P. Heath, *The English Parish Clergy On the Eve of the Reformation*, Toronto 1969, 196; C. Haigh, 'Anti-Clericalism and the English Reformation', *History* lxviii, 1983, 391–407 suggests that the Reformation changes exacerbated anti-clericalism.

relationship between parish clergy and pre-Reformation gilds is illustrated by clerical membership of these groups. Many clergy, including parish priests of Cambridge and the surrounding district, were named in the late thirteenth- and early fourteenth-century bede rolls of St Mary's Gild, Cambridge. The fifteenth-century Cambridge gild statutes, the sixteenth-century St Katherine's Gild register, Holy Trinity parish, Cambridge, and the Statutes of St James's Gild, Dullingham, all record priests as members. Out of the sample of approximately 2,000 wills, 7% were made by clergy and 8% of those testators who mentioned gilds were clergy.[131]

Conclusion: Orthodoxy and The Avant-Garde

It might be inferred, wrongly, from this chapter that gilds or fraternities were central to lay people's experience of late medieval Catholicism. For some this may have been true: many more were too poor to participate in them but would have been aware of their general contribution to religious practice. It has been necessary to emphasise that contribution to compensate for their comparative neglect. Beyond the confines of the parish, monastic foundations still enjoyed a certain amount of patronage. Monasteries were originally founded by noble or knightly families, who had sole rights to their spiritual resources and commemorative powers. The wills which contain bequests to over sixty houses of canons, monks and nuns in England and abroad, are nearly all drawn from among the 11% of the sample of approximately 2000 wills proved in the Prerogative Court of Canterbury. Patronage of these institutions was confined to gentry, such as the Ingaldesthorp family of Burgh, and to wealthy townsmen and yeomen such as the Masse family of Wisbech.[132] Except for local houses, few received more than one bequest. These were often made to a named person there, generally specified as a relative. Most bequests asked for prayers, few for masses. Monasteries lacked the flexibility of other institutions which had become popular in the later Middle Ages. Over twenty-five houses of friars in sixteen different towns, in London, East Anglia and Yorkshire were patronised, once again by those

[131] A. Kettle, 'City and Close: Lichfield in the Century before the Reformation' in C.M. Barron and C. Harper-Bill, *The Church in Pre-Reformation Society*, Woodbridge 1985, 158–69, esp. 161, 7% clergy membership recorded.

[132] PRO, Prob 11/2a/20, fos 157r and v, 158r, 1409 will of Katherine de Burgh, widow of Sir John de Burgh, left money and household goods to Margaret Brunne, nun of Denney, and also to Margaret Brunne, nun of Swaffham Bulbeck. Both these houses in Cambridgeshire attracted a number of bequests. Her descendant Elizabeth, widow of Lord John Ingaldesthorp of Burgh, patronised local nuns and monks at Swaffham Bulbeck, Anglesey Abbey and Crabhouse in Norfolk, PRO, Prob 11/2b/53, fos 417v, 418, 1421; ECC HK2791/A/96, fos 34r and v, 35r, 1454 will of Alicia Masse, wife of the Alderman of the Trinity Gild, Wisbech, left 20*d* to the Master of St John's House in Lynn, Norfolk.

wealthy enough to have their wills proved in the Prerogative Court of Canterbury. As regular priests, the friars were able to provide the temporary chantries, trentals and funeral masses increasingly demanded by larger numbers of laity in the fifteenth and sixteenth centuries.[133] The Cambridge Colleges and other chantry foundations at Ely, Oxford, Eton, Fotheringay, Wingham and Plessey also attracted benefaction. To say that support for the monasteries was in decline on the eve of the Reformation is a misrepresentation: they were now merely one provider of religious services to the laity, along with newer institutions, including the gilds, which had become widespread in the later Middle Ages.

Alongside the demands of lay testators for 'an honest priest' to sing commemorative masses, is evidence of their relationships with secular priests. In 1532 Alicia Stukyn of Chesterton left a pair of sheets to her 'ghostly father' to pray for her soul, and in 1554 William Gardner left 'to the vicar of the parish of St Andrew in Histon for his pains and business 10*s*'.[134] Hermits too, particularly in the fens, were left bequests in return for prayers and masses.[135]

Women gave more details in their wills about personal items and thus indirectly about their piety. The wealthier of those whose wills were proved in local diocesan courts, gave sets of beads, or rosaries made of semi-precious stones, to relatives and close friends, references to which disappear from wills between 1546 and 1557. In 1544 Madlyn Rychardson of Ely left a pair of red coral beads and her collection of devotional silver to her son.[136] In 1557 Alice Holmes, widow, of Chesterton, left 'to my son John, five new painted cloths hanging in the chapel chamber'.[137] Less wealthy women left less valuable devotional items. In 1546 Agnes Ayghton, widow, of Littlington, left 'to Mother Peter my best black gown that I wear on Holy days', and a number of Holy day kerchiefs to her daughter and her son's daughters.[138]

Books were rare in this society: most were owned by clergy. Titles were not generally given in wills, except by priests, who described these possessions in more detail. Overall, only four wills provide evidence that their writers, three gentlemen and a hermit, John Wodsowle of St Mary Heldirnale, a chapel in the fens, had been influenced by the new devotional ideas emanating from

133 For detailed discussion of funeral and commemorative rites, see ch. 4.

134 ECC (1/3/15); (5/2/1).

135 PRO, Prob 11/2b/54, fos 426v, 427r, 1422 will of Peter Palmer, Chaplain of Wisbech, left 6*s* 8*d* to the Hermit of Walsoken; Prob 11/15/19, fos 153v, 154r and v, 1506 will of Richard Buckworth of Wisbech, left 'Sir George Harmytt' 10s for a trental; ECC (2/5/13) 1545 will of John Portare, priest sometime hermit.

136 ECC (2/2/20) 1544 will of Madlyn Rychardson.

137 ECC (6/5/12) 1557 will of Alice Holmes of Chesterton. Painted cloths were the ancestors of today's oil paintings on canvas, see Anon., *East Anglian N. & Q.*, new series xiii, 1909–10, 371–3, 'A Painted Cloth, dated 1596, with Memorials of Ely and Armorial Lists of Imprisoned Recusants'.

138 ECC (3/1/2) 1546 will of Agnes Ayghton.

Syon Abbey and Carthusian houses.[139] There is no further evidence that the intense individual piety of the *Devotio Moderna*, which passed over into later puritan spirituality, had affected the members of yeomen, husbandmen and other tenant farming families, by whom the vast majority of the wills were made. Surprisingly, there is little evidence for the spread of new continental devotions in this wealthy area of the country. A small number of gilds and lights were dedicated to the Name of Jesus.[140] The image of Our Lady of Pity had begun to appear in churches and a handful of sixteenth-century wills requested masses for the five wounds of Our Lord and the seven sorrows of the Virgin. In wills proved in the diocesan courts, bequests for the education of boys began to occur in 1546. The Communication of the Gospel to the laity was ensured in Sawston in 1552 by Robert Lockton who left 20*s* to found six sermons in the church.[141] In 1558 Thomas Bedell of Waterbeach left money for sermons at Braintree, Bocking and Bardfield in north Essex, an area where Protestant ideas had already taken root. He also left money to the poor in those places and in Black Notley, Duxford and Fairstead.[142] From Willingham, one of the communities explored by Margaret Spufford, where Protestantism was established early, comes evidence of anti-clericalism. In 1553 William Parkarr left his daughter a cow called Holyman.[143]

Professor Dickens' division of will preambles into three categories, 'Protestant', 'neutral' and 'Catholic', as a thumbnail sketch of the spread of Protestantism, treated with overmuch reverence by subsequent writers, proves very little other than that 'confessional faith', whether Protestant or Catholic, was held by only a tiny minority in the years of uncertainty between the 1530s and the 1580s. By far the largest category were the 'pragmatists', who both concealed their religious allegiances, and preserved their goods from confiscation, by a radical reduction in bequests to devotional and communal purposes.[144] From about 1540 there was a marked decline in traditional Catholic bequests to church ornaments, images, vestments, books, torches and lights. From 1547 to 1556 these ceased completely. More surprisingly, mundane bequests for maintenance of the church fabric, bells and the highways dwindled to single figures in Edward's reign, not to begin recovery until 1556.[145]

139 ECC, HK2791/A/117, fo 40r, 1454 will of Johannes Wodsowl.

140 PRO, Prob 11/15/30, fos 240r and v, 1507 will of Philippe Odame of Wisbech, states that there is a light to the Mass of the Name of Jesus in the church of Saints Peter and Paul.

141 ECC (4/6/3) 1552 will of Robert Lockton.

142 ECC (8/1/14) 1558 will of Thomas Bedell.

143 ECC (4/7/6) 1553 will of William Parkarr; M. Spufford, *Contrasting Communities: English Villages in the Sixteenth and Seventeenth Centuries*, Cambridge 1974, chs 5 and 13.

144 Dickens, *The English Reformation*, 266; V.R. Bainbridge, 'Religious Devotion in Cambridgeshire 1500–1558', paper presented at the Tudor and Stuart Seminar, Institute of Historical Research, London, 27 October 1986.

145 'Churchwardens' Bills or Returns for the Deanery of Barton, Cambridgeshire for Michaelmas 1554', ed. W.M. Palmer, in *Cambs. & Hunts. Arch. Soc.* v, 1937, 257–65,

The gilds, colleges, chantries and hospitals were abolished in 1547. The last hopeful bequest to a gild is found in 1548 and such bequests did not reappear in Mary's reign.[146]

How then had late medieval piety, as expressed by gild practice, prepared the majority of the population for acceptance of the Reformation? The feast of Corpus Christi and the cult of the Name of Jesus exemplified the process of change from religious images to abstract concept, which was immeasurably intensified by the print explosion of the written word. As evidence, the central role of the priest changed from that of providing the Eucharist to that of preaching the word. The mission to extend the model of monastic piety to the laity in the world had begun in the towns of thirteenth-century southern Europe. However, as the puritans found, this calling to the inner life of prayer was not to everyone's taste and the majority, the 'lukewarm', retreated behind the anonymous conformity of Anglican ritual. In reality, however, few people in this society, so different from our own, had 'control over their own lives', one of the key myths of individualism in our own time.[147] The relative powerlessness and lack of financial resources at a level below gentry meant that religious choice was a luxury unavailable to the majority: ultimately led by the yeomanry they had to conform to the settlement imposed by their political superiors. Our sources do not describe the change in their individual faith. Only the material culture of late medieval Catholicism gives any clues. This was the product of custom, the expression of collective identity and was as important to social structure and local economy as it was to religious life. The laity had made a substantial investment in the traditional faith on many levels, both as individuals and collectively through such organisations as gild and parish. This explains the slow erosion of Catholic practice, its readoption under Queen Mary, despite the confiscations of gild and parish property under Edward VI, and, with the fading of living memory over three generations or so, the very gradual rise to ascendancy of the Anglican Protestant compromise.

most churches still lacked basic liturgical equipment; Whiting, *The Blind Devotion of the People*, 159–61, there was no substantial investment in new liturgical vessels in the south-west until the 1570s.

146 ACE (2/6/4), 1548 will of John Basse the Elder of Gamlingay.

147 C. Richmond, 'Religion and the Fifteenth Century English Gentleman' in *The Church, Politics and Patronage in the Fifteenth Century*, ed. R.B. Dobson, Gloucester 1984, 193–208; J. Catto, 'Religious Change under Henry V' in *Henry V: The Practice of Kingship*, ed. G.L. Harriss, Oxford 1985, 97–115.

4

Death as a Mirror of Society: Commemoration and the Afterlife

The men and women of the late Middle Ages were as fearful as we are of what lies on the other side of death.[1] They too were afraid of dying, afraid of what was beyond, of their own aloneness in facing death. They too had their euphemisms for the process of dying. Some went the way of all flesh, 'Viam universe carnis ingredi', while others migrated from this light, or from this age, to the Lord, 'ab hac luce migraverit', 'ab hoc saeculo emigraverit', 'ad Dominum migraverit'.[2] To comfort themselves they held up a mirror to their own society, which reflected the network of relationships which bound them in life to their lords, their tenants and servants, their families and benefactors, their fellow religious, their fellow gild brethren, townsmen and parishioners. This image they projected into the void beyond the grave.[3]

Unlike us, consensus of opinion in their society over preceding centuries of Christianity had mapped out the continents of hell, purgatory and heaven, and the path through purgatory to the presence of God and eternal

1 I am grateful to the Ecclesiastical History Society for permission to inlcude this chapter, a previous version of which appeared as 'The Medieval Way of Death', in Prophecy and Eschatology, Studies in Church History Subsidia x, Oxford 1994, ed. M. Wilkes. Scholarly interest in the subject of death grew out of the work of art and literary historians on such striking representations as 'The Dance of Death' and the 'Ars Moriendi', for example, A. Tenenti, 'La Vie et la Mort à travers l'Art du xve Siècle', *Cahiers Des Annales* 8, Paris 1952; A Tenenti, *Il senso Della Morte e l'Amore della Vita Nel Rinascimento*, Turin 1957. The debate widened to the discussion of western attitudes towards death and dying, and many publications on this subject followed P. Ariès, *Western Attitudes towards Death*, Baltimore 1974; P. Ariès, *L'Homme devant la Mort*, Paris 1977, translated as *The Hour of our Death*, New York 1981.

2 PRO, C47/38/7; C47/38/14, 15, 24, 36; PRO, C47/38/3, 20, 23, 33; C47/38/8; Bateson, 24, St Mary's Gild prayer for the dead; J. Chiffoleau, *La Comptabilité de l'Au-delà: Les Hommes, La Mort et la Religion dans la Region d'Avignon à la fin du Moyen Age vers 1320 – vers 1480*, Collections de L'Ecole Français de Rome, 47, Rome 1980, 114.

3 S. Reynolds, *Kingdoms and Communities in Western Europe 900–1300*, Oxford 1984, confirms the importance of collective activity in the Middle Ages; J. Bossy, 'The Mass as a Social Institution 1200–1700', *P&P* c, 1983, 29–61, esp. 37–46, the obligation of the living to pray for the dead to whom they were bound. D.L. d'Avray, *Death and the Prince: Memorial Preaching before 1350*, Oxford 1994.

salvation.[4] This map enabled them to make the crude assumption that the vast majority of people who had been neither very bad nor very good must be living out their sentences in purgatory.[5] Thus, it was imperative for the living to do all in their power to ensure that the sentences were curtailed, particularly for those to whom they were bound by ties of loyalty and fellowship. The significance of the bond between the living and the dead has now become almost a commonplace of social history.[6] The belief that the deeds of the living can affect the progress of their dead in the afterlife is extremely ancient, and is to be found in many cultures.[7] Images of the afterlife in western Christendom were deeply rooted in the common stock of Indo-European mythology[8] and some ideas may have been renewed with the Crusades and greater contact with the East. Historians influenced by sixteenth-century church reformers are apt to take too rationalist an approach to medieval Catholic practice.

Social obligations were as pressing at the moment of death and beyond as they had been in life. Mortmain licences and the foundation documents of chantries; wills and the records of the corporate devotion of gilds or boroughs, cite prayers for the sovereign, the founders' feudal lords and other benefactors or relatives as the recipients of the spiritual fruits of the chantry or other commemorative practices.[9]

The obligation to provide prayers for the departed members of a family was passed down together with the title to the estate. The commemoration of the

4 P. Camporesi, *The Fear of Hell: Images of Damnation and Salvation in Early Modern Europe*, Oxford 1991, esp. ch. 1 on the organic horrors of hell; J. le Goff, *The Birth of Purgatory*, Chicago 1984; C. McDannell and B. Lang, *Heaven: A History*, Yale 1988.

5 Le Goff places the emergence of the third place where venial sins were sloughed off in the 12th century; A.H. Bredero, 'Le Moyen Age et le Purgatoire', *Revue d'Histoire Ecclesiastique* lxxviii, 1983, 429–52, a review and useful counter-balance to Le Goff. This emphasises the period between antiquity and the 12th century when prayer for dead monks and laymen evolved in monasteries; when a money economy and towns emerged, where the doctrine of purgatory developed from the 11th century and was popularised through preaching and indulgences from the 13th century on; C. Burgess, ' "A fond thing vainly invented": an Essay on Purgatory and Pious Motive in Late Medieval England', in *Parish, Church and People: Local Studies in Lay Religion 1350–1750*, ed. S.J. Wright, London 1988, 56–84, esp. 56–70; E. Duffy, *The Stripping of the Altars: Traditional Religion in England c.1400–1580*, Yale 1992, section D, 299–376.

6 Bossy, 'The Mass', 29–61, esp. 42; J. Bossy, *Christianity in the West 1400–1700*, Oxford 1985, esp. 26–34.

7 R.J.E. Boggis, *Praying for the Dead: An Historical Review of the Practice*, London 1913, traces the history of this practice from Judaism to the Reformation; *Death and the Regeneration of Life*, ed. M. Bloch and J. Parry, Cambridge 1982, Introduction 10–11. Such beliefs are still widespread in 20th century Western-society.

8 *The Tibetan Book of the Dead*, ed. W.Y. Evans-Wentz, Oxford 1957, 3rd edn paperback 1960, Introduction v, xiii–xiv, xx; the Tibetan judgement, xxx–xxxiii, 165–9; pain experienced in the spiritual body after death, lxxix.

9 PRO, C47/38/24; J. Bossy, 'The Mass', 36–46, the spiritual power of the mass could be directed to confer benefit on friends, and indeed to harm enemies.

ancestors, both through the endowment of monastic houses and lesser foundations such as chantries, was an important aspect of the maintenance of family tradition and identity.[10] Ancestor worship pre-existed Christianity among the German peoples and is one of the strands from which the custom of praying for the dead emerged.[11] In a primarily oral culture, just as the heralds were witness to aristocratic lineage and noble prowess, so the monks and mass-priests embodied the memory of ancestral souls and their spiritual deeds. This may be seen in the wills of the gentry family of Ingaldesthorp of Burgh in Cambridgeshire. In 1456 Sir Edmund Ingaldesthorp requested his executors to amortise a manor in Burwell 'for my chantry in Burgh, according to the intention and effects of the last will of Lady Catherine de Burgh' his ancestor who had died in 1409, 'for two suitable chaplains, to pray in perpetuity for my soul, and for the soul of the said Lady Catherine and the souls of our parents'.[12] The accretion of obligations to dead forbears multiplied as they were handed down from generation to generation, and the living were obliged to re-endow foundations which had become impoverished. The duty to continue these observances was passed on by will to the executors, who often included the heir, and even to the executors of the executors.[13]

Sir Thomas Randis, chantry priest of Our Lady Gild in Tydd St Giles left a messuage and garden to 'the priest serving the Gild of Our Lady and to his successors without end' on condition that he kept an anniversary mass and obit for him.[14] John Savage, chaplain and fellow of King's College Cambridge, left a breviary for the use of Master John Hogekyns. He was to give this and a psalter to Nicholas Burnham *alias* White, when he became a priest, who was to pray especially for John Savage's soul and the souls of Thomas Brown and John White. On his death he was to leave the breviary to another priest who was to do likewise for the term of his life, and he to another priest for his, on pain of excommunication.[15] There was a passing on of spiritual obligations with material wealth, for the priesthood just as for the laity. A priest would expect spiritual services from the inheritor of a spiritual position, or of religious books or ornaments.

10 J. Rosenthal, *The Purchase of Paradise: Gift Giving and the Aristocracy 1307–1485*, London 1972, 16, table 1; L. Goff, *Purgatory*, 11–12, 233, for the strength of family and corporate ties; 293, the likeness of the bond between living and dead to 'feudo-vassalic' contracts. *Person und Gemeinschaft im Mittelalter*, ed. G. Althoff, D. Geuenich, O.G. Oexle and J. Wollasch, Sigmarinen 1988, provides an introduction to the important work of a group of German historians on the subject of *Memoria*, or the commemoration of the dead.

11 A.H. Bredero, 'Le Purgatoire', 448.

12 PRO, Prob 11/4/7, fo 54r, 1456.

13 M. Hicks, 'Chantries Obits and Almshouses: the Hungerford Foundations 1325–1478', in *The Church in Pre-Reformation Society*, ed. C.M. Barron and C. Harper-Bill, Woodbridge 1985, 123–42, esp. 124–36.

14 PR0, Prob 11/14/32, fos 255r and v, 1504.

15 KCC, fo 78r, 1474.

It was not only kinsmen for whom people were bound to pray, but also their benefactors: all those who had shown them favour, whose patronage had assisted them in the life of this world. In 1472 Geoffrey Sprynge, citizen and draper of London (with connections with Downham in the Isle of Ely) expressed his obligations in this way:

> To have an honest and well-disposed priest for to pray and sing for my soul all divine service, as such priests ought for to do: with the Great Trental of St Gregory with all manner of prayers, fastings and other observances belonging, and also to pray for the souls of John and Agnes, my father and mother *and in especiall for the souls of all them that I am most bound to pray for*, and all christian souls.[16]

Duties to the dead not only bound one to those above in the social hierarchy, but also to those below. Sir John Ingaldesthorp, who died in 1420 ordered his executors to distribute money among his tenants 'in order that they might pray for me'.[17] Nicholas Hughson left two of his grandchildren 'five marks to pray for me and for their mother',[18] and Master Robert Fowlmere, rector of Fowlmere and canon of Westminster, left money for five priests to pray for one year 'for my soul, my parents, all faithful departed, my benefactors, and for the souls of my parishioners'.[19]

It is easy for us in our individualistic society to focus on the desire of individuals to be commemorated, particularly when so much evidence comes from documents such as wills.[20] It must be remembered, however, that the will was only the written record of a public act which took place, in ideal circumstances, at the deathbed of the testator surrounded by his or her family and household.[21] Those bequests not immediately coming into effect, for example those to be made when children reached adulthood, would generally be administered by the dead person's family and the expenses for funeral and commemorative rites would come out of property which would otherwise have been theirs.[22] In some cases an element of coercion was necessary: some

16 PRO, Prob 11/6/15, fos 114r and v, 1472; R.W. Pfaff, 'The English Devotion of St Gregory's Trental', *Speculum* xlix, 1974, 75–90.

17 PRO, Prob 11/2b/48, fo 379, 1420.

18 PRO, Prob 11/17/20, fo 160r, 1512.

19 PRO, Prob 11/2a/1, fos 7r and v, 1401.

20 M.M. Sheehan, *The Will in Medieval England*, Toronto 1963; C. Burgess, 'By Quick and By Dead: Wills and Pious Provision in late Medieval Bristol', *P&P* ccccv, 1987, 837–58. Wills give only incomplete evidence for pious provision.

21 G. Duby, *William Marshall: The Flower of Chivalry*, London 1986, 3–27. The biography of William Marshal depicts an ideal death-bed scene, with the hero divesting himself of his worldly possessions one by one to members of his family and household.

22 Hicks, 'Hungerford Foundations', 126: some bequests were never paid due to the financial embarrassment of the testator; Burgess, 'By Quick and By Dead', 844, 855. Objections by relatives to the alienation of property for commemorative rites led to

sixteenth-century testators reminded their children that they would answer before God on the day of judgement for the fulfilment of their parent's dying wishes.[23] This illustrates that although they might break these, the responsibility was held in some awe. These wishes were performed for the dead as members of kin groupings which had sustained them in life and now did so in death.[24]

Commemoration was a collective activity carried out by the various groups to which people had belonged during the course of their lives: the family; those so-called surrogate families: brotherhoods, fraternities, gilds;[25] and trade or professional groupings.[26] Some of these represented the ties of neighbourhood and social or occupational status, and others cut across such divisions thereby lending cohesion to the society of town or parish.[27] Commemoration at once affirmed corporate identity, transcending the boundary between the living and the dead, and issued a direct challenge to the negation of human endeavour by the finality of the grave.

Entry into the fellowship of a gild or other society might entitle new brethren to have their names registered on a bede roll. These documents, sometimes inadequately described as membership lists, were not drawn up primarily for administrative convenience, but so that those named would receive the prayers of their parent institutions.[28] The accounts of St Mary's Gild, Great St Mary's Church, Cambridge, 1298–1319, record the entry fines paid by the living on admission to the fraternity, and paid on their behalf for the dead. The three rolls of the same period record the same practice. Single women, men, priests, husbands and wives, and family groups joined the fellowship, and along with them were joined dead parents, spouses, and

their endowment in the testator's life-time rather than relying on their last will being carried out.

23 There are 22 examples in Ely Consistory Court Wills 1544–1558 and one in Ely Archdeaconry Court in 1546. Nine of these come from Willingham, a village where Protestant ideas took root early in the 16th century and were the work of particular scribes; see M. Spufford, *Contrasting Communities: English Villages in the Sixteenth and Seventeenth Century*, Cambridge 1984, 320–44.

24 Ariès, *Western Attitudes*, ch. ii. Ariès, and those who follow him, perhaps overlook the extent to which commemoration was a collective activity.

25 Chiffoleau, *La Comptabilité*, ch. 3. One of his theses is that fraternities grew up as people moved away from their families to the towns of the 11th and 12th centuries; Westlake, 9, asserts that the chief function of the fraternities was to pray for their dead.

26 C. Gross, *The Gild Merchant: A Contribution to British Municipal History*, 2 vols, Oxford 1890; E. Coornaert, 'Le Ghildes Médiévales (Ve–Xive Siècles) Définition-Évolution', *Revue Historique* cxcix, 1948, 22–55, 208–43.

27 R.F.E. Weissman, *Ritual Brotherhood in Renaissance Florence*, New York 1982; R.C. Trexler, *Public Life in Renaissance Florence*, New York 1980.

28 N. Orme, 'The Kalendar brethren of the City of Exeter', *Report and Transactions of the Devonshire Association for the Advancement of Science, Literature and Art* cix, 1977, 153–69; A. Kettle, 'City and Close: Lichfield in the Century before the Reformation' in *The Church in Pre-Reformation Society*, 143–157, esp. 161.

others who had been important to them.[29] In 1389 the gild of St John the Baptist, Wisbech, 'ordained that the priest of the fraternity should have a tablet on which were written the names . . . of the living and the dead, so that he might pray for both at mass and in his prayers'.[30] Ten Cambridgeshire gilds at this date specified that the living and the dead were to be prayed for together at festive occasions. This was also the case in the statutes of three fifteenth-century gilds in the town of Cambridge: St Clement's, Saints Peter and Paul and All Saints, in the parishes of those names. They had special arrangements with the priests of their respective churches:

> Also it is ordained by all our common assent that every year the vicar of the foresaid church shall have 3*s* 4*d* for a centene (100) of masses, that is to say to have in mind both the quick and the dead every Sunday in the year and also to pray every Sunday at the beads time for all the company, both for them that be living and also for them that be passed out of this world.[31]

The dead and the living were prayed for together: they stood as one company before God.[32]

Like the family, societies such as gilds or fraternities, town councils and parishes, religious houses and colleges of secular priests had a collective identity which would survive an individual member. In this respect they enshrined not only the memory of that individual's existence and his or her deeds and benefactions, but also provided an administrative framework through which memory could be carried forward into future generations. This was recognised in England by the legislative authorities in the application of the statute of mortmain to lands alienated from crown control: first in 1279 to monastic foundations and chantries; in 1391 to corporate bodies such as gilds merchant, town corporations and fraternities; and in 1536 to the parish.[33] The extension of legislation indicates which bodies were most popular for administering commemorative bequests at each time.

A bede roll or *liber vitae* was monastic in origin and carried the names of dead brethren to sister houses where they would also receive prayers.[34] As the

29 Bateson, 1–13 minutes, 14–25 bede rolls; J.R. Banker, *Death in the Community: Memorialisation and Confraternities in an Italian Commune in the Late Middle Ages*, Athens, Georgia 1989, 59–68. There are far fewer women than men on the bede rolls of the Confraternity of San Sepolcre 1269–1309. Banker thinks that they are widowed heads of households which suggests a different system of memorialisation, 64.

30 PRO, C47/38/39.

31 BL Add Ms. 5846, pp. 5–13, St Clement's Gild Statutes 1431; Cambridge University Library MM1 36: Baker Mss. vol. 25, Item 10, pp. 361–6, Saints Peter and Paul Gild Statutes 1448; pp. 367–71, All Saints Gild Statutes 1473 quoted, spellings modernised.

32 Duffy, *Stripping of the Altars*, 334–7.

33 S. Raban, *Mortmain Legislation and the English Church 1279–1500*, Cambridge 1982, 170; A. Kreider, *The English Chantries: The Road to Dissolution*, Harvard 1979, 84. The crown was hostile to the alienation of lands for intercession, even before the abolition of intercessory institutions in the mid-16th century.

34 G.H. Cook, *Medieval Chantries and Chantry Chapels*, London 1963, Introduction 1–6.

Eucharist took on a central role in later medieval Christianity, the emblem of Christ's passion for mankind and his triumph over the grave, that ancient theme of love and death, became a vehicle for transferring spiritual power to the dead when celebrated in their name.[35] Institutions which were more typical than monasteries as the administrators of commemorative rites in the later Middle Ages were chantry colleges and gilds or fraternities.[36] They provided services for those with less wealth and social connections on a sliding scale, according to the resources of the departed.

In Cambridgeshire this may be seen in the practices of the colleges of the university. These were primarily endowed as chantries for the souls of their benefactors and only secondarily as educational establishments, a fact that is often overlooked due to their secularisation at the reformation. They included the college of Corpus Christi, which had been founded by two gilds of Cambridge burgesses and their aristocratic associates: the gilds of St Mary and Corpus Christi in 1352.[37] They followed the pattern of all chantry colleges at this time, a group of secular priests living a common life, and commemorating, through their prayers and masses, their benefactors and their fellow priests. Wills proved under the peculiar jurisdiction of King's, one such college, give evidence of this.[38] Clergy wills have an advantage over the wills of the laity for our understanding of beliefs about the afterlife, as they are in general more articulate where religious ideas are concerned.

In 1509 Richard Hatton, fellow of King's College, left books for his soul 'in recompensiam omnium neglectorum aut male gestorum et perpetratorum per me in adolscentia mea'.[39] A priest there was to say masses for him and his benefactors for one year. He was also a fellow of the chantry college of St Mary and St Stephen, Westminster, where he was to be buried and an anniversary kept. In 1517 John Sampson, who described himself as 'indignus sacerdos et peccator penitens', commended his soul into the hands of the Trinity, the Blessed Virgin, Jesus Christ his redeemer, a number of saints whom he named, all other saints and the elect of God, 'that through their holy prayers and through the passion of Jesus Christ, I might gain remission of all my sins'. His body he commended to Christian burial.[40] He was not taking any chances for he continued:

35 Bloch and Parry, *Death and the Regeneration of Life*, Introduction 1; J.G. Fraser, *The Golden Bough*, London 1890; M. Eliade, *The Myth of the Eternal Return*, Princeton 1965; Bossy, 'The Mass', 29–61; M. Rubin, *Corpus Christi: The Eucharist in late Medieval Culture*, Cambridge 1991.

36 G.H. Cook, *English Collegiate Churches of the Middle Ages*, London 1959.

37 Bateson, Introduction; *VCH Cambs*., iii, 371–6; J. Josselin, *Historiola Collegii Corporis Christi et Beatae Mariae Cantabrigiae*, ed. J. Willis, *Publn Camb. Antiq. Soc.* xvii, Cambridge 1880.

38 KCC, King's College ledger book 1451–1558 contains 39 wills in this period, on the whole made by Fellows of the College with some college servants and their widows.

39 KCC, fos 219v–20v.

40 KCC, fos 247v–8r.

> I will that immediately after my death there shall be celebrated for my soul 30 masses according to the order of the Trental of St Gregory;[41] and 5 masses for the 5 wounds of Jesus Christ at a certain altar at *Scala Celi*;[42] and . . . that a priest shall celebrate for a whole year for the safety of my soul and all those souls whom I hold dear; . . . and that two fellow priests shall celebrate in college for a year . . .; if it happens that I die in Cambridge there are to be due ceremonies on the day of my death, and a mass the following day at which the officiating priest shall have 12*d*, each fellow 8*d*, each priest 6*d*, clerks and scholars 4*d*, choristers 2*d*, and in alms to the poor 10*s*.

In 1528 Robert Hacumblen, provost[43] commended his soul

> into the hands of the Holy Trinity and Jesus Christ my saviour, by whose bitter passion, and through continually worshipping His five wounds I trust mercifully to be saved . . . and through the intercession and prayer of the Blessed Virgin . . . (and other named saints) . . . through whose prayers and the long worshipping and devotion which I have had of them, God willing the same I trust verily to obtain everlasting joy.

His body was to be buried in the new church (King's College Chapel) and the goods given to him by the grace of Almighty God went to the college in return for provision for his soul, including a gilt chalice and patten engraved with 'Orate pro Anima R.H.' On the day of his burial or within two days, a trental was to be sung with *placebo* and *dirige*.[44] A *dirige* was to be held in the university at which the vice-chancellor, doctors, priests, regents and non-regents, and bedels were to have sums of money graded according to their status to pray for him. A *dirige* was to be kept in the college by his 'company', at which the vice-provost, fellows, undergraduates, priests, clerks, choristers, ringers of bells and college servants likewise were given money. At the burial, the executors were to provide torches and eight poor men to carry them, each to have for his labour a black gown and 8*d* in money. Other mourners were to be dressed in black gowns to the sum of 26*s* 8*d*, and £6 13*s* 4*d* was to be

41 Pfaff, 'St Gregory's Trental', 75–90. A custom based on St Gregory's release of his mother's soul from purgatory, through his intercession, having just seen a vision of her in torment pleading for help, and afterwards, a beatific vision of her release and subsequent joy.

42 Duffy, *Stripping of the Altars*, 375–6. *Scala Celi* was in Rome.

43 KCC, fos 278v–9r.

44 A Trental (from Latin *triginta* and French *trente*) was 30 masses; *placebo* (from the first Latin word of the service) was evensong; and *dirige* (from the first Latin word of the service) mattins; Burgess, 'By Quick and By Dead', 840–1; R.C. Finucane, 'Sacred Corpse: Profane Carrion: Social Ideas and Death Rituals in the Later Middle Ages', in *Mirrors of Mortality: Studies in the Social History of Death*, ed. J. Whaley, London 1981, 40–60, provides a brief summary of funeral rites.

distributed to the poor in alms for his soul. A 'month day', or mass thirty days after death was to be kept, and there was provision for other prayers as well.[45]

These three wills illustrate the extensive range of late medieval funeral and commemorative rites. Jacques Chiffoleau comments on the multiplication of masses and prayers which went hand in hand with the computation of the number of years one was likely to spend in purgatory, and the remission these were likely to provide.[46] Robert Hacumblen's death was commemorated by his college and the university, as he had been a member of both institutions, and Richard Hatton's by both colleges to which he had belonged.

Gilds or fraternities provided funeral and commemorative rites for their dead and records of their rituals reveal much about contemporary belief and practice. Early gild historians described them in the language of their times. Toulmin Smith likened them to the 'burial clubs' or funeral savings schemes of the nineteenth century.[47] His critic Westlake, asserting that pious motives were uppermost, labelled them 'co-operative chantries'.[48] Both descriptions are limited and thus misleading. They were not simply the 'poor man's chantry' but one type of social group which kept alive the memory of those who had died in their company: the wealthier the company, the more elaborate the range of practices they were able to provide.

According to the royal survey of these institutions in 1388–9, 39 (65%) Cambridgeshire gilds undertook some service for their dead brothers and sisters. Attendance at these occasions was compulsory in 21 (35%) gilds, enforced by a system of fines to ensure company solidarity, ranging from 1*d* to 1*s*, or 1 pound of wax paid to the light burning before their patron saint. Members were summoned to funerals by a gild officer, sometimes with the title of dean or apparitor.[49] The tasks of the apparitor of the Purification Gild, Great St Mary's Church, Cambridge, were

> to inform brethren of funeral services, meetings and other gatherings; to preside over the offices of the dead and to organise the torches and the carrying of the body to the church.[50]

45 *New Catholic Encyclopaedia*, vol. 12, McGraw Hill, New York etc. 1967, 384. Requiem mass was usually celebrated the day after burial, and on certain other days, the third, seventh, thirtieth days after death and the anniversary; Burgess, 'By Quick and By Dead', 840–1; Boggis, *Praying for the Dead*, chs viii and ix.

46 Chiffoleau, *La Comptabilité*, part II, 'le Mathematique du Salut'.

47 Toulmin Smith, Introduction by L. Toulmin Smith, xxxvi.

48 Westlake, 40–44, contradicts the 'burial club' idea and labels them 'co-operative chantries'.

49 E. Durkheim, *The Elementary Forms of the Religious Life*, translated by J.W. Swain, 2nd edn, London 1976, 399, 'when someone dies the family group to which he belongs feels itself lessened and, to react against this loss, it assembles'.

50 PRO, C47/38/9.

The fraternity of the Assumption of the Virgin in Tydd St Giles had a 'Bellman' who was

> to go around the village ringing his bell to cause men to pray for the soul of the departed and to cause all brothers to come to the funeral rites . . .[51]

both eliciting prayers from the community at large at the time the soul left the body and reinforcing a sense of gild identity by the special summoning of the brethren to the gild rites.[52] Other companies expressed their solidarity by wearing gild livery or badges on such occasions.

Thirty-two (53%) gilds stated that they organised funerals for their members. This included the provision of lights or torches and in one case a hearse.[53] Thirty-four (57%) organised commemorative rites, 15 holding requiem masses or prayers for the group as a whole, often on the feast-day of their patron saint. Nine organised commemoration of individual members, a requiem mass, a trental of masses or an anniversary mass, but these were more likely to be for founders or substantial benefactors of the gild. At such occasions, it was obligatory for the brethren to offer soul pennies or ha'pennies or for the alderman to do so on behalf of the company. Thus funeral and commemorative rites re-enforced notions of hierarchy as well as collectivity.

People with more money had greater opportunity for commemoration.[54] The statutes of Holy Trinity Gild, Holy Trinity Church, Cambridge, a fraternity for the wealthy elite of the town and surrounding area, offered the whole spectrum of funeral and commemorative rites.[55] On the death of a member of the gild, lights stood around the body to ward away evil spirits at the night's vigil kept by mourners. Brethren were to attend the *placebo* on the eve and the *dirige* and mass on the day of burial. They were to accompany the body in a solemn procession to the church and there to make prayers and offerings for the soul, at mass on the day of burial, and on the seventh and thirtieth days following. Elsewhere prayers were said on the third day after burial. The soul was believed to remain in proximity to the body for a few days after its separation at death; the appropriate rites and prayers at this liminal point aided its journey to the other world.[56] The Trinity Gild supported a chaplain to say one hundred masses for each departed member and to celebrate mass

51 PRO, C47/38/36.

52 A. Van Gennep, *The Rites of Passage*, translated by M.B. Vizedom and G.L. Caffee, London 1977, esp. ch. viii, 165, 'convocation by drum crier or messenger gives the meal even more of the character of a collective ritual'.

53 PRO, C47/38/6. The small sums left to gilds in wills of the 15th and 16th centuries were probably to pay for the hire of such things.

54 The medieval view was that they also had greater opportunities for sin and therefore less chance of redemption, as exemplified in the story of Lazarus and the rich man, Luke 16, vv. 19–31.

55 PRO, C47/38/10.

56 Toulmin Smith, 194 Statutes of the Palmer's Gild, Ludlow; alternative folk customs are described.

daily for its brothers and sisters. The gild purchased two indulgences from the Bishop of Ely. One in 1378 granted forty days' remission from purgatory to its benefactors, and one in 1384 another forty days' remission to benefactors or to those who took part in the gild celebration of the feast of the Holy Trinity 'Mente pia' with pious intent.

The Holy Trinity Gild, Wisbech, was another wealthy gild.[57] It acted as *de facto* corporation for the town with the approval of the bishops of Ely, for whom Wisbech was the administrative centre of many of their estates.[58] In 1389 the gild employed various chaplains and clerks to sing commemorative masses for brethren and benefactors in its private chapel in the church of Saints Peter and Paul.[59] Income from land endowed these services, and by the time of its abolition in 1547 the gild employed four perpetual chaplains, one of whom had additional responsibilities as local schoolmaster.[60] The gild purchased a mortmain licence for various bequests of land in 1453 under the aldermanship of John Masse,[61] who left the gild, among other things, the sum of 5 marks to purchase an indulgence from the Pope.[62]

The smaller and poorer fraternities offered a narrower range of funeral and commemorative practices according to their funds. Not all could support a perpetual chaplain and so contented themselves with hiring a priest for particular occasions when funds allowed, or relying on the intercession of their patron saint for whom they burned a light in the church.

Within a gild, some funeral and commemorative customs were performed for all brothers and sisters, and others only for certain individuals according to a number of factors: age, gender, status and wealth. The gild, like a microcosm of society at large and like other social groups, made a greater public display of mourning people, generally men, who had played a larger part in public life.[63]

Trentals of masses were celebrated only for the brothers and sisters of the Assumption Gild, St Mary's Church, Ely, who were aged over sixteen, and according to a 1504 addition to its statutes, All Saints Gild, All Saints Church, Cambridge, provided five priests to sing *dirige* and mass for departed brothers and only two for sisters.[64] In 1389, although eight gilds buried poor brethren at gild expense, this was an act of charity, akin to burying strangers, rather than an automatic right. The Assumption Gild, Holy Trinity Church,

57 *VCH Cambs.*, ii, 92, 320, 327; iv, 254–6.

58 WCR1. This document started life as the Trinity Gild Register and became vol. 1 of the corporation records on the town's incorporation in 1547.

59 PRO, C47/38/43.

60 PRO, Prob 11/20/8, fos 55v, 56r and v, 1520, will of Robert Smythe; Prob 11/20/24, fos 190v–2r, 1521, will of Thomas Wyth, gentleman.

61 PRO, C66/478, 32 Henry VI, membrane 23, patent roll licence to found a chantry.

62 PRO, Prob 11/5/14, fos 112r and v, 113r, 1466, will of John Masse.

63 Bloch and Parry, *Death and the Regeneration of Life*, Introduction 4; Van Gennep, *Rites of Passage*, 148, mourning is greater for those of higher social standing.

64 PRO, C47/38/17a, b; CUL, MM1 36: Baker Mss. vol. 25, item 10, p. 371.

Cambridge, expressed the reduced status of brethren whose funerals were paid for from gild funds by burning only two candles at the offices of the dead, not the customary four.[65]

So that a brother might not be buried as a stranger in another town, 12 (20%) gilds in 1389 made arrangements to counter this. If a brother died within ten leagues of Stretham, the warden and two brothers of the Assumption Gild would bring the body back to the town, where it was to be buried among the brothers of the fraternity with due ceremony.[66] Other gilds in the rural communities of Stretham, Stowe Cum Quye and March also imposed a distance limitation on such activities, whereas the gilds of the major towns of the county, Cambridge, Ely and Wisbech, took it for granted that some members would die while away on business. This is also a feature of gilds in the trade centres of Norwich and Lynn in Norfolk.[67] The statutes of St Katherine's Gild, St Simon and St Jude's Church, Norwich, provided for the body to be buried wherever lawful, illustrating the practical as well as the religious aspects of dying away from home. Gilds in the larger towns had members from the surrounding region,[68] who gained limited benefit from the burial customs. Attendance at their funerals was not compulsory, although two Cambridge gilds, the Annunciation, Great St Mary's Church, and St Katherine's, St Benet's Church, arranged for mass to be held as if the corpse were present.[69] Membership of a gild in a town where a man had business dealings such as Thomas Gladman's membership of the fraternity of St Thomas the Martyr at Bruges would ensure commemoration and burial appropriate to his status if he died there.[70]

The widows of the brethren of the Purification Gild, Great St Mary's Church, Cambridge, who had fallen into poverty, were denied burial at gild expense.[71] Poverty brought no recompense for the status they had once enjoyed as the wives of the wealthy burgesses of Cambridge. Women generally received individual commemoration only as the wives of founders, or as widowed benefactresses.

Founders undertook the expense of setting up a gild, in part for their own commemoration, but over the course of time, these institutions came to need re-endowment. Men who had been prominent in gild affairs, such as John Masse, alderman of Holy Trinity Gild, Wisbech, often made substantial gifts so that memory of their deeds would continue. Some commemorative practices were assured on payment of a certain sum: 40*s* for an anniversary mass for

65 PRO, C47/38/5.
66 PRO, C47/38/32.
67 Toulmin Smith, 19–20, statutes of St Katherine's Gild, church of Saints Simon and Jude, Norwich; 51–53, statutes of St Leonard's Gild, St James Church, Damgate, Lynn.
68 PRO, C47/38/4, 9.
69 PRO, C47/38/4, 7.
70 PRO, Prob 11/3/33, fos 257v, 258r, 1443 will of Thomas Gladman of Northamptonshire.
71 PRO, C47/38/9.

brothers and sisters of St Clement's, Saints Peter and Paul, and All Saints Gilds in fifteenth-century Cambridge.[72] Some commemorative practices were administered by the gild on behalf of a wealthy person who had made an endowment for that specific purpose. Lord Robert de Scales of Haslingfield endowed the Assumption Gild in order to administer his chantry in 1344, and Thomas Whiskyn in 1528 left 12*d* a year for twelve years to the Resurrection Gild, Chesterton, for a mass and *dirige*.[73]

Wills are an additional source of material to augment the scant records which most of the fraternities leave behind. Out of a sample of around 2,000 Cambridgeshire wills (1383–1588), around 1,000 were proved prior to the abolition of the gilds or fraternities in 1547. Only 150 (14%) mentioned gilds or fraternities. Sixty-seven of these wills were proved nationally in the Prerogative Court of Canterbury and so were made by richer people who could afford to pay for a number of forms of commemoration. Indeed, 82 did request commemoration by groups apart from the gilds to which they had belonged. Wills illustrate multiple membership of the gilds, especially in the later fifteenth and early sixteenth centuries. This caused no apparent conflict of loyalty but merely increased opportunities for commemoration. In 1529 Margaret Pepis of Cottenham left 8*d* to every gild within the town keeping a light within the church, 'So that they come with their banners to bring my body to burial'.[74]

Town corporations such as that of Cambridge were nominated in the wills of their former aldermen and burgesses, as the guardians of their memory and administrators of their commemoration. These follow the same pattern as the exequies kept by the university and the colleges for their fellows.[75] Just as the small sums of money given to participants in the ritual imitate the monastic *pitancia* given to the monks for their prayers, as money or extra food at the anniversary of a benefactor, so also the gradation of the sums disbursed reflected the ordering of the social hierarchy of the town. In 1545 John Chapman 'one of the Aldermen of the town of Cambridge' died.[76] After the death of his wife he requested that his messuage and tenement be sold, and the money delivered to the mayor and burgesses on condition that they kept an annual obit,[77] with *placebo* and *dirige* and a mass of requiem for his soul, those of his wife, their friends and all Christian souls. On that occasion the parish priest was to have 8*d*; every fellow of the same house 4*d*;[78] the mayor or

72 BL Add. Ms. 5846, pp. 5–13; CUL MM1 36, Baker Mss., vol. 25, pp. 361–6, 367–71.

73 PRO, C47/38/24; ECC (1/3/4) 1528.

74 Palmer, 348 cites this will. Multiple membership seems to contradict the emphasis in the 1389 Ordinances on loyalty and keeping gild secrets; Chiffoleau, *La Comptabilité*, part II.

75 P. Michaud-Quantin, *Universitas: Expression du Mouvement Communautaire dans le Moyen Age Latin*, Paris 1970.

76 ACE (2/1/12), 1545, will of John Chapman.

77 Obit – commemorative services on the anniversary of a death.

78 I.e. College of the University at which the priest resided.

deputy being present 3*s* 4*d*, the aldermen present 20*d*, with 2*d* or 1*d* for their offerings; 16*d* to the town clerk and the town sergeant, with 1*d* for their offerings; and 4*d* for the bell-ringers, and 12*d* for lights about the hearse. The poor were to feast on 13*s* 4*d* worth of bread, 7*s* worth of cheese, and 2*s* worth of ale, while the mayor and corporation were to be entertained to a breakfast or dinner costing 5 marks a year.

Colleges, gilds or borough corporations were the preserves of the elites of town or village. The parish was an institution to which technically every person belonged. It emerged into prominence in the course of the later Middle Ages, in recognition of which the Tudor dynasty endowed it with greater local powers. Nearly everyone was buried in the parish churchyard, their funerals conducted by the parish clergy. The parish church possessed a stock of liturgical ornaments and paraphernalia donated by the parishioners over the years, and, like that owned by the gilds, hired out for funeral and these commemorative rites. The churchwardens of Holy Trinity Church, Cambridge, administered the rental of small tapers, great tapers, standers, lights, and torches at various prices, a hearse purchased collectively in 1515, and vestments for mass priests who doubtless could also be hired in the town.[79] Elsewhere parish coffins and palls were available. The rural parishioners of Bassingbourne seem to have had less choice. There the only such payments recorded were for the hire of the torches.[80]

The parish was a repository for collective memory, and furthermore, provided continuity of administration for memorials to its dead. A wealth of detail on the administration of anniversaries or 'obits' is found in Bassingbourne churchwardens accounts and the evidence of wills augments the sparse survival of such documents. Most commonly, wills requested the administration of commemorative rites by family members, executors who were generally family members or men prominent in parish affairs, and churchwardens. For example, in 1416, Sir Thomas de Skelton of Hinxton, left a tenement to be administered by the churchwardens there 'custodi operis ecclesie predicte et successoribus suis'. They were to arrange an anniversary mass for him for twenty years following his death and to distribute 40*d* on the anniversaries of each of his three wives.[81] As with the gilds, age, gender, status and wealth determined the extent of commemoration. In Norwich at this time

> Notice is given of the death of such a person by the great bell of the parish where the deceased dwelt and died . . . continued a greater or less time according to the estate and reputation of the deceased, and for persons of

[79] CCRO, P22/5/1, churchwardens' accounts, Cambridge, Holy Trinity Parish 1504–1558, fo 6r, et passim. A hearse was a stand to support lights placed over the body at the exequies, and a pall was a decorative cloth which could be placed over this.
[80] CCRO, P11/5/1–2 Bassingbourne churchwardens accounts 1490–1540, passim.
[81] PRO, Prob 11/2b/34, fos 270v–1r, 1416 will of John de Skelton, knight, of Hinxton.

> note half an hour or more; for poor persons only a short time. Also less for children than men or women . . . the bell thus ringing is by some called a soul bell . . .[82]

Because such 'superstitious' practices lingered on, the removal of church bells was under way, when Edward VI died in 1553.[83]

Out of the sample of 2,000 wills, 627 (32%) made specific requests for certain funeral or commemorative rites. Added to this a further 499 (25%) left details of such arrangements in the hands of their executors, bringing the total to 57%.[84] The will itself was intimately associated with the death of the testator: most were written when people were on their death-beds, judging by the short time between the date of the will and the date of probate, and many testators refer to themselves as 'sick in body but of good and perfect remembrance.'[85] The standard bequests of a few pennies to certain causes listed below the preamble, sometimes dismissed as convention, must be viewed in association with the death of the testator. The sums left to the mother church, or the churchyard or fabric of the parish church were to pay for burial; to the bells and torches for their hire at the funeral. Bequests for tithes forgotten were to ensure that the soul would not be hampered on its journey. Bequests to altars, lights or gilds within the church invoked the intercession of the saints for the soul, and bequests to secular or regular clergy invoked their prayers. All these disappeared from wills between the mid-1540s and the mid-1550s.

Chantries have received much attention in recent research. They have been studied primarily as architectural or institutional forms and in relation to the aristocratic or gentry families with which they were associated.[86] This has concealed the variations in their administration and their connections with other aspects of late medieval life.

Work on perpetual chantries in Cambridgeshire by Edward Ventris, supplemented by information in the Victoria County History, records sixty-six, founded between the late thirteenth and early sixteenth centuries.[87] This figure includes two chantry colleges: one at Newton St Mary and one at

82 W. Rye, 'The Order of Funerals, Ringings etc. at Norwich', *The East Anglian, N. & Q.* new series, ii, 1887–8, 389–92. The number of strokes would inform the hearers of the exact status of the deceased.

83 P. Collinson, *The Elizabethan Puritan Movement*, London 1967, 370–1.

84 J. Scarisbrick, *The Reformation and the English People*, Oxford 1984, 5–6; two-thirds of testators in the 1530s requested some prayers for their soul.

85 This phrase is more common in the 16th than the 15th century.

86 Cook, *Medieval Chantries and Chantry Chapels*; K.L. Wood-Leigh, *Perpetual Chantries in Britain*, Cambridge 1965; Rosenthal, *The Purchase of Paradise*, ch. 3; M. Hicks, 'The Piety of Margaret, Lady Hungerford', *JEH* xxxviii, 1987, 19–38, an excellent study of the pious motivation of a foundress.

87 *VCH Cambs.* ii–vi, viii; E. Ventris, 'Notes upon Chantries and Free Chapels', *Proc. Camb. Antiq. Soc.* i, 1859, 201–40.

Ely,[88] but does not take into account the many colleges of Cambridge University, endowed primarily as chantries.

Early chantry foundations were administered by monasteries, either within their precincts or by providing chaplains to celebrate in a parish church. This was the case in Barton where, from 1278, two canons of Barnwell Priory lived, serving God and St Mary and saying masses for their benefactors.[89] By the later Middle Ages other corporate bodies, gilds or fraternities, parishes or townships were being entrusted with chantry management; ten (15%) were either wholly or partly funded by fraternities. Henry Cyprian of Whittlesford had endowed a chantry there, but failed to obtain a mortmain licence: the township, its administrators, recovered the land and put it to other use.[90] Perpetual chantries were expensive; an option open only to the extremely wealthy who could guarantee landed income in perpetuity to sustain them. There has been much debate on whether they were in decline on the eve of the reformation.[91] However, Alan Kreider has demonstrated that the further away they were from their date of foundation the greater the likelihood of their decline.[92] For example, the chantry at Barton had fallen into abeyance by the late-fourteenth century. There was a pragmatic approach to uneconomic institutions: once the founder had been forgotten, unless there was re-endowment by a new benefactor, as for 8 (12%), of the Cambridgeshire chantries, the foundation was dissolved and the revenues transferred elsewhere.[93]

For perpetual chantries to be fully understood they must be set within the context of temporary chantry provision, as revealed in wills and parish records. Out of 254 wills proved in the Prerogative Court of Canterbury, drawn from twenty sample parishes, 98 (38%) requested some form of chantry.[94] The late medieval church catered for every pocket. Great wealth bought 'perpetual' commemoration: 14 (5%) people requested perpetual chantries to be administered respectively; one by Walsingham Priory, Norfolk; one by a Cambridge college; five by family or executors; six by religious gilds; and one by the Hedborowes, or officers of the township of Chesterton. Those with moderate wealth could pay 8 marks a year for a secular or regular priest to say mass for them daily,[95] 37 (15%) people requested the services of one or more priests

88 The 'Cantarie de la Grene' at Ely is not mentioned in either of the above, and is known only through wills. See for example, EDA, HK2791/A, fos 10v, 40r, 46v.

89 *VCH Cambs*. v, 172.

90 *VCH Cambs*. vi, 272.

91 J.A.F. Thompson, 'Piety and Charity in Late Medieval London', *JEH* xvi, 1965, 178–95; R.B. Dobson, 'The Foundation of Perpetual Chantries by the Citizens of Medieval York', *SCH* iv, 1967, 22–38. Both argue against this line.

92 Kreider, *English Chantries*, 89.

93 Dobson, 'The Foundation of Perpetual Chantries', 22–38.

94 Burgess, 'By Quick and By Dead', 837–8, esp. 840, 842 reminds us of the limitations of wills as a source. Nevertheless they express intention if not actuality.

95 EDA, HK2791/A, fos 56v–57r, 1458 wills of Margaret Ffarnham. A priest to sing for a year cost 8 marks. Other examples show this to have been the usual price.

for between two and twenty years, and 47 (18%) for one year. Thirty-three (13%) people endowed an anniversary mass or obit for a number of years. These varied in expense and elaboration and were a fashionable practice particularly in the early sixteenth century, often in addition to other commemoration.[96] For those with lesser means a trental costing about 10*s* could be sung shortly after death.

Others had to content themselves with a mass of requiem at their funeral, or the prayers of their friends and the poor who had enjoyed the funeral dole. Countless others went to their graves with none of these spiritual resources, but were remembered, nevertheless, by the wealthier who made provision for all Christian souls along with those to be specifically commemorated. The same groups which administered perpetual chantries administered temporary ones. These were less cumbersome than the perpetual institutions, which may partly explain their popularity. Their numbers and the diversity of commemorative practices attest not only to the vitality of pre-Reformation Catholicism, but also to the resources available to comfort medieval men and women facing bereavement.[97]

Commemorative activities were not merely for the benefit of the dead, but to assist those left behind with their grief.[98] The different stages of the funeral, the vigil, the *placebo* and *dirige*, and mass and burial; and of the commemorative rituals, the third, seventh and thirtieth days and anniversaries may be seen as markers in the passage of grief.[99] Indeed, the commemoration of the dead by the living was an affirmation of their continuing affinity. This may be seen with particular clarity in the commensality or sharing of food provided by the dead at their funeral or commemoration.[100] Wills show that bread and ale and sometimes cheese or barrels of herrings were regularly consumed, sometimes by all who were gathered there and sometimes specifically by the poor, those on the margins of society who represented the dead at the feast. Colleges, gilds, towns and parishes ate and drank the health of their dead on appointed days, the expenses of which they recorded carefully in their accounts. In Bassingbourne, a herd of 'obit cows' and 'obit lands' funded

96 C. Burgess, 'A Service for the Dead: the Form and Function of the Anniversary in Late Medieval Bristol', *Transactions of Bristol and Gloucester Archaeological Society* cv, 1987, 183–211.

97 Ariès, *Western Attitudes*, ch. iv, draws on recent sociological studies to underline the impoverishment of 20th-century Western society in this respect.

98 E. Kubler-Ross, *On Death and Dying*, New York 1969; E. Kubler-Ross, *Death: The Final Stage of Growth*, Englewood Cliffs, New Jersey 1975.

99 Bloch and Parry, *Death and The Regeneration of Life*, Introduction 3–4, the two phases of mortuary rituals enable society to recover and to locate death, an arbitrary event, within time; Van Gennep, *Rites of Passage*, 147, mourning is a transitional rite for the survivors.

100 Bloch and Parry, *Death and The Regeneration of Life*, 28, commensality is associated with sexuality and therefore birth with death; Van Gennep, *Rites of Passage*, 164–5, commensality unites the survivors with the dead.

the anniversaries of those who had left them for this purpose.[101] The cows were hired out as milk beasts and breeding cattle to the poor and the lands to those who could afford them, thus becoming a feature of agricultural life in the community. Grain left as pious bequests to the church was regularly brewed and consumed at 'church ales' to make money for parish funds. In these ways the commemoration of the dead and their gifts to the living were part of the tissue of communal life and endeavour, rather than confined to the elaborate carved forms of the chantry chapel.

The performance of funeral and commemorative rituals was a deed of charity done for the souls of the dead by the living, who in return would gain spiritual reward in the next life. These rituals contained the enactment of the dead divesting themselves of their material goods through the distribution of food, thus symbolizing the complex reciprocities between the living and the dead. For the population in general the Reformation period was a time of doctrinal change and uncertainty which had a profound effect on this nexus of relationships.

In the 1520s the doctrine of purgatory and the belief that the living could help the dead began to be discredited, along with the authority of the papacy, under the attacks of continental reformers. In the early 1530s legal changes prevented the foundation of perpetual chantries.[102] In 1536 Henry VIII issued a declaration against purgatory and by 1540 institutions which had catered for commemoration, not only monasteries but friaries which had been popular for prayers, trentals and other masses, had gone. Other commemorative groups – gilds, colleges, chantries and hospitals – were to follow them in 1547.

In wills this is reflected in changes to the pattern of bequests.[103] From the late 1530s, money for prayers, masses and anniversaries was entrusted to family or executors in preference to public bodies such as gild or parish, presumably due to fear of confiscation. Some anniversary doles to the poor shifted from the date of death of the testator into association with Christ's death and were made during Lent, at Easter, or at Christmas. Prior to these religious upheavals, on average one-third of the will was taken up with the disposal of the testator's material wealth for the health of his or her soul. By the mid-1540s, testators requested elaborate funerals and commemoration only 'if it be lawful'. By 1547 and the more thorough-going Protestantism of Edward VI's reign all this was absent from the will and the testators' personal

101 CCRO, P11/5/1–2, Bassingbourne churchwardens' accounts 1490–1540, passim.

102 Kreider, *The English Chantries*, 84–85, the end of chantry foundation; chs iv and v, on the demise of purgatory.

103 From work on the sample of 2,000 Cambridgeshire wills, it appears that they are not suitable for measuring the growth of confessional faith, whether Protestantism or post-Reformation Catholicism, as too many testators used neutral wording at this difficult period. They do show, however, the broad outline of response to government initiatives on religious matters.

tastes were marked by the opaque phrases 'at the discretion of myne executors', 'according to the laudable custom of the realm'. Between the mid-1540s and mid-1550s the only continuity was of bequests to the poor at the funeral to pray for the dead man or woman, and annual doles for a number of years after death, with no explicit request for prayers, but perhaps with the hope among those who still held the old beliefs that the poor held them also. However, even this relationship was interrupted by the mediation of 'the poor mens' box' into which many bequests now went, thus severing the link between donor and recipient. Traditional Catholic funeral and commemorative bequests reappeared in wills after Mary I had returned England to papal allegiance, but only in any numbers from 1556, and even then fewer in proportion and for a shorter number of years than before.

It seems that medieval belief about the nature of the afterlife had been struck a mortal blow in the one or two generations since the outset of the Reformation. More importantly, all the bodies, except the family, which had administered commemorative practices, both the small number of perpetual institutions and the rich undergrowth of temporary provision, had either been secularized or were simply no longer there.

When attempting to understand late medieval perceptions of death, certain things are plain. There is no sense in which death was an annihilation of the individual: he or she was merely translated to the other side of a divide, retaining the status and identity once held in life. The dead were still a part of the various bodies to which they had belonged in life and these communities mourned their forbears as their social standing required and to the extent that their resources allowed.

The swift and apparently uncontested decline in practices identifiable with the belief in purgatory is less well understood. John Bossy suggested that the system became an overwhelming burden on the living and simply collapsed under its own weight.[104] This is a practical suggestion, but does not go far enough to explain the changes in mentality which accompanied it. The tearing apart of death and charity, the reciprocity between the living and the dead, and the poor, their substitutes, struck a blow at the very core of medieval concepts of community.[105]

There were some continuities however: those benefactions which were not confiscated by the Crown were re-absorbed and re-deployed by the secular groups which administered them: the family, secular colleges, the town, the parish.[106] The 'elect', once petitioned for spiritual succour on behalf of the faithful departed, were now the champions of the Protestant faith: they hoped to be saved by 'the merits of Christ's passion' and 'his

104 Bossy, 'The Mass', 29–61.
105 Duffy, *Stripping of the Altars*, 8.
106 C. Kitching, 'The Quest for Concealed lands in the Reign of Elizabeth I', *TRHS* 5th series, xxiv, 1974, 63–78.

redeeming blood' just as these very symbols had been central to the devotional practices of a generation before.[107] The poor were still given alms at funerals and on church festivals as a pious memorial to the wealthy, who still commissioned elaborate effigies of themselves, now with their eyes open as if alive, rather than closed as if in sleep.[108] Death remained a preoccupying theme for the writers of Jacobean tragedy and metaphysical poetry, and death itself, through plague or famine or other mishap, continued to carry many to an untimely grave.

So, whither purgatory? How deep-rooted had belief ever been among the laity and how far just an insurance policy? We must view these things in the *longue durée*. Historians such as Ariès and le Goff may have under-estimated the cyclical nature of eschatological belief.[109] The renewed emphasis on the imminence of the last judgement which accompanied the Protestant Reformation supplanted the temporary judgement of souls newly arrived in eternity and waiting out their sentences for that last great distant moment. This must be set against the long-term decline in belief in the supernatural. The existence of purgatory became widely doubted in the course of the sixteenth century; also the existence of hell by the late seventeenth century.[110] The supernatural itself became less able to intervene in everyday life; a realm increasingly remote from the cosmology of the early modern world.

107 The use of these phrases in the preambles of wills takes on a particular ambiguity in the 1540s and 1550s.

108 P. King, 'The Iconography of the Corpse', paper delivered at the Institute of Historical Research, London 29 May 1991.

109 McDannell and Lang, *Heaven: a History*, 353–8, describe the cyclical prominence of various beliefs about the afterlife at different times. Ariès and le Goff tend to view changes on a linear model.

110 R. Wunderli and E. Broce, 'The Final Moment before Death in Early Modern England', *Sixteenth Century Journal* xx, 1989, 259–75, 275 cite D.P. Walker, *The Decline of Hell: Seventeenth-Century Discussions of Eternal Torment*, Chicago 1964. By the late 17th century belief in hell had declined, by the 18th century it was under open attack; Camporesi, *The Fear of Hell*, part I, gives details of the outrageous descriptions of hell the Jesuits made in the 18th century to try to gain the attention of sophisticated audiences.

5

Poverty, Charity and the After-Life

The medieval concept of charity was far broader than the definition of the word today.[1] The modern term 'charity' means benefaction to the poor: the gracious bestowing of surplus goods by the morally and socially advantaged on those less fortunate than themselves. The dependent status of the poor was enshrined in the Elizabethan Poor Laws of 1598 and 1601.[2] Until the enactment of the New Poor Law or Poor Law Amendment Act of 1834, the sixteenth-century legislation was the foundation on which all charitable activity was based, and so has fundamentally determined modern attitudes and definitions.[3] However, much Victorian scholarly writing on charity was influenced by the prolonged crisis in the social conditions of the poor, caused by industrialisation, which the 1834 legislation failed to solve.[4] Concepts current at the time were applied to the study of poverty and charity in late medieval and early modern culture. This is also true of the work which has shaped much current debate, W.K. Jordan's monumental, if problematic, study of *Philanthropy in England 1480–1660*, most notably in the borrowing of the nineteenth-century term 'philanthropy' to unlock the attitudes of a previous age.[5]

Early studies of medieval charity emphasised its institutional forms.[6] During

1 M. Mollat, *Les Pauvres Au Moyen Age: Etude Sociale*, Paris 1978; J.A.F. Thompson, 'Piety and Charity in Late medieval London', *JEH* xvi, 1965, 178–95.

2 P. Slack, *The English Poor Law 1531–1782*, London 1990; J. Pound, *Poverty and Vagrancy in Tudor England*, London 1971; E.M. Hampson, *The Treatment of Poverty in Cambridgeshire 1597–1834*, Cambridge 1924.

3 A.L. Beier, *The Problem of the Poor in Tudor and Early Stuart England*, London 1983, 1.

4 B. Tierney, *Medieval Poor Law: A Sketch of Canonical Theory and its Application in England*, Berkeley, Los Angeles, 1959, 44–54 offers a critique of 19th-century historians of medieval poor law.

5 W.K. Jordan, *Philanthropy in England 1480–1660: A Study of the Changing Patterns of English Social Aspirations*, London 1959, esp. ch. vi, 'The Impulse'; W.K. Jordan, *The Charities of London 1480–1660: The Aspirations and Achievements of the Urban Society*, London 1960; W.K. Jordan, *The Charities of Rural England: The Aspirations and Achievements of the Rural Society*, London 1961; D.C. Coleman, 'Review: W.K. Jordan, Philanthropy in England', *EcHR*, series 2 xiii, 1960–1, 113–15, is an example of the criticism which Jordan's methodology has received.

6 R.M. Clay, *The Medieval Hospitals of England*, London 1909; W.H. Godfrey, *The English*

the course of the later Middle Ages, increasing numbers of charitable institutions were founded: hospitals and almshouses,[7] and a new development in the sixteenth century, workhouses.[8] The wholesale dissolution of the monasteries from 1536 to 1539, and hospitals, along with gilds, chantries and colleges from 1545 to 1547, organisations which had previously assisted the poor, necessitated a refoundation of charitable institutions on a grand scale in the later sixteenth century.[9] This process, identified by Jordan's survey, was well-documented, as it coincided with the explosion of written records which characterised early modern administrative activity.

In medieval times, certain motives for founding an almshouse or hospital might today be identified as 'secular', for example, the glorification of the founders and their families,[10] and the alleviation of poverty and sickness. The inmates were likely to have been among the retainers of the founders' families and their admission therefore represented a reward for loyalty. Almshouses and hospitals, however, epitomised the aspirations of late medieval piety, which was one of the reasons for their abolition. Corporate activity revolved around prayer for the souls of founders and benefactors, and provided the opportunity for small numbers of the respectable poor, often the symbolic number of thirteen, to live a semi-monastic life, according to a rule.[11] Medieval charitable institutions therefore illustrate the lack of distinction between the religious and the secular and the inter-relation of ideas concerning poverty, charity and the afterlife during this period.[12]

Institutional provision for the poor, like institutional provision for the souls of the dead, was underpinned by a vast mass of informal benefaction: this is comparatively poorly documented and thus visible, for example, only through numerous small bequests in the wills of yeomen, husbandmen and modest town-dwellers, proved in local diocesan courts; or through gild statutes,

Almshouse, London 1955; Jordan, *Philanthropy in England*, 23, 146–7, wrongly identifies monastic and other almsgiving as the most representative form of medieval charity, probably because it is better documented and therefore more easily quantified.

7 C. Dyer, *Standards of Living in the Later Middle Ages*, Cambridge 1989, 242–6, esp. 244; A. Kreider, *English Chantries: The Road to Dissolution*, Cambridge, Massachusetts, 1979, ch. 3. As with the chantries, the highest numbers of hospitals and almshouses are documented after the 1279 mortmain legislation and by the surveys prior to their mid-16th-century dissolution.

8 Beier, *The Problem of the Poor*, 25, 34–35, Bridewell, the first workhouse founded in London in 1553, provided a model for this type of institution.

9 Jordan, *Philanthropy in England*, 146–7.

10 J. Rosenthal, *The Purchase of Paradise: Gift Giving and the Aristocracy 1307–1485*, London 1972, ch. 7.

11 Clay, *The Medieval Hospitals*; Godfrey, *The English Almshouse*; M. Rubin, *Charity and Community in Medieval Cambridge*, Cambridge 1987, focuses on the Hospital of St John the Evangelist in Cambridge; Dyer, *Standards of Living*, 243–4.

12 Thompson, 'Piety and Charity', 180; M.G.A. Vale, *Piety, Charity and Literacy among the Yorkshire Gentry 1370–1480*, York 1976, 7. Both these authors assert that piety and charity were indistinguishable in the Middle Ages.

which claimed to aid their brethren when they fell on hard times. It is necessary to examine this evidence more closely to find a more exact definition of medieval charity. Two main principles governing medieval charitable benefaction emerge. The first was the obligation laid upon those with surplus wealth to distribute the excess to the needy,[13] which affirmed notions of hierarchy through the imbalance in social status between donor and recipient.[14] The second was reciprocal support among equals, which the nineteenth century called 'self-help'.[15] The history of collective charitable provision through the communal bonds of neighbourliness has only recently begun to be explored. It is far more elusive, leaving fewer records, but as Judith Bennett states, it was fundamental to the survival of the poor.[16]

By the later Middle Ages, the interaction of Canon Law, the accretion of case-law and interpretation which had grown up around passages from scripture and the Church fathers, had shaped both popular attitudes towards poverty and charity and early poor laws enacted from the mid-fourteenth century.[17] In the sixteenth century secularisation of many aspects of social life previously overseen by the church led the state to take over responsibility for the system of poor-relief.[18] The focus of change in this profoundly important shift in mentality may be located more exactly. During the course of the Reformation period, there was a gradual dissolution of the tie between death and charity. At the beginning of the period under discussion, all charitable activity, all giving to the poor in this life, aided the soul along the path towards salvation.

In 1449 William Roskyn, a layman, and probably a college servant of sufficient standing to be granted the privilege, had his will proved in King's College Peculiar Court. He left 20*s* to be distributed among the poor and the sick for tithes and oblations he had not paid the church, and 8*s* to be distributed among the same 'per rebus illicite perquisitis ac de pauperibus retentis', 'for things illicitly acquired and withheld from the poor'.[19] At worst, then, the poor were perceived as a sponge or a towel on which to wipe away sin, or as John Doget, a priest of King's College, put it, 'sicut aqua extinguit ignem, ita elemosina peccata extinguit', 'just as water extinguishes fire, so alms extinguish sin'.[20] Directives within the body of Canon Law contradicted

13 Tierney, *Medieval Poor Law*, ch. 2, esp. 33–38.
14 F. Heal, 'The Idea of Hospitality in Early Modern England', *P&P* cii, 1984, 66–93, esp. 90.
15 Toulmin Smith, xiv.
16 B. Hanawalt, *The Ties that Bound: Peasant Families in Medieval England*, Oxford 1986, an impressive analysis of interdependence in peasant society; J. Bennett, 'Conviviality and Charity in Medieval and Early Modern England', *P&P* cxxxiv, 1992, 3–41, esp. 22–23, 41; Jordan, *Philanthropy in England*, 146–7.
17 Tierney, *Medieval Poor Law*, 5–6, 128–31.
18 Tierney, *Medieval Poor Law*, 131.
19 KCC, fo 1r, 1449.
20 KCC, fos 177r–8v, 1500; M. Flynn, *Sacred Charity: Confraternities and Social Welfare in*

this lenient view: motives for benefaction had to be pure. The soul would not acquire merit from gifts of property which had either been stolen or which were inspired by vainglory.[21] Nevertheless, the hour of death was the last time at which men and women could themselves perform acts of piety which might release them from hell or a long purgatorial sentence, and it is often the only time at which the historian may pry into the mind of the past. The original purpose of the will was to ensure the testator's state of grace at death, rather than to dispose of worldly property.[22] From the early Middle Ages, the poor had held a special role in the rituals associated with death: their prayers were efficacious in assisting the souls of the dead at this dangerous time, as they migrated towards the other world.[23]

Charity and the Affirmation of Hierarchy

In 1505 Richard Stevyns died, a young scholar at King's College Cambridge. As a priest he would have been expected to expound the moral and religious teachings of his society. Instead they were inscribed in his will:

> . . . because Jesus Christ accepts temporal goods distributed to the poor as given to himself according to the Evangelist Matthew, and because also according to the Apostle, this is of the greatest assistance to God, I will that on the day of my death, loaves may be distributed among the poor, to the sum of 20*d*.[24]

The passage from St Matthew's gospel, to which Stevyns referred, formed the guidelines for much of the charity which the rich bestowed upon the poor in the Middle Ages.

> When the Son of Man comes in his glory, and all the Angels with him, he will sit on his throne in heavenly glory. All the nations will be gathered before him, and he will separate the people one from another as a shepherd separates the sheep from the goats. He will put the sheep on his right and the goats on his left. Then the King will say to those on his right, 'Come, you who are blessed by my Father; take your inheritance, the Kingdom prepared for you since the creation of the world. For I was hungry and you gave me something to eat (1), I was thirsty and you gave me something to drink (2), I was a stranger and you invited me in (3), I needed clothes and you clothed me (4), I was sick and you looked after me (5), I was in prison and you came to visit me (6).' Then the righteous will answer him, 'Lord

Spain 1400–1700, London 1989, 45, quotes this phrase from a fraternity document. This was obviously a stock formula.

21 Tierney, *Medieval Poor Law*, 49–53.

22 M.T. Clanchy, *From Memory to Written Record*, London 1979, 183.

23 M.M. Sheehan, *The Will in Medieval England*, Toronto 1963, 11–14.

24 KCC, fo 201v, 1505.

> when did we see you hungry and feed you, or thirsty and give you something to drink? When did we see you a stranger and invite you in, or needing clothes and clothe you? When did we see you sick or in prison and go to visit you?' The King will reply, 'I tell you the truth, whatever you did for one of the least of these brothers of mine, you did for me.' Then he will say to those on his left, 'Depart from me, you who are cursed, into the eternal fire prepared for the devil and his angels.'[25]

This, then, was the Last Judgement as represented in the many *dooms* painted and carved in pre-Reformation churches, often with St Michael the Archangel, weighing the souls and the Virgin Mary interceding for them before her son.[26] The moral of the story was clear: those who had obeyed the Church's injunction to assist the poor through the seven works of bodily mercy, the burial of the dead being the seventh, would go to heaven: those who had not done so would be led away by demons into Hell, depicted as the mouth of a huge monster. Luther's doctrine of justification by faith alone initiated a swingeing attack on the necessity of good works for salvation, so that although the same passage was alluded to in the preamble to the 1601 Law of Trusts and in subsequent writings on charity, puritan authors were careful to distance themselves from any link with the seven works of mercy.[27]

Maureen Flynn in her important analysis of *Sacred Charity: Confraternities and Social Welfare in Spain 1400–1700* includes all medieval charity within the definition of religious ritual: its primary purpose was symbolic, not the alleviation of need.[28] Like other religious rituals, the dispensation of charity reflected the structure of society. The provision of food and the provision of drink, the first two works of mercy, were the most common expressions of charity. Here there was a distinction between commensality, the consumption of shared provisions among equals and those occasions to which the poor were invited by their social superiors. The bread, ale and other food provided by the feudal lord for his *famuli* or household servants and tenants in return for labour services, represented a charitable ideal which was held by

25 Matthew 25, vv. 31–41 (Gideon's Translation), see also vv. 42–46; J. Ryan, 'Charity and Charities', *The Catholic Encyclopaedia*, vol. 3, 15 vols London 1907–12, 592–3.; Tierney, *Medieval Poor Law*, 45–46; Flynn, *Sacred Charity*, esp. chs 1–2.

26 C.E. Keyser, 'On Mural Paintings and Other Coloured Decorations at Chippenham Church, Cambridgeshire', *Proc. Camb. Antiq. Soc.* vi, 1884–8, 321–9, esp. 324–5, 328–9; M.R. James, 'On the Wall Paintings in Willingham Church', *Proc. Camb. Antiq. Soc.* ix, 1894–8, 96–101, esp. 96–97, 100; H.J.E. Burrell and G. Montagu Benton, 'The English Alabaster Carvings of Cambridgeshire, with Special Reference to Fragmentary Examples at Wood Ditton Church', *Proc. Camb. Antiq. Soc.* xxxiv, 1934, 78–83, esp. 81; *Ickleton Cambridgeshire*, ed. R.L. Bristowe, Parochial Church Council of St Mary Magdalen Ickleton, n.d., pamphlet available at the church, section 3, 'The Wall Paintings in the Church', by T. Sladen, no page nos.

27 Pound, *Poverty and Vagrancy*, 56; Heal, 'The Idea of Hospitality', 72.

28 Flynn, *Sacred Charity*, 5; Jordan, *Philanthropy in England*, 58–61; Heal, 'The Idea of Hospitality', 72.

contemporary authors to be in decline by the sixteenth century.[29] Such hospitality illustrates a fundamental point about the nature of medieval charity: that there was some element of reciprocity, however uneven the relationship between donor and receiver.[30] Charity was one of the affective bonds which tied individuals and groups together into the fabric of society. Contemporaries also perceived a decline in the hospitality, or provision of food for the poor, by the parish clergy of the fifteenth and sixteenth centuries.[31] Originally the laity had been entitled to claim a quarter of what was paid in tithes for the relief of the poor.[32] The appropriation of at least half of all parishes to monastic houses in the later Middle Ages created a body of impoverished chaplains paid only a small stipend out of the tithes, making it impossible for them to help their parishioners in times of need.[33] Monastic disbursement of food and other alms to the poor did not compensate for this loss, although recent research suggests that such aid was far more substantial than was once thought.[34]

The later Middle Ages, especially the period following the Black Death, was a time of immense demographic, economic and social change. Alongside the declining incomes of nobility, gentry, monasteries and clergy,[35] there emerged greater extremes of wealth and poverty among the peasantry, with the rise of wage-labour and industrialisation.[36] As a result the existing mechanisms for addressing the problem of poverty were no longer adequate.[37]

The large number of gilds recorded during this period both reflect the

29 G.C. Homans, *English Villagers of the Thirteenth Century*, Cambridge, Massachusets, 1941, ch. xviii.

30 M. Mauss, *The Gift: Forms and Functions of Exchange in Archaic Societies*, London 1966, 1–3.

31 Heal, 'The Idea of Hospitality', 66 raises the issue of nostalgia, which should not be overlooked in this context.

32 J.R.H. Moorman, *Church Life in England in the Thirteenth Century*, Cambridge 1945, 138–9.

33 Moorman, *Church Life*, 39–42, at least half of English parishes were appropriated by the end of the 13th century; 139, the effect on poor relief was very serious; Jordan, *Philanthropy in England*, 58–61; Tierney, *Medieval Poor Law*, 67–84, appropriation was partly to blame for the demise of the traditional system of poor relief.

34 Beier, *The Problem of the Poor*, 19–20, esp. table p. 20. Beier suggests that poor relief probably did not make up the amount of charitable provision lost on the dissolution of the monasteries; Pound, *Poverty and Vagrancy*, 16–24, esp. 24.

35 G.A. Holmes, *The Estates of the Higher Nobility in the Fourteenth Century*, Cambridge 1957, provides examples of the problems of some landlords at this time, although this particular point has been the subject of debate.

36 L. Poos, *A Rural Society After the Black Death: Essex 1350–1525*, Cambridge 1991, part v, esp. 181.

37 M.K. McIntosh, 'Local Responses to the Poor in Late Medieval and Tudor England', *Continuity and Change* ii, 1988, 209–45; M.K. McIntosh, 'Local Change and Community Control 1465–1500', *Huntingdon Library Quarterly* xlix, 1986, 219–42; M.K. McIntosh, 'Social Change and Tudor Manorial Elites' in *Law and Social Change in British Society*, ed. J.A. Guy and H.G. Beale, London 1984, 73–85.

greater surplus incomes of the wealthy and moderately wealthy peasants and town dwellers and their efforts at insurance against greater economic uncertainty. Traditionally gilds have been seen as important providers of charity to the poor.[38] On closer inspection this is found not to have been the case. Entry-fees were high, limiting membership, and the charity they gave out was primarily to their own brethren.[39] Unlike the great *scuole* of the Italian cities, they did not administer a religious welfare system through which rich members redistributed their wealth to the deserving poor within the fraternity.[40] Nevertheless, in northern Europe the poor, as outsiders, did serve a ritual purpose at gild occasions. The statutes of the Trinity Gild, St Peter's Church, Ely, proclaimed that the Brethren were to find thirty poor and very needy people to dine with them each year on the feast of the Holy Trinity.[41] Only eleven (18%) of the sixty 1389 statutes extant for Cambridgeshire gilds recorded charitable donations to people outside the gild. Apart from the example cited above, all the other donations were made in association with the funeral and commemorative rites of gild brothers and sisters. The Brethren of the Assumption Gild, Tydd St Giles, were each to give a penny to the poor for the soul of a departed member at the funeral.[42] Collectively they were to give a further thirty pennies to the poor for the soul, either in money or in bread.

The poor as outsiders represented the dead at the feast or at the funeral dole.[43] The reciprocity in the relationship is located in the expectation that the poor would pray for the souls of the dead in return for food. On the evidence of wills, funeral doles were common, and usually took the form of bread, sometimes with ale, herrings or cheese. Sometimes a few shillings' worth of small change or 'penny dole' were dealt out.[44] Grain was one of the forms of currency used in the countryside and so doles of barley, malt, or corn to plant were also made, especially by the men and women of moderate wealth, whose wills were proved in diocesan courts, rather than nationally. In cases where doles were not explicitly linked with the funeral, their distribution soon after the death of the testator would still ensure the customary prayers of the poor.

In 1494 William Bretton the Elder of Dullingham in the Isle of Ely, willed: 'that there be disposed and distributed every lent by the space of five years, six shillings and eight pence among the poor people of the said town of Dullingham'.[45]

38 J.J. Scarisbrick, *The Reformation and the English People*, Oxford 1984, 20–21.
39 Dyer, *Standards of Living*, 246; C. Gross, *The Gild Merchant*, 2 vols, Oxford 1890, i, 36.
40 B. Pullan, *Rich and Poor in Renaissance Venice*, Oxford 1971; J.S. Henderson, *Piety and Charity in Late Medieval Florence*, Oxford 1994.
41 PRO, C47/38/23(5); Toulmin Smith, xxxvii.
42 PRO, C47/38/36.
43 Sheehan, *The Will*, 11–14.
44 This is a standard phrase which occurs in 16th-century wills.
45 PRO, Prob 11/10/22, fo 174v, 1494.

The annual distribution of alms at Christmas, Lent, Holy Week, Easter and Whitsunday illustrates a trend which was to become more popular in the course of the sixteenth century. The initial inspiration for the shift in emphasis from the death of the individual to the death of Christ, derived from the focus of late medieval piety on Christ's passion. This shaded over neatly into Protestant formulations of faith current in the latter years of Henry VIII's reign, and especially under his son Edward, who came to the throne in 1547. After this date such provision became much more common.

In 1547 Thomas Baesley of Toft made this bequest:

> I bequeath to George Baesley my younger son, seven acres of land in 'Woddefyld' and will also that the said George Baesley bestow twelve pence in herring, to be given to poor folk dwelling in the parish of Toft, every lent during the term of thirty years next ensuing.[46]

Several points may be made here. Alms to the poor had always been a prominent feature of an obit described previously. By the early 1540s, Cambridgeshire testators who requested annual charitable distributions over a number of years, were more likely to leave lands, cows or money to support them in the hands of relatives, rather than the churchwardens or the township as in past times. This practice suggests fear of confiscation as the Reformation progressed. It seems most likely that such provisions were the vestiges of medieval Catholic commemorative practice, despite their association with the high feasts of the Church's year. While living memory of the old beliefs survived among the poor, they would have continued to say prayers for the donor's soul in return for the food. Thus although there was a marked decline in requests for prayers for the souls of the dead from the mid-1540s and a halt to such practices during the reign of Edward VI, the secular impulse described by Jordan did not take over straight away.[47] It is possible to see the old beliefs behind a change in practice. Bequests of alms associated with funeral and commemorative rites returned in Mary's reign, although never with the same force.

Sources on charity are remarkably silent about giving hospitality to strangers, the third work of bodily mercy. There was little help for those outside the various overlapping groups which constituted medieval society. There was general suspicion of strangers. *Forinseci* or foreigners was the name given, even to men from the next town, who had limited rights outside their own community. Paradoxically, it was a far more mobile society than is commonly supposed. This may be adjudged by the attempts of landlords through manorial custom, labour legislation enacted after the Black Death and later the 1662 Act of Settlement, to stem ordinary people's mobility.[48] Well-to-do

46 ACE (2/5/3) 1547.
47 W.K. Jordan, *The Charities of Rural England*, 176–80 for comparison with Norfolk.
48 By this Act poor relief was only payable in a person's parish of origin.

households, both monastic and secular, offered hospitality to those of their own social condition who needed lodgings while travelling. For those who were not wealthy there existed a type of hostel, the *Maison Dieu*, about which little is known. In 1464 Thomas Blower stated in his will:

> I will that out of my goods, through the discretion of my executors, a certain house in Wisbech may be made suitable to give hospitality to the poor men and women who come to the said town.[49]

Such institutions were generally short-lived and references to no other Cambridgeshire *Maisons Dieu* have been found. Marjorie McIntosh describes the competition between local people and itinerant strangers over basic resources, once population recovery was under way in the latter half of the fifteenth century.[50] Sixteenth-century anxieties about vagrants are reflected in wills of the time. In the 1540s and 1550s increasing emphasis was laid on distributing alms to the poor of the parish, a system formalised by the 1662 parish settlement legislation. Such poor were not strangers, but they were neither fully inside, nor fully outside, the community, as they participated in the collective rituals of feast or funeral. They were not powerful enough to undermine the social order, but their malevolence and potential disruptiveness had to be propitiated.[51] The distinction between the deserving and the undeserving poor was defined more exactly in the course of the later Middle Ages;[52] like the emphasis placed on the acquisition of an honest priest to say masses for a departed soul, the prayers of the deserving poor, like the sacraments of a clean-living priest, were judged more efficacious. The distinction between the deserving and undeserving poor was not just a utilitarian standard for the division of meagre resources: it had its roots in the desire for salvation. In these circumstances though, the poor were the known poor, not poor strangers.

'Charity begins at home' was a sentiment which was endorsed by the Canon Law.[53] The fourth work of bodily mercy was the clothing of the poor. Death was a suitable time to pass on garments that were no longer required. Best clothing was given to relatives and friends, but garments that were for everyday use or were old and worn would be given to poor people, often to those known by the donor. Jone Hunter of St Giles parish, Cambridge, having left a smock and three petticoats to various women, left another petticoat 'to some

49 PRO, Prob 11/5/6, fos 48v–49r, 1464; P.H. Cullum, '"For Pore People Harberles": What was the Function of the Maisons Dieu?', paper presented at the Fifteenth Century Conference, Manchester University, July 1989, publication forthcoming.

50 McIntosh, 'Social Change and Tudor Manorial Elites', 79–85.

51 Flynn, *Sacred Charity*, 78.

52 Rubin, *Charity and Community*, 72–73, describes the development of this attitude in the late 13th and 14th centuries; Tierney, *Medieval Poor Law*, 59.

53 Tierney, *Medieval Poor Law*, 57.

other poor body within my parish'.[54] Annes Deyn of Connington left 'to Dorant's wife one petticoat'.[55] Richard Algar of St Botolph's parish, Cambridge, left 'unto Bryand the almsman a buxleyng doublet and fourpence . . . and to William Maneyng of St Andrew's Parish a shirt [and] a pair of high shoes'.[56] Raffe Bell of Gamlingay left 'To "Old Bentun" my second coat, and to the povertie of Gamlingay 3*s* 4*d*',[57] and Robert Garret, fellow of Queen's College, Cambridge, left 'To the poor woman which is in the chamber above Master Froote, called Besse, my long frise coat and my old shirt'.[58] It is seldom possible to identify deeds of charity to individuals unless it is specified that they were poor: occasionally, as with some of these examples, this may be judged from the context. It is likely that many of the bequests of small sums of money, grain, livestock and clothing in wills, were made on a charitable basis.

Just as those of middling wealth cast off some of their old clothes to the poor, so those who were significantly wealthier were able to provide new clothes for the poor. It was customary at the most lavish funerals, among the *tableaux vivantes* which accompanied the mourning of a great personage, for a number of paupers, suitably dressed, to attend the dead man or woman.[59]

In 1391 William Fulbourne, lord of the village of Fulbourne St Vigor, requested in his will: 'I would like to have five candles, each containing twelve pounds of wax and six torches, and poor tenants to hold the said torches, each having a tunic and a cap'.[60] In 1409 Katherine de Burgh, Lady of Burgh and Swaffham Bulbeck, pictured the scene of her funeral thus:

> I leave six virgates of russet cloth sufficient in width that they may be placed over my body on the day of my burial, and afterwards to be given to one of the poor friars minor to pray for my soul; ten pounds of wax for two tapers on the day of my burial; six torches of wax; and six paupers holding the torches around [my body] clothed in russet cloth . . .[61]

The same customs applied to the funerals of the leading citizens of towns. In 1413 William Marchford, Citizen and Mercer of London, with lands in Doddington in Cambridgeshire, requested particularly elaborate funeral observances. He left the sum of three pounds to purchase thirty virgates of black cloth to clothe ten torch-bearers. All executors, apprentices, servants and others who came to the funeral, and all those who came on business that day, were to wear black.[62] In 1556 William Bryssyn, burgess of Cambridge,

54 ACE (2/2/7) 1545.
55 ACE (2/3/12) 1546.
56 ACE (2/6/1) 1548.
57 ACE (3/2/1) 1552.
58 VCC (1/1/20) 1557.
59 Rosenthal, *The Purchase of Paradise*, 104, 106–7.
60 PRO, Prob 11/1/8, fos 60r and v.
61 PRO, Prob 11/2a/20, fos 157r and v, 158r.
62 PRO, Prob 11/2a/28, fos 223v, 224r and v, 1413.

required his executors 'to give unto six poor men at their discretion on the day of burial, six black gowns and 4*d* in money'.[63] Such *largesse* says as much about the ostentation customary among those of higher rank as it does about their attitude to the poor. It is not known whether the poor continued to languish in their funeral livery. Flynn believes they would have done so, thereby acting as a living *memento mori*.[64] Certainly tenants and servants may have worn them out of loyalty, but the poor without such ties might have sold them on for the money.[65]

The fifth work of bodily mercy was caring for the sick. As today, the sick came in a wide variety of categories, unable to fend for themselves for numerous reasons. Leprosy was dying out in England by the beginning of the period under study.[66] In 1392 John de Donewich, Master and Warden of Clare Hall, left 2*s* to the lepers outside Trumpington Gate and in 1418 John Herrys, burgess of Cambridge, left 6*s* 8*d* to the same hospital.[67] By this date leper hospitals were treating patients with other skin complaints or general illnesses. Many had been abandoned, like St Mary Magdalene's at Stourbridge on the other side of Cambridge, and their revenues appropriated as at Ely, where the revenues of the hospitals of St John the Baptist and St Mary Magdalene had fallen into the hands of the Bishop.[68] New foundations of hospitals and almshouses in the fifteenth and sixteenth centuries took the place of institutions which had perished.[69] During that time Cambridgeshire testators made bequests to institutions in Cambridge, Ely, Wisbech, Great Linton, Newton, Whittlesey and Royston just over the border in Hertfordshire. They also patronised institutions in other towns where they had connections, London, Arundel, Worcester, York, Lincoln and Lynn. These were institutional remedies, generally in urban centres, to a need far vaster than they were able to assist. In towns the mechanisms for collective self-help among the poor were weaker due to immigration, and the distinction between the deserving and undeserving poor was enforced more strictly.[70] The sick were among the deserving and provided a standard by which other categories of

63 ACE (3/6/12) 1556.

64 Flynn, *Sacred Charity*, 77.

65 *EHD* ii, 1042–1189, ed. D.C. Douglas and G.W. Greenaway, 1953, 820–1, is an example of the poor selling on the clothes of St Thomas Becket, given to them after he had been martyred.

66 P. Richards, *The Medieval Leper and his Northern Heirs*, Cambridge 1977, 11. In the 13th and 14th centuries at the peak of the disease in England there were approximately 200 leper hospitals.

67 PRO, Prob 11/1/6, fos 45v, 46r and v; Prob 11/2b/44, fos 346r and v.

68 W.M. Palmer, 'The Hospitals of St John the Baptist and St Mary Magdalene at Ely', *Proc. Camb. Antiq. Soc.* xxxvi, 1935, 76–108, esp. 86; L. Cobbett, 'The Hospitals of St John the Baptist and St Mary Magdalene at Ely', *Proc. Camb. Antiq. Soc.* xxxvi, 1935, 58–75, architectural remains; Rubin, *Charity and Community*, 111–46.

69 Dyer, *Standards of Living*, 244.

70 Rubin, *Charity and Community*, ch. 4, esp. 72–73, 98.

poor might be judged for assistance. Fifteenth-century wills specified that doles of small change or foodstuffs were to be given to the 'pauperes et egeros', 'the poor and sick'; 'pauperes ac debiles personae', 'the poor and weak'; 'pauperes, debiles ac paraliticos', 'the poor, weak and paralysed'.[71] Such people, especially the bed-ridden, could have been less able to attend funerals. Thus visiting the sick, as in the Biblical imperative, would have been necessary, and some discrimination on behalf of the executors as to who should receive alms. During the sixteenth century it became less common for the sick to be singled out, presumably because such discrimination had now become commonplace. In 1551 Christopher Brown, fellow of St John's College, Cambridge, left money to be distributed among 'the halt, the lame, and the blind and others that have as great need',[72] and in 1557 Sir John Huddylston of Sawston left £20 'in alms to the most poor and needy people: sturdy beggars and vagabonds as much as may be avoided'.[73] Other facets of charity were essentially urban, such as the sixth work of mercy, visiting people in prison. At this time people resided in prison at their own expense, and so were dependent on those outside for food and other support. Throughout the period under study there are a few bequests to the prisoners in the Castle and the toll booth at Cambridge, and in Ludgate, Newgate and King's Bench in London.

So far the gifts of the dead to the living, through the mechanism of the will, have been emphasised. The last work of corporal mercy was the burial of the dead and their commemoration was a further deed of charity. The final section of the will, beginning 'The Residue . . .' included a plea to the executor, generally a relative of the dying man or woman, 'ut disponat pro salute anime mee', 'that he or she might dispose [of the residue] for the salvation of my soul', sometimes adding the phrases 'sicut eis melius videbitur fieri' or 'sicut eis melius videbitur Deo placere et anime mee prodesse', 'as it seems best to him, to the pleasure of God and the wealth of my soul'.[74] Requests for prayers for the souls of benefactors, parents, friends and all Christian souls could be included here, as the dead passed on their duties to the living. Many testators requested their bodies to be 'brought honestly to the ground', leaving the details of the funeral to the executor's discretion. This phrase was still used in the 1540s, when references to the soul had already disappeared. This suggests that those who adhered to medieval Catholic belief and custom, while not advertising the fact, would in so far as it was possible receive the old funeral and commemorative practices from a sympathetic executor.

71 These are regularly occurring phrases in the wills of the 15th century.
72 VCC (1/1/5) 1551.
73 PRO Prob 11/40/5, fos 39v, 40r and v, 1557.
74 These phrases and their English translations are common in 15th-century wills, but become less so as the 16th century progresses, especially from the 1530s.

In the influenza epidemic of 1558, Agnes Campion of Ely left her 'godson John Symond, one sheet if he be alive. If he be dead, then I give the said sheet unto the next poor body that dies and wants a winding sheet'.[75] In the same year, Agnes Hancock said in her will 'I give to five poor folk where need is in Swaffham Bullbeck aforesaid after my departing, five sheets to bury them in'.[76] In the last three years of Mary's reign some medieval Catholic practices returned. This included the devotion to the five wounds of Our Lord with which this second bequest is associated, although the extremely high mortality in 1557 and 1558 was the major factor prompting the bequest of winding sheets.[77]

The evidence of wills focuses attention too closely on the benefactor as an individual. People were buried and commemorated by the various groups to which they had belonged in life, primarily by the family. The town corporation, the gild, the parish, and other groups which provided funerals and commemoration for their dead members also administered charitable provision made by them.

Charity and the Lateral Bonds of Society

Charity which affirmed the lateral bonds of society, directed towards other members of a particular group was far more important to the well-being of medieval society than the ritualised dispensation of alms by those of higher social standing. In an urban context charity took many forms. Here there were particularly complex relations between the hierarchies, which controlled town life and groups within the community concerned with mutual charity. The Borough Corporation of Cambridge administered both commemorative rituals and charitable endowments for its members. In 1545 John Chapman, alderman, left the monies from the sale of a messuage and tenement in the hands of the mayor and burgesses to support a perpetual obit.[78] During Edward's reign such endowments were not made, but in 1558 Christopher Frank, alderman, left the revenue from three booths at Stourbridge Fair in the hands of the mayor, bailiffs and burgesses, expressing renewed confidence in Catholic practice in the final years of Mary's reign.[79] Meanwhile, John Richardson, burgess, left the revenue from six booths in the hands of his brother and heirs. If this went against the custom of the borough, the mayor, bailiffs and burgesses were to enter into a £100 obligation to provide a similar annual dole to the poor in St Clement's parish, where he

75 ECC (8/3/2).
76 ECC (8/5/14).
77 Out of 1,909 wills in the sample, 502 were made in 1557–8, 26% overall.
78 ACE (2/1/12) 1545.
79 ACE (4/2/14) 1558. These two obits are examined in ch. 4; see also ACE (3/3/4) 1553, will of Hugh Chapman, probably written much earlier.

had lived and in whose church he was buried.[80] This illustrates the interrelation between town and parish in urban communities. James Fletcher, another alderman, was concerned with the welfare of his fellow burgesses who had become impoverished. He left money to be put in Andrew's hutch, or loan chest, to be lent out yearly to give poor burgesses at the discretion of the mayor and two chief aldermen on provision of sureties.[81]

Over the centuries, the burgess and ecclesiastical oligarchies had presided over the institutional structure of charity in the town.[82] New Testament injunctions to assist widows and orphans were influential in the Middle Ages, when those suffering from what historians now term 'life-cycle poverty', were classed among the deserving poor.[83] In 1467 Roger Merston, a scholar of King's College Cambridge 'legavit cuidam vidue paupercule unum superlectum coloris viride', 'left to a certain poor little widow, a green coloured coverlet'.[84] In 1548 there were a number of widows dwelling in the almshouse by Queens' College, to whom Richard Algar left 4*d* each.[85] In 1500 John Doget, fellow of King's College, a man of wealth and immense if eccentric piety, was almost exclusively concerned with religious and charitable bequests in his will. Having already made bequests to a number of hospitals and prisons, he left

> to the poor lying sick and other beggars £6 13*s* 4*d* to be distributed on the day of my burial according to the discretion of my executors. I will that on the same day £5.00 may be distributed among needy widows and the poor remaining indoors; and £5.00 among young girls who are almost nubile, so that each may have 20*s*.[86]

William Massey, a priest of St Clement's parish, Cambridge, left his pewter to be distributed among young unmarried maidens.[87] In 1528 pewter was still something of a luxury, although it was more widely owned as the century wore on. Due to their poverty, the maidens would have little chance of marrying. Instead, they might enter into temporary liaisons which produced illegitimate children, to the detriment of themselves and the community.[88] Support was therefore extended to young people to ensure that they fulfilled

80 ACE (5/7/8) 1556.
81 ACE (3/5/5) 1555.
82 Rubin, *Charity and Community*, 146–7, identifies three main phases of charitable benefaction by the leading inhabitants of Cambridge.
83 1 Timothy 5, vv. 3–16.
84 KCC, fo 58r, 1467.
85 ACE (2/6/1) 1548.
86 KCC, fos 177r and v, 178r, 1500.
87 ECC (1/3/3) 1528.
88 M. Spufford, 'Puritanism and Social Control?', in A. Fletcher and J. Stevenson, *Order and Disorder in Early Modern Europe*, Cambridge 1985, 41–57; Flynn, *Sacred Charity*, 79, although often girls from established families were chosen, as it was an honour to get one of these dowries.

their obligations to society as they grew to maturity. In rural communities it is likely that gifts of animals, grain or money to household servants, godchildren and other young people functioned in the same way.

Both the charitable endowment of apprenticeship schemes and the funding of education stem from the same root: a concern to integrate the unruly young into the social order through the disciplined acquisition of trades and skills.[89] Widespread literacy and education was new in the later Middle Ages. It was not until the mid-sixteenth century that Cambridgeshire testators began to show concern for the education of their sons or other boys they knew. However, in Cambridge, support for poor scholars had long been seen as an act of charity. In 1352 Corpus Christi College was founded by the gilds of St Mary and Corpus Christi. The poor scholars of Cambridge were the regular recipients of alms on a smaller scale, such as those who resided at St Nicholas' Hostel in the sixteenth century. In 1552 John Walker, a baker, of St Andrew's parish left 'all my apparel to be sold and 20s of the money to be given to the poor scholars, being in those colleges which I do serve with bread'.[90] Other benefactors established loan chests for scholars on a similar line to Andrew's hutch for poor burgesses.[91] Books could be used as surety for securing the loan.[92]

The four Cambridge houses of friars, the *Pauperes Christi*, the poor of Christ, were recipients of much charity. The evidence of wills makes quite clear the merits attributed to their prayers. Right into the sixteenth century substantial numbers of testators, the wealthy particularly, whose wills were proved in the Prerogative Court of Canterbury, left goods to the friars in return for masses and prayers. They also patronised friars in fourteen other towns, locally in East Anglia and further afield, London, the Midlands and Yorkshire.

Although much urban charity affirmed the hierarchical bonds of society, it also strengthened the bonds of community by reducing tensions within the town. For the town to function efficiently as an economic and social unit, each member had to play their allotted part. The oligarchy of burgesses controlled much of the charity, as they did every other aspect of town life. For

89 S. Brigden, 'Youth and the English Reformation', *P&P* xcv, 1982, 37–67, esp. 37–38, control of youth and their elders' fear of their energy; Jordan, *Philanthropy in England*, 40–53, places the endowment of apprenticeship schemes in his 'Social Rehabilitation Category' and the endowment of schools and scholarship under 'Education'. This is a 19th-century class-based analysis. For details from Norfolk see Jordan, *The Charities of Rural England*, 130–43 Apprenticeship, 150–69 Education.

90 VCC (1/1/20) 1552.

91 J.W. Clark, 'On the Charitable Endowments in the University Called Chests', *Proc. Camb. Antiq. Soc.* xi, 1903–6, 78–101; R. Lovatt, 'Two Collegiate Loan Chests in Late Medieval Cambridge', in *Medieval Cambridge: Essays on the Pre-Reformation University*, ed. P. Zutshi, Woodbridge 1993, 129–65.

92 G. Pollard, 'Medieval Loan Chests in Cambridge', *BIHR* xvii, 1939–40, 113–29, esp. 113.

example, Christopher Frank, alderman and mayor in 1539 and 1551, who died in 1558, also held office as churchwarden of Holy Trinity parish in 1521–2, and as master of St Katherine's Gild in the same parish in 1524–5. He was one of the leading men in parish affairs throughout the 1520s and 1530s.[93] The burgesses were just one of many overlapping groups whose mutual charity illustrated the lateral bonds within society. Aside from allocating charity to others, the burgesses assisted each other, through such mechanisms as Andrew's loan hutch, when they fell on hard times.

A number of burgesses belonged to St Clement's fraternity, whose 1431 Statutes recorded the annual celebration of their obits in return for a 40*s* donation.[94] In common with the fifteenth-century Statutes of St Peter and Paul and All Saints' Cambridge gilds, each brother and sister was to pay 2*d* for their pension at each of the two morrow speeches each year. On entry they were to find two sufficient pledges, that they could pay 40*d* to the gild, 1*d* to the clerk and 1*d* to the dean within the year. As a result of these payments, and the careful financial assessment of new entrants, in old age or great poverty each brother and sister was to have 4*d* a week. If there was more than one needy member, the sum was to be divided between them. This was only to occur as long as the gild possessed 40*s* or more, hence the need for the 40*s* obit donations.

The gild was a status group within a community: its members bound together through mutual interest to maintain their social position. Nowhere can this be seen more clearly than in the provision of charity. In this respect the comparison made by Toulmin Smith is correct: the medieval gilds were like the nineteenth-century friendly societies, which provided some form of insurance for those with enough surplus income to pay their fees.[95] In 1389 twenty-one (35%) gilds made provision for members in need, although there were strict caveats on the circumstances in which this could be given.

Members of the eight Cambridge gilds had to prove that they had fallen into poverty, without fault, by God's will, or through ill-fortune and not through vice or loose-living. For the gild of St Katherine, St Andrew's Church, Cambridge, members were to have kept gild secrets, thus making loyalty a further criterion for payment.[96] For the gilds of St John the Baptist and Holy Trinity Wisbech, members were to have fallen into poverty through fire, the sea or robbers.[97] The Holy Trinity Statutes went on to say that brethren must have been reduced to a state where they could not survive

93 J. Milner Gray, *Biographical Notes on the Mayors of Cambridge*, Cambridge 1922, 24, 26; CCRO, P22/5/1, fo 63r; P22/5/15, fo 15v et passim.

94 BL Add. Ms. 5846, pp. 4–8, 10, Statutes of St Clement's Gild and commentary; CUL, MM1 36, Baker Mss. vol. 25, pp. 361–6, Statutes of St Peter and Paul Gild; MM1 36, Baker Mss. vol. 25, pp. 367–71, Statutes of All Saints' Gild.

95 Toulmin Smith, xiv.

96 PRO, C47/38/6.

97 PRO, C47/38/39, 43.

without begging, and be able to prove this to the fraternity, before being granted aid.[98] Another gild which gave the impression that members' circumstances must be extreme before assistance was given was Corpus Christi Gild, Stretham; its brethren were to have lost their eyes, feet or other limbs so that they were unable to support themselves.[99] A number of gilds required brethren seeking charitable assistance to make a formal request to the gild. On the assent of the officers and majority of the brethren, the officers were empowered to distribute aid. The rigorous application of such 'means tests' to discriminate between deserving and undeserving cases, and the distribution of charity by the officers may be seen as a fore-runner of the later system of parish poor relief under the vestry and the overseers of the poor.

Benefits included exemption from gild payments while poor; an amount of money each week, varying from 10*d* to 3*d*; a new garment annually and, in the case of the two gilds of Stretham, a pair of shoes as well;[100] and also burial at gild expense. Four gilds or fraternities stated that where there was more than one poor member, the money was to be divided equally between them each week. Several fraternities stressed that charity was to be given only while the recipient's hardship lasted, 'durante sua inopia', and no further, 'et non ultra'. Aid was a temporary solution to sudden calamity or misfortune, intended either to enable brethren to recover their former status fairly shortly, or to die with some dignity. It must have put a strain on collective resources because six fraternities gave out charity only while there was enough money: two gilds at Littleport added a further qualification, indicating other priorities, only as long as there was enough money to sustain the light.[101]

Fraternity statutes give no indication of how the system worked in practice, but the fifteenth-century accounts of St Katherine's Gild, Holy Trinity parish, Cambridge, offer some information. In correspondence with the Statutes of the three fifteenth-century Cambridge gilds or fraternities, brethren paid in sums towards their pensions at meetings.[102] Pensions were paid out to brethren from the annual increases, or profit, which accrued from lending out communal stock to the substantial men involved in running the gild.[103] In addition, money paid back from old debts, such as the surety owed by George Ffoyster, pledge to Harry Cressewell, who had died while holding stock, were used for the same purposes.[104] The 'Election' or group of stock-holders decided how the increase should be apportioned.[105] Between 1514 and 1517 Lynsey's wife, or Mother Lynsey, was paid a pension which worked out at

98 PRO, C47/38/43.
99 PRO, C47/38/31.
100 PRO, C47/38/31, 32.
101 PRO, C47/38/26(1), (2).
102 CCRO, P22/5/15, fos 5r, 6v.
103 CCRO, P22/5/15, fos 13r, 14r; W. Tate, *The Parish Chest*, Cambridge 1951, 87.
104 CCRO, P22/5/15, fos 12r and v.
105 CCRO, P22/5/15, fos 17v, 19v.

between 1¼*d* and 2*d* a week depending on how much money was available.[106] Only 12*d* was paid to her in 1516–17, so presumably she died in that year. In 1520–1 two widows, Alice Wortewell and Margaret Burwell, were given 4*s* each for the year, paid quarterly,[107] thus sharing the allowance of around 2*d* a week. Alice Wortewell, the widow of William Wortewell who had been prominent in Holy Trinity parish affairs,[108] does not appear in the accounts again. Margaret Burwell continued to receive the annual pension until 1527–8, being joined by Margaret Fenton in 1524–5, who was also ordered to receive 2*d* a week out of the debt owed by George Ffoyster.[109] The increase and debts also paid for more general deeds of charity: the mending of St Katherine's banner in 1520;[110] general church uses in 1521;[111] in 1524 the mending and in 1527 the purchase of new torches, both paid for by George Ffoyster.[112] The repayment of debts for new purposes was also a feature of wills at this time. The use of debts in this way may help to explain some of the inconsistencies in medieval accounts. St Katherine's Gild, Cambridge, was a wealthy social group attached to Holy Trinity Church. Judging by the membership of substantial burgesses and their expenditure on regular feasts,[113] they were well able to give support to impoverished members.

There are no references to the payment of pensions in the register of the Holy Trinity Gild of Wisbech, the most important commercial centre of the Isle of Ely. Clearly such payments were also made indirectly.[114] In 1453 the Trinity Gild purchased a chantry licence which mentioned their obligation to assist certain poor weak men according to the Statutes.[115] The gild, under the authority of the Bishop of Ely, acted as the informal corporation of the town. With this status and the revenue from large holdings of land, it undertook to administer many activities which fell under the broad medieval definition of charity. Besides religious devotions which it maintained within the church, and a hall used for both gild and general civic functions, one of the chaplains taught a grammar school.[116] The gild maintained chapels at Murrow and the high Fendyke which assisted both parish worship and repair

106 CCRO, P22/5/15, fos 21r and v, 22v.
107 CCRO, P22/5/15, fos 12r and v.
108 CCRO, P22/5/1, fos 20r, 21v, 22v, 33r, 1511–12 William Wortewell died. He had lights and torches at his burial.
109 CCRO, P22/5/15, fos 13r, 14r, 16v; 17v reference to Margaret Fenton, fo 19v.
110 CCRO, P22/5/15, fo 11v.
111 CCRO, P22/5/15, fo 12v.
112 CCRO, P22/5/15, fos 16v, 19v.
113 CCRO, P22/5/15, fos 20r–22r.
114 C.M. Barron, The Parish Fraternities of Medieval London', in *The Church in Pre-Reformation Society*, ed. C.M. Barron and C. Harper-Bill, Woodbridge 1985, 13–37, esp. 26–27; B. McCree, 'Charity and Gild Solidarity in Late Medieval England', *Journal of British Studies* xxxii, 1993, 195–225, finds little evidence of charitable payments by Norfolk gilds.
115 PRO, C66/478, 32 Hen VI, membrane 23.
116 WCR1, pp. 106–8. The grammar school was refounded under King Edward VI.

of defences against the sea.[117] In justifiable fear of the confiscation of their properties in 1549, the officers of the gild spent the sum of £74 5*s* 6*d* on municipal betterment.[118] The projects undertaken were repair of local banks and ditches, repair of the market cross and the paving of the market place. Having bought back their lands after the dissolution of the gild, the oligarchy of officers became the town corporation, and their role in the community continued undiminished. The charity of the Trinity Gild extended beyond assistance to fellow brethren. As the most important institution in Wisbech, they were able to impose their own model of charity on the rest of the community.

Maureen Flynn sees the gild or confraternity as the most fundamental institution of medieval charity: one which could be replicated simply, not through expensive benefaction, but through the collective energies of the laity.[119] Mutual support was the essence of the charity which gilds provided for those who belonged. This was one of the ways in which the better off among the one third to a half of the population classed as poor survived.[120] In 1389 the gild of Corpus Christi, Stretham, maintained a common chest from which members could borrow, using the money for trade and profit.[121] St Katherine's Gild, Elm, hired out twelve cows.[122] This was their stock: the increase, or calf, went to support the light before the saint in the church, the milk to the person who had hired out the cow. This would have made a real difference to the middling peasantry who made a modest surplus in a good year and very little in a bad year, and so would have helped to prevent them from falling into poverty.[123]

In wills there are numerous bequests of agricultural stock given to be administered by gilds, lights and the parish. In 1506 Richard Buckworth of Wisbech left either a cow or 6*s* 8*d* each to St Peter's, Our Lady and St George's Gilds.[124] In 1507 Nicholas Smyth a butcher of Wisbech left 'to the light of St Martin, a bull or 6*s* 8*d* in money, Whither of both [i.e. whichever] the keepers of the light will have'.[125] John Herner's will of 1546 left 'to the church two beasts yearly to be prayed for; and two poor folk to have them after the discretion of the executors, to be let for 2*s* a year'.[126] John Atkyn's will of 1552 included the bequest

117 WCR1, p. 107.
118 WCR1, pp. 109–10. They pointed out that this exceeded the sum raised from the sale of their plate by £29 3*s* 2*d*.
119 Flynn, *Sacred Charity*, 73–74.
120 Bennett, 'Conviviality and Charity', 20.
121 PRO, C47/38/31.
122 PRO, C47/38/16; Toulmin Smith, xxxv–xxxvi.
123 Dyer, *Standards of Living*, 130.
124 PRO, Prob 11/15/19, fos 153v, 154r and v, 1506.
125 PRO, Prob 11/15/31, fos 251v–52r, 1507.
126 ECC (3/2/6) 1546.

> Item I will that my part of the bull which John Jaklynge and I did buy together shall be to the use of the poor people in Haslingfield; and they shall pay nothing for my part of the same bull: and if the bull be sold, then I will that all my part of the money shall be distributed and divided among the poor people in Haslingfield.[127]

John London of Burrough left wax from his beehives to burn before the Trinity and John Sleg of Great Shelford left 'to St Anne's Gild, a swarm of bees'.[128] Churchwardens' accounts provide further details of these practices. The church accounts of Leverington 1497–1600, an area of rich grazing in the fens, were largely a list of cows hired out to parishioners both before and after the confiscations of the 1540s.[129] In Bassingbourne, the churchwardens were administering a small herd of 'obit cows'. The accounts of 1498 to 1540 record details of their hiring-out, the spending of revenues on obit or anniversary celebrations and the occasional sale of skins.[130] The same township possessed a 'common bull'. Sums were paid for his 'wintering' and 'fetching home', and fees received for his services to local cows.[131] The use and increase of the animals served a dual purpose, firstly the support of religious activities and the commemoration of the dead, and secondly the benefit of the community through the assistance of certain weaker members chosen by the administrators.[132] Due to their association with medieval Catholic practices, herds of cows and sheep, along with 'obit lands', were confiscated by the Crown under the Edwardian regime.[133] This not only severed the link with the old religion, but also struck a serious blow to the system of mutual charity in rural society.

Church ales were held frequently in Bassingbourne. There were ten in 1497–8 and twelve in 1499–1501. This was a period when the parish was saving up for new bells and these events were a very successful fund-raising activity.[134] Ales too were related to the commemoration of the dead. Every year money from lands left by Thomas Heynes to support his obit was put towards one of the church ales held in May.[135] Ale was brewed from the bushells of grain bequeathed for church purposes by dead parishioners, donated by wealthier individuals, 'gathered in the township', and occasionally bought

127 ECC (4/5/1) 1552.

128 ECC (1/3/2) 1528, will of John London; Palmer, 397, cites the will of John Sleg.

129 WFM, Microfilm 8, item 1, Leverington Church Accounts 1497–1600.

130 CCRO, P11/5/1–2, 1498–1540, vol. 2, for example, fos 46r, 47r, 59v, 63v, 65v.

131 CCRO, P11/5/1–2, vol. 1, fo 9v; vol. 2, fos 22r and v, 24r, 27v, 28r. These are the initial few references. There are many more.

132 Tate, *The Parish Chest*, 87, sheep and cows were lent out to 'reputable' parishioners.

133 'Cambridgeshire Church Goods', ed. J.J. Muskett, *East Anglian N. & Q.*, new series ix, 1901–2, 311–14.

134 CCRO, P11/5/1–2, vol. 2, fos 14r and v, 17r and v, and many more references; Bennett, 'Conviviality and Charity', 26–28.

135 CCRO, P11/5/1–2, vol. 2, fo 14r, 1498; fo 35v, 1511, subsidy payment; fo 75v, 1540, Terrier of Heynes obit lands; and annual entries.

by the churchwardens. By the 1520s, large sections of the churchwardens' accounts were devoted to the administration of 'obit lands', left by substantial men of the town: Master Richard Lynn, gentleman, Thomas Heynes, William Andrews and Cropwell.[136] Cropwell's obit was held in Lent and William Andrew's on Good Friday itself, according to the spiritual fashion of the time.[137]

Unlike more formal and more widely studied charitable institutions, the obit formed a part of the tissue of communal life and agricultural endeavour. Obit customs made a charitable contribution on a number of levels: to the memory of the dead; to gild and parish revenues; to those who hired lands and cows; and to all those who attended the annual rites at the church, and afterwards to consume the bread and ale. The food and drink at obits and funerals was not just for the poor, but also for kin and neighbours. In this way the wealthy and the not so wealthy among the living drank the health of the dead and celebrated their contribution to the community.[138]

In c.1182 Walter Map had remarked upon buildings which would now be called 'village halls', 'such a one as the English have as drinking houses, one in each parish called in English "*Ghildhus*" '.[139] These were erected in increasing numbers by the wealthier sectors of the peasantry in the era after the Black Death. The feoffees of one such hall, built at Fressingfield in Suffolk in 1407, stated their reasons in a memorandum of 1509,

> For the more reverence of God and in avoiding of eating and drinking and other abusions in the church . . . for the keeping of church ales, gild yeardays, burials, and other drinkings necessary to the profit of the said church or parish . . . thirty days, seven days or burials.[140]

Parish or gild houses were usually built on land belonging to the lord of the manor, or on land held collectively on behalf of the community, as at Fressingfield.[141]

Ale brewed by gilds for fund-raising and merry-making is mentioned in 1389 by the Ressurection Gild, Chesterton;[142] by the three fifteenth-century

136 CCRO, P11/5/1–2, vol. 2, fos 34v, 35v, 37r, 61r and v.
137 CCRO, P11/5/1–2, vol. 2, fos 41r, 66v.
138 C. Burgess, 'The Benefactions of Mortality: The Lay Response in the Late Medieval Urban Parish', in *Studies in Clergy and Ministry in Medieval England*, ed. D.M. Smith, York 1991, 65–86; C. Burgess and B. Kümin, 'Penetential Bequests and Parish Regimes in Late Medieval England', *JEH* xliv, 1993, 610–30.
139 W. Map, *De Nugis Curialium*, translated by M.R. James and others, London 1923, 82–83. The gildhall appears in one of the stories of Edric Wild which Map recounts.
140 J.J. Raven, 'A Parish House for Church Ales and Other "Drynkynggs" ', *East Anglian N. & Q.*, new series vi, 1895–6, 49–50; P. Cowley, *The Church Houses: Their Religious and Social Significance*, London 1970; CCRO, P11/5/1–2, vol. 2 fo 33r, 1511, Bassingbourne gildhall mentioned.
141 Palmer, 352.
142 PRO, C47/38/13.

Cambridge gilds; and by St James's Gild, Dullingham, in 1517.[143] In this rare survival of Statutes from so humble a gild, there is evidence that collective enterprise went a stage further. The alderman, elected every quarter, was paid 16*d* to brew and bake and was to provide lodgings for the Mastrick [sic] and the cook, if they were strangers. There was also a steward and caters [caterers?]. Activities must have revolved around a gildhall, although its existence is not mentioned in the document. It seems that dinners were cooked there every weekend and brought to the sick who were unable to attend. Assets included donations of malt and a herd of cows let out at 2*s* each a year. Both halls and contents, and lands and cows, were concealed from crown confiscation from the 1540s on, evidently seen as the legitimate property of either the communities or individuals who had given them. At Bassingbourne in 1546, plates, furnishings and cooking utensils belonging to the Trinity Gild were worth 46*s* 8*d*. By 1554–5 many of these things had disappeared back into the community: what remained was worth only 17*s* 8*d*.[144] In the same document of 1554/5 other concealed goods had been rooted out, belonging to gilds at Chesterton, Gamlingay and Downham, along with charity and free chapel property. Two hundred and sixty-three cows and 119 obit sheep had also been found.[145] Concealed lands, gildhalls and other property continued to come to light until well into the next century,[146] for example a pair of andirons and two spits were found in the hands of Joan Blanks, widow of Ickleton in 1570, formerly gild property.[147]

The Dissolution of the Medieval Bonds of Charity

Just as there were collective assets, there were collective responsibilities. Medieval charity extended to cover the maintenance of common properties: churches, highways, causeways and bridges. Many of the middling ranks of villagers left bequests of a few pennies each to such causes in their wills, the work being overseen by churchwardens and executors.[148] Apart from one or two bequests a year, for the upkeep of essential roads and causeways, such bequests dwindled away during the confiscations of Edward's reign. The worsening economic situation of the mid-Tudor period may also have been a

143 CUL, MM1 47, Baker Mss., vol. 36, pp. 161–2.
144 Palmer, 367–8.
145 Muskett, 'Cambridgeshire Church Goods', 311–14.
146 C. Kitching, 'The Quest for Concealed Lands in the Reign of Elizabeth I', *TRHS*, 5th series xxiv, 1974, 63–78.
147 Palmer, 374.
148 CCRO, P11/5/1–2, vol. 2, fo 36a, mending of the bridge. These changes outlined are based on the sample of 2,000 Cambridgeshire wills, with particular reference to those proved in the diocesan Courts.

factor. This hastened the use of new solutions to the age-old problem of the poor.[149]

New remedies were applied in a piecemeal fashion, ranging from town to town and village to village. In 1502, in Chesterton, the local government of the twelve Hedborowes were hiring the poor as labour.[150] In 1517 the churchwardens of Holy Trinity parish, Cambridge, were paying small sums to the poor for cleaning the church and churchyard.[151] In 1556 in Swaffham Bulbeck, the poor were being paid 2*d* a cart load for stones gathered to mend the highways.[152]

During the sixteenth century, the limits within which assistance would be given to the poor were defined more and more strictly. On the evidence of wills this process intensified from about 1544, in line with more general changes to the pattern of bequests to communal purposes, to church repair and the highways. Wills increasingly stipulated that charity was to be given to the poor of the parish; and within the parish, to poor householders to cottagers; to the poor charged with children; the poor that had no cow, no plough, or no corn of their own growing. In Cambridgeshire in the early sixteenth century, donations to the poor men's box begin to appear in wills.[153] This custom was built on an old precedent, as parish chests had long been used to collect alms for specific purposes.[154] The anonymity of the poor men's box, used increasingly from the mid 1540s, alienated the giver from the receiver. The medieval ideal of reciprocity expressed through the prayers of the poor for the salvation of the donor, was now no longer relevant. The poor, always viewed with some suspicion during the period under study, 'pauperi venienti et querenti elemosinas', 'the gathering of the poor, clamouring for alms',[155] were now purely a burden to society: they now had nothing to give, not even their prayers.

Prominent in medieval society was the institutional charity provided by the wealthy, whether the foundation of hospitals and almshouses, or the ritualised public alms giving of royalty, nobility, clergy or gentry. Charitable institutions are easily identified in the towns but in the countryside, they are less easy to see. There the institutions were of a different nature, woven into the fabric of the community. *Misericordia*, or pity, characterised the charity dispensed by the social hierarchy: its purpose was largely symbolic and its effect, although useful, was limited. *Caritas*, the charity most characteristic of

149 McIntosh, 'Local Responses to the Poor'; Mark 14, v. 7.
150 PRO, Prob 11/13/17, fos 146v and 47r, 1502, will of Thomas Martyn, yeoman.
151 CCRO, P22/5/1, 1517, fos 53v, 54r.
152 PRO, Prob 11/38/21, fos 140v–42r, 1556 will of Thomas Rudston, gentleman.
153 ECC (1/2/2) 1509, will of William Parker of Dullingham is the earliest reference to the 'common box of the poor'.
154 Tate, *The Parish Chest*, 36.
155 PRO, Prob 11/2b/41, fo 322r, 1418 will of Robert Scalton of London and Wendy, Cambridgeshire.

the Middle Ages, was expressed through the lateral bonds of society. Mutual aid of a practical nature was given through ales and obits administered by family, town, gild or parish. Kinship, whether of blood or artificially created through godparenthood or gild membership, could help to alleviate the harshness of sudden misfortune on individuals.[156]

Neighbourliness and the bonds of community were under attack in the changed economic circumstances following the Black Death.[157] The manorial system, which had traditionally given some shelter to the old and disabled, was in decline,[158] and the complexities of the land-market and the rise of wage-labour were polarising rich and poor, the yeomen and the landless labourers among the peasantry. The destruction of the link between death and charity at the Reformation and, more significantly, the confiscation of the assets of gild and parish associated with the commemoration of the dead, also destroyed the framework of medieval charity.[159] The Protestant shift away from a religion of good works towards a more abstract theology was paralleled by the greater impersonality of the Elizabethan Poor Law system.[160] However, continuities between medieval and early modern approaches to poverty and charity may be found on an administrative level among the yeoman oligarchy of gild and parish, who had already presided over the increasingly exact distinction between the deserving and undeserving poor.

156 J. Bossy, 'Blood and Baptism: Kinship, Community and Christianity in Western Europe from the Fourteenth to the Seventeenth Centuries', *SCH* x, 1973, 129–43, esp. 133; R. Dinn, 'Baptism, Spiritual Kinship and Popular Religion in Late Medieval Bury St Edmunds', *Bulletin of John Rylands Library* lxxii, 1990, 93–106.

157 K. Thomas, *Religion and the Decline of Magic*, Harmondsworth 1978, chs 16, 17, esp. pp. 669–80.

158 F.M. Page, 'The Customary Poor Law of Three Cambridgeshire Manors', *Cambridge Historical Journal* iii, 1929–31, 125–33.

159 S. Brigden, 'Religion and Social Obligation in Early Sixteenth Century London', *P&P* ciii, 1984, 67–112, esp. 110–12.

160 Flynn, *Sacred Charity*, 70.

6

The Contribution of the Gilds to Local Government

Many details of the workings of local government in the Middle Ages are obscure, in part due to the diffusion of power among a kaleidoscope pattern of overlapping jurisdictions: town, parish; merchant, craft and social gild; manor, borough or leet court; church and assize court; the office of Justice of the Peace and sheriff, according to regional variations.[1] To chart the history of the so-called religious or social gilds is to chart one strand of local administration.[2] Because they interacted in different situations with all other organs of local government, gilds illuminate their activities, and also the process of change by which the parish replaced the manor as the basic unit of local administration, which is only now beginning to be understood.[3]

It is important to see the extension of central government control over local affairs, particularly associated with the Tudor administration of the sixteenth century and the Reformation period, as the culmination of a process with long antecedents. By the later fourteenth century, developments in the economic status and political role of the knightly classes had resulted in their greater powers over local government at the expense of the magnates, under the King in Parliament.[4] In 1361 the powers of the 'keepers' or 'Justices of the Peace' were ratified by the statute of Westminster.[5] In 1368 they were made

1 M.K. McIntosh, 'Social Change and Tudor Manorial Elites', in *Law and Social Change in British Society*, ed. J.A. Guy and H.G. Beale, Royal Historical Society Studies in History, no. 40, London 1984, 73–85, esp. 75; J.P. Dawson, *A History of Lay Judges*, Cambridge, Massachusetts, 1960; W.O. Ault, *Private Jurisdiction in England*, Newhaven 1923.

2 Toulmin Smith, xxii–xxiii; Westlake, ch. x; C. Gross, *The Gild Merchant*, 2 vols, Oxford 1890, chs 5 and 6, the role of merchant gilds in the development of town government.

3 Marjorie McIntosh in the article cited above and elsewhere has been at the forefront of this process.

4 C. Given-Wilson, *The English Nobility in the Late Middle Ages: The Fourteenth Century Political Community*, London 1987, 16–19.

5 PRO Justices of the Peace 1361–1961: Exhibition of Records, HMSO 1961; E.A.L. Moir, *Justices of the Peace*, Harmondsworth 1969; *Proceedings before the Justices of the Peace in Fourteenth and Fifteenth Centuries, Edward III-Richard II*, ed. B. Puttnam, London

responsible by Parliament for the enforcement of the statute of labourers.[6] In an effort to shift the burden of taxation from themselves to the peasantry, the Commons, in association with central government, initiated various experiments in taxation, beginning in 1371 with the parish tax.[7] These continued with the poll taxes of 1377–81 and the income and land taxes of the early fifteenth century.[8] Concern shared by both the Crown and gentry led to the censuring of local institutions or gatherings which were seen as potentially subversive. In 1388 there was legislation against the playing of games such as camping, a violent mixture of all-in wrestling and football played between different parish teams, for which much evidence survives from East Anglia. This prefigures a similar clamp-down on game playing in the late sixteenth and early seventeenth centuries.[9] The commons petition to the Cambridge Parliament in the same year, 1388, expressing anxieties about gilds, the enforcement of labour and wage legislation and other matters of importance to themselves, was ratified in legislation.[10] This legislation led to the royal survey of religious and craft gilds in 1388–9 and their inclusion within the scope of the statute of mortmain in 1391. Many of these measures were passed at a time of great government insecurity in the wake of the Peasants' Revolt of 1381, but they also illustrate an increasing national intervention in local affairs through legislation, enforced by the knightly classes.

England was already divided into units for the collection of the lay subsidies required with greater frequency in the fourteenth century to finance the war with France.[11] These units were based on the 'vill' or 'township', a settlement sometimes with outlying hamlets, in some places coterminous with parochial or manorial boundaries and elsewhere unrelated to them.[12]

1938; A. Verduyn, *The Politics of the Creation of Justices of the Peace Under Edward III*, paper at the Late Medieval Seminar, Institute of Historical Research, London 25 Jan. 1991; *EHD* iv, 1327–1485, ed. A.R. Myers, London 1970, 533–45.

6 *EHD* iv, 542.

7 C. Fenwick, 'The English Poll Taxes of 1377, 1379 and 1381: A Critical Examination of the Returns', London School of Economics, London Ph.D. 1983, 19, 20.

8 W.M. Palmer, 'A List of the Cambridge Subsidy Rolls 1250–1695', *East Anglian N. & Q.*, new series vii, 1897–8, 362–6, 379–81; viii, 1899–1900, 24–26, 44–47.

9 D. Dymond, 'A Lost Social Institution: the East Anglian Game of Camping' (unpublished paper), 4, 8.

10 J.A. Tuck, 'The Cambridge Parliament 1388', *EHR* lccciv, 1969, 225–43, esp. 228.

11 M.W. Beresford, *The Lay Subsidies and Poll Taxes*, Canterbury 1963; B. Hanawalt, *The Ties that Bound*, Oxford 1986, 4, the parish and township developed as units of taxation; 15, parish legislation.

12 Fenwick, 'The English Poll Taxes', 62; P. Vinogradoff, *The Growth of the Manor*, rev. edn, London 1911, 144–9, 150–64, the *tun* or township was the most ancient social unit; H.M. Cam, 'The Community of the Vill', in *Medieval Studies Presented to Rose Graham*, ed. V. Ruffner and A.J. Taylor, Oxford 1950, 1–14; E. Britten, *The Community of the Vill*, Toronto 1977; W.O. Ault, 'The Village Church and the Village Community in Medieval England', *Speculum* xlv, 1970, 197–215; W.O. Ault, 'Manor Court and Parish Church in Fifteenth Century England', *Speculum* xlii, 1967, 53–67.

The collection of the parish tax of 1371 was thus a variant on already existing practice. Fifteenth- and sixteenth-century wills attest to the overlap of identity between the terms parish, vill or township, which testators used to describe their place of residence. The term gild was also used to express some aspects of civic identity.[13] The medieval equivalent of the village hall or community centre was the church house, the gild hall or house or the town house. Bequests of land, cows, money or agricultural produce were made to parish, gild, town or common stock for the use of the commonalty or specific sections of it such as the poor. Bassingbourne churchwardens' accounts describe their community, seemingly interchangeably, as parish or township. In Chesterton it was the Hedborowes of the leet court who undertook the administration of common stocks to support communal, devotional or commemorative activities.[14] The overlap or confusion expressed in these documents is not to be teased out into coherence: it existed in the minds of contemporaries. Just as the terms light, altar, image, chapel and gild described similar devotional activities, so terms for corporate identity reflected the complex inter-relation of different facets of communal life.

Gild and Parish

Westlake called the gilds which existed for religious and social purposes in many of the towns and villages of England 'parish gilds' because of their association with the parish church. However, they were associated as much with place-name and settlement and their identities shifted with the different balance between parish, township and manor as this varied according to place and time. The Cambridgeshire gild returns to the survey of 1388–9 give little indication of their relationship with the parish, despite their association with a particular church.[15] But from other evidence it is plain that gilds acted in parallel with other groups of laity, such as light-wardens and churchwardens, engaged in the administration of devotional and practical aspects of community life. From the Cambridgeshire evidence it is possible to discern three broad types of relationship between gild and parish: those gilds which were of importance within one parish, sometimes under the control of the churchwardens; those gilds which existed between parishes, administering chapels of ease in outlying hamlets, or free chapels at the intersection of several settlements; and those gilds whose influence extended beyond the confines of one particular

13 S. Reynolds, *Kingdoms and Communities in Western Europe 900–1300*, Oxford 1984, ch. 3, Fraternities and Gilds, ch. 4, The Parish, and ch. 5, Villages and Rural Neighbourhoods, are particularly useful here.

14 CCRO, P11/5/1–2 Bassingbourne Churchwardens' Accounts 1498–1540; PRO, Prob 11/13/17, fos 146v, 147r, 1502 will of Thomas Martyn, yeoman, left land to the hedborowes to keep an annual obit for him.

15 Only nine (15%) mention the parish, and six of these are from the town of Cambridge.

parish to become of regional and occasionally national, importance.[16] To an extent these three types of gilds were drawn respectively from the compact parishes of the shire of Cambridge; the marshlands of the Isle of Ely; and the urban centres.

(1) In the first category may be included those gilds whose existence was in some way identified with that of the parish. Marjorie McIntosh describes the extended role of manorial leet courts in the fifteenth century undertaking new administrative tasks at a time of jurisdictional change.[17] It seems that other local institutions such as gilds also stepped into the gaps left by the decline of the manorial structure, to act as the forerunners of later parish councils.[18] An indication of this role is given when a gild shared the same dedication as the parish church, such as three fifteenth-century gilds in the town of Cambridge: St Clement's, Saints Peter and Paul, and All Saints'. Elsewhere their title might be more general: in 1525 the 'village gild' of Whittlesford owned a stock of £3,[19] and in the fifteenth and sixteenth centuries a gild known simply as 'the brotherhood' dominated Gamlingay. Gamlingay was a small market town on the western edge of the shire. The main landlord was an absentee, Merton College, Oxford, which had perhaps enabled the Holy Trinity Gild to attain its powerful position. It left no documents but, on the evidence of manorial records and wills, it held substantial amounts of land, built a 'church-house', employed a priest as assistant to the vicar, and enjoyed the patronage of prominent yeomen families.[20] Its functions, such as the upkeep of the 'town-house', were taken over by the parish in the later sixteenth century.[21] In general, gilds of the Holy Trinity were likely to have the function of unofficial local councils.[22] In France, according to Pierre Duparc, it was fraternities of the Holy Spirit which fulfilled this role. The houses of the Holy Spirit often became the town halls of the sixteenth century and later.[23]

16 Westlake, ch. x.
17 McIntosh, 'Social Change and Tudor Manorial Elites', 76–77.
18 M.K. McIntosh, 'Local Change and Community Control 1465–1500', *Huntingdon Library Quarterly* ixl, 1986, 219–42. Her main argument is that due to social and economic change, greater burdens were put on local government to the extent that people in charge of each community were later willing to accept the endorsement of their power through Tudor legislation.
19 *VCH Cambs*. vi, 272.
20 *VCH Cambs*. v, 83, the gild held a gildhall, malt mill, messuages, crofts, and over 60 acres of land; PRO, Prob 11/24/23, fos 176 r, v, 1532 will of Thomas Aucton *alias* Malton left the gild a one-third share in a boat and 40s towards the building of the 'church house'.
21 J. Brown, *Gamlingay: 600 Years of Life in an English Village*, London 1989, 125.
22 Gross, *The Gild Merchant*, i, 34, says this was a favoured dedication of merchant gilds.
23 P. Duparc 'Confraternities of the Holy Spirit and Village Communities in the Middle Ages', in *Lordship and Community in Medieval Europe*, ed. F.L. Cheyette, New York 1975, 346–9.

The primary purpose of the gilds was to fund lights in the parish church.[24] In some places they had grown beyond this original intention, in others the parish acted as an umbrella organisation for smaller groups of laity, gilds and lights, creating multiple foci for worship and involvement within the community. In 1542 ten gilds or lights in the church of Whittlesea St Mary and two in Whittlesea St Andrews were assessed to pay between 6*d* and 2*d* in taxation.[25] Bassingbourne was a prosperous market-town on the Hertfordshire border in the later fifteenth and early sixteenth centuries. It was of ancient demesne and one of the manors held by Margaret Beaufort, King Henry VII's mother. The Holy Trinity Gild, a wealthy and influential local body, is conspicuous by its absence from the churchwardens' accounts 1498–1540, apart from the fact that the gild priest John Hobard wrote them until his death in 1518. However, there are references to other groups which contributed money to parish funds, the 'singlemen' who held stocks for the roodloft lights; the 'wives' who made an annual collection at the Hocktide games; and for lights before Our Lady, the chancel, the Sepulchre, St Nicholas and St George.[26] In the churchwardens' accounts for the parish of Holy Trinity, Cambridge, 1504–58, two wardens for each of the four lights were 'elected' at the same time as the churchwardens. The same names recur year by year, the same men passing office from one to another, and their wives taking turns as mistresses of Our Lady's light. Several of these men, for example Harry Cressewell, John Wortwall, George Ffoyster and Richard Dale, were also tenants of messuages, barns and stables belonging to the parish.[27] They formed an oligarchy associated with the organisation of parish life, for whom self-interest may have been an important consideration, anticipating the vestry system of the seventeenth century. Once again the gilds of St Katherine and St George are only shadows in the Trinity churchwardens' accounts. The rare survival of St Katherine's Gild accounts 1514–37 show that they were administered separately, but some of the same names occur as officers of both gild and parish affirming oligarchic control.[28]

(2) The second type of relationship between gild and parish may be seen where there was no formally constituted body of parishioners.[29] In a chapel of

24 B.A. Hanawalt, 'Keepers of the Lights: Late Medieval English Parish Gilds', *Journal of Medieval and Renaissance Studies* xiv, 1984, 21–37.

25 Palmer, 355; *VCH Cambs*. iv, 133.

26 CCRO, P11/5/1–2. vols 1–2; singlemen, vol. 1, fo 8v; vol. 2, fos 29v, 32v; wives, vol. 2, fos 20v, 69v; various lights, vol. 1, fo 10a; St George's stock, vol. 2, fo 34b.

27 CCRO, P22/5/1, fo 36r, enrolment of deeds including leases, and passim.

28 CCRO, P22/5/15, 1514–37, St Katherine's Gild accounts; M. Siraut, 'Accounts of St Katherine's Gild at Holy Trinity Church, Cambridge, 1514–37', *Proc. Camb. Antiq. Soc*. lxvii, 1977, 111–21.

29 D.M. Owen, *Church and Society in Medieval Lincolnshire*, Lincoln 1971, 10–19, free chapels in the fens; C.J. Kitching, 'Church and Chapelry in Sixteenth Century England', *SCH* xvi, 1979, 279–90.

ease or a free chapel, a gild might perform the same functions of upkeep of the fabric and religious ornaments as the parishioners of a parish church. The gild structure gave a group of men and women in an outlying hamlet, or those associated with an isolated chapel, a coherence and a framework for organising necessary tasks.

Gilds were associated with about half (25, 51%) of the 49 chapels traced during the period of this study.[30] Roughly half (21, 43%) the chapels were located in the shire and half (28, 57%) in the Isle of Ely. The Isle was less densely populated, with large parishes and scattered hamlets. Here there was a larger number of gilds and a larger number of them were associated with chapels. Overall there were six chapels to which gilds are known to have been attached in the shire and eighteen in the Isle. In the majority of these cases the role of the gilds in their administration is unknown, but where there is more evidence, some were indeed controlled by gilds. In 1389 seven chapels had gilds associated with them, one in the shire and six in the Isle.[31] In Tydd St Giles the chapel of the Holy Cross by the Sea was administered by the gild of the Holy Cross; in March the gild of St Wendreda administered the chapel of that name. March was a settlement on one of the gravel islands in the fens at a considerable distance from the mother church at Doddington, making a chapel necessary.[32] It was probably the gild which purchased a papal indulgence for pilgrims in 1343 and supervised the re-building of the chapel, recently completed when the gild made its return in 1389.[33] Although the chapel functioned in many ways as a parish church, in terms of size, religious services and benefaction, for example in the addition of one of the finest surviving late medieval angel roofs in the country,[34] like its neighbour, St Mary's chapel in the Wisbech hamlet of Fennend, it did not gain full parochial status until the nineteenth century.[35] This seems to have been merely a formality. The parochial system in England was largely fixed by the thirteenth century but chapels in secondary settlements played a decisive role in

30 This figure is drawn from secondary sources and the sample of about 2,000 wills.

31 PRO, C47/38/12a Chatteris convent; C47/38/17, 18, 19 Ely St Mary; C47/38/23(1–3) Ely Holy Trinity; C47/38/24 Haslingfield chapel of Our Lady in the parish churchyard in the shire; C47/38/25 Leverington chapel of Our Lady in the parish church; C47/38/27 March chapel of St Wendreda; C47/38/34 Tydd St Giles chapel of Holy Cross by the Sea. This illustrates the variety of types of chapels.

32 *VCH Cambs*. iv, 119–20; E. Miller, *The Abbey and Bishopric of Ely*, Cambridge 1951, 12 and map between 76 and 77; A. Kreider, *The English Chantries: The Road to Dissolution*, Cambridge, Massachusetts, 1979, 43–44, on the need for chapels in difficult terrain.

33 CCRO, P116/1/4, p. 63; T.A. Bevis, *The Memorial Church of St Wendreda, March*, Chatteris, no date, a leaflet available at the church gives further details on its history and architecture.

34 The wealth in this area in the late Middle Ages is evident: there are similar roofs in the St Nicholas Chapel, King's Lynn, and Upwell St Peter, where Dorothy L. Sayers set her novel *The Nine Taylors*. Both these parishes are nearby in Norfolk.

35 *VCH Cambs*. iv, 234–6, St Mary's was rebuilt as a substantial church in the 14th century.

later parish formation, as Dorothy Owen has demonstrated for the region of Kesteven in the Lincolnshire fenlands.[36] Gilds administered a number of chapels which became parishes in the course of the Middle Ages: at Coton in Granchester in the shire; and in the Isle at Welney in Upwell; at Parsondrove in Leverington; and at Wimblington in Doddington parish.[37] All of these gilds erected gildhalls, which demonstrates their significance to these communities.

Gild officers, like churchwardens, also co-ordinated the upkeep of bridges, banks and ditches along with the chapels on the sites of these public amenities.[38] This was the case at St Catherine's bridge, Hauxton in the shire; and in the Isle, Tritton bridge at Tydd St Giles; Stathedyche in Walsoken; and the high fendyke at Murrow in Wisbech parish.[39] The gilds and chapels disappeared at the Reformation and the continuation of such provision shifted to the officials of other local bodies, sometimes the same men in different guise.[40]

(3) In the third category may be included certain urban gilds whose influence transcended parish boundaries, and became of regional or national importance. Holy Trinity Gild, Wisbech, is an example.

Gild and Diocese

If gilds may be viewed in relation to the parish, what then was their relationship with the diocese? Great gilds tended to spring up in urban communities

36 D.M. Owen, 'Chapelries and Rural Settlement: An Examination of Some of the Kesteven Evidence', in *Medieval Settlement: Continuity and Change*, ed. P.M. Sawyer, 1976, 66–71.

37 *VCH Cambs*. v, 189 Coton. Palmer, 400; PRO, Prob 11/19/27, fos 26v–27r, 1519 will of Humphrey Gardener; Welney. *VCH Cambs*. iv, 195; PRO, Prob 11/16/20, fo 152r, 1509 will of William Lambert; Parsondrove. Palmer, 388; ECC HK2791/A/40, fos 14v, 15r, 1456 will of William Payne, Wimblington.

38 Kreider, *English Chantries*, 69; *Walberswick Churchwardens' Accounts AD 1450–1499*, ed. R.M. Lewis, no date, but Preface 1947, pp. iii; 24, building of a new quay and haven.

39 *VCH Cambs*. viii, 204, there was a chapel and gild at St Catherine's bridge, Hauxton. *VCH Cambs*. iv, 231, chapel and gild of St John Baptist at Tritton bridge, Tydd St Giles; 'Fifteenth Century Visitation Records of the Deanery of Wisbech', ed. W.M. Palmer, *Proc. Camb. Antiq. Soc*. xxxix, 1938–9, 73–74. PRO, Prob 11/6/20, fos 148r and v, 1475 will of Thomas Jecson, chaplain and warden; Prob 11/10/10, fos 78r and v, 1493 will of Edward Artor of Wisbech; both these wills refer to Walsoken chapel and gild of Holy Trinity by Stathedyche, which chapel was technically in Norfolk, but was much patronised by Cambridgeshire residents. *VCH Cambs*. iv, 235; WCR1, pp. 107–8; J.J. Muskett, 'Cambridgeshire Church Goods', *East Anglian N. & Q*., new series ix, 1901–2, 311–14, esp. 312; all refer to Murrow Chapel, Wisbech.

40 Wisbech corporation, formerly the Trinity gild, took over the upkeep of Murrow fendyke.

where ecclesiastical control impeded incorporation by the Crown. Examples of this may be seen in East Anglia: at Bury St Edmunds in Suffolk; at King's Lynn in Norfolk, called Bishop's Lynn until granted the royal charter of 1537; and at Wisbech in Cambridgeshire.[41] These religious or social gilds, composed of the leading citizens of the town, took on the role of town government. Because their power was derived from their ecclesiastical overlord, that relationship was characterised by periodic conflict over control of the town. This tension was of course also apparent in royal or seignorial towns.[42] With the extension of royal authority through the Common Law in the high Middle Ages, powerful gilds attempted to play off episcopal against royal authority to their own advantage. In 1299 a group of London metal workers were prosecuted by the crown for using the ecclesiastical courts in preference to the royal courts, thus eroding the royal prerogative.[43] In 1347 the Great Gild or Trinity Gild of Lynn took advantage of the imprisonment of the Bishop of Norwich at His Majesty's pleasure to extend its privileges.[44] Unfortunately the Bishop clawed these back on his release in 1350.

In 1389, in response to royal probings into their affairs, five gilds from the town of Cambridge placed themselves firmly under the jurisdiction of the Bishop of Ely.[45] They emphasised their religious activities and three had taken the precaution of having their statutes examined and confirmed by the Bishop.[46] Brethren who brought their gilds into disrepute through unseemly or immoral behaviour, who refused to obey the statutes or to pay fines for the ones they had broken, were to be handed over for discipline to the diocesan machinery. St Katherine's Gild, St Andrew's Church, refused to allow appeals to Civil Law and the Purification Gild, Great St Mary's, to either Civil or Canon Law.[47] Other gilds went out of their way to declare that, although their brethren made certain promises, they were not bound by oath,[48] or that this did not conflict with their obedience to secular or ecclesiastical authority.[49] These injunctions make explicit the uneasy balance between the

41 M.D. Lobel, *The Borough of Bury St Edmunds*, Oxford 1935; R.S. Gottfried, *Bury St Edmunds and the Urban Crisis 1290–1539*, Princeton 1982; A. Kettle, 'City and Close: Lichfield in the Century before the Reformation' in *The Church in Pre-Reformation Society*, ed. C.M. Barron and C. Harper-Bill, Woodbridge 1985, 158–69, esp. 160–2, town government, 164 joint administration by the cathedral and the leading gild of a loans fund for the poor.

42 G.O. Sayles, 'The Dissolution of a Gild at York in 1306', *EHR* lv, 1940, 83–98.

43 N. Fryde, 'Gilds in England before the Black Death', *Vorträge und Forschung* xxix, 1985, 221–2, ecclesiastical authority over towns, 223–4, London metal workers.

44 D.M. Owen, *The Making of King's Lynn: A Documentary Survey*, British Academy Records of Social and Economic History, new series ix, London 1984, Introduction 1–65, esp. 34–37.

45 PRO, C47/38/5, 6, 9, 10, 11.

46 PRO, C47/38/5, 9, 10.

47 PRO, C47/38/5, 10.

48 PRO, C47/38/3(1–7), 33(1–4).

49 PRO, C47/38/17.

usefulness of gild self-regulation to seignorial power as a means of social control, and the threat it represented to seignorial jurisdiction.

A rare fragment of a fifteenth-century visitation survives for the deanery of Wisbech.[50] Here the Bishop's influence was immense. He held all the manors in the region and his power was an amalgam of ecclesiastical, manorial and baronial jurisdictions.[51] The churchwardens and sidesmen of the parishes of Newton, Wisbech, Leverington, Elm and Tydd St Giles presented gild brethren largely for debts owing to lights or gilds, but also for refusal to obey officers and ordinances. The gilds in this area, while largely autonomous, were ultimately answerable to both parochial and diocesan administration.[52]

Gild and Manor

The manorial system also exercised authority over recalcitrant gild brethren where internal remedies had failed. In 1385 at the court baron of the manor of Dorking in Surrey, William Elmeshale and his associates presented Roger Bachelor and Thomas Caas, who owed them 4*s* each, promised for the salary of a chaplain. Later evidence reveals a gild of the Blessed Virgin there.[53]

Manorial records are a neglected source of information on local gilds. The historiographical tradition has focused on feudal, economic, and demographic questions in the late twelfth and thirteenth centuries, when the manorial system was at its most cohesive, rather than on the era of its disintegration after the Black Death. In *English Villagers of the Thirteenth Century*, published in 1941, George Homans, the sociologist, pioneered broader approaches to local community life. His ideas were later developed by Ambrose Raftis and the 'Toronto School'. More recently the role of gilds in rural communities has been included in the scope of work by Barbara Hanawalt and Christopher Dyer.[54] Manorial records provide two main types of information, on individuals

50 W.M. Palmer, 'Fifteenth Century Visitation Records of the Deanery of Wisbech', *Proc. Camb. Antiq. Soc.* xxxix, 1938–9, 69–75.

51 E. Miller, *The Abbey and Bishopric of Ely*, Cambridge 1951, 154, the bishops were more than economic or religious authorities; they held the honour of St Etheldreda 'per baroniam' as a feudal unit; 269, in the Middle Ages an administrative act took the form of a legal act – a judgement, a verdict, or a declaration of law and custom.

52 Kettle, 'City and Close', 168–9. In Lichfield gild and cathedral were jointly responsible for policing citizens' morals.

53 Arundel Castle Ms. 734, 12 June, 8 Richard II; 3 July, 9 Richard II; meetings of the Court Baron; PRO, Prob 11/5, 1464 will of Henry Sond of Dorking. I am grateful to Mrs Vivien Ettlinger for this information.

54 G.C. Homans, *English Villagers of the Thirteenth Century*, New York 1941; J.A. Raftis, *The Estates of Ramsay Abbey*, Toronto 1957; J.A. Raftis, *Tenure and Mobility: Studies in the Social History of the Medieval English Village*, Toronto 1964; E.B. Dewindt, *Land and People in Holywell Cum Needleworth*, Toronto 1972; Britton, *The Community of the Vill*; B. Hanawalt, *The Ties that Bound: Peasant Families in Medieval England*, Oxford 1986, 262–5 passim; Dyer, *Standards of Living*, 24; R.M. Smith, 'Modernisation and the

known to have belonged to particular gilds, and on the land and goods of the gilds themselves.

In the later fourteenth century Bottisham was a medium sized village in south-east Cambridgeshire: 392 adults paid poll tax here in 1377.[55] Jurisdiction was divided among five manors,[56] with the main settlement at Bottisham and a hamlet at Bottisham Lode. In 1389, the year of the survey, this village supported seven gilds.[57] These gilds were of a simple type of organisation consisting of a warden or *custos* and a group of stock-holders who held goods for the use of the gild in their hands, in this case sums of money ranging from 10*s* to 64*s* per gild. There are no other references to gild activity in Bottisham during the period of this study.[58] However, twenty-eight men and one woman are named as wardens or stock-holders in the 1389 certificates, and they may be traced in other contemporary sources to reveal more about these gilds.

In the records of the honour and general courts of Bottisham manor for 1386–90,[59] twenty-one of these twenty-nine people are mentioned. Most references find them acting as pledges, and exchanging small parcels of land, sometimes with each other. Some of them, or their wives, paid fines for brewing, and a few are worthy of special comment. Johanna Noble was the wife of John Noble and held stock for All Saints' Gild. Robert Aleyn and Reginald Leverington were both priests, although this fact is not mentioned by the gild of the Nativity of the Virgin for whom they held stock. Of Robert Aleyn, nothing further is known. Reginald Leverington was a member of the Bishop of Ely's household at the time of the clerical poll tax in 1379,[60] and had perhaps recently come to Bottisham, as in 1386 he became tenant of a messuage and seven acres of land formerly held by Thomas FitzRichard and Richard Atteslo, both chaplains,[61] and recorded as resident in Bottisham, in 1379. In that year Bottisham supported one rector and three chaplains:[62] in

Corporate Medieval Village Community in England: Some Sceptical Reflections', in *Explorations in Historical Geography*, ed. A.R.H. Baker and D. Gregory, Cambridge 1984, 140–79, an important and wide-ranging synthesis of ideas in this field.

55 Fenwick, 'The English Poll Taxes', 290.

56 National Register of Archives: Manorial Registers, Index vol. i, A–H, see Cambridgeshire. The five manors were Allington Vauxes, Anglesey, Bottisham, Tunbridge, Tunbridge Hall.

57 PRO, C47/38/3(1–7).

58 The documents relating to the dissolution of the gilds in 1547 and the hunt for concealed lands give an indication of continued gild activity in Bottisham, but supply no details; E. Hailstone Junior, *The History and Antiquities of the Parish of Bottisham and the Priory of Anglesey in Cambridgeshire*, Publns Camb. Antiq. Soc. no. 14, Cambridge 1873; and *Supplement* no. 16, Cambridge 1878, 10; Palmer, 374.

59 PRO, SC2/155/53, fos 1–5, Bottisham Court Rolls: honour and general courts 10–17, 21, 22 Richard II (1386/7–1393/4, 1397/8, 1398/9).

60 W.M. Palmer, 'A List of Cambridgeshire Subsidy Rolls 1250–1625', *East Anglian N. & Q.*, new series xiii, 1909–10, see Appendix no. xii, 'The Clerical Poll Tax of 1379 in Cambridgeshire', esp. 224.

61 PRO, SC2/155/53, fo 1r.

62 Palmer, 'A List of Cambridgeshire Subsidy Rolls', 191.

the 1380s one vicar and seven chaplains are recorded in the court rolls. Probably a number of the chaplains were employed by the gilds, although this was not mentioned in the certificates of 1389.

In 1389 Walter Rous was warden of two fraternities, Holy Trinity and the Nativity of the Blessed Mary; Thomas Mittilweye of Corpus Christi; William Osbern of All Saints; William Stoker of St Peter; and John Christemasse of St James. Three of these five men are known to have held manorial office. In 1389 Walter Rous became a marsh warden. He paid two fines for brewing, a common activity for gild social events, and in 1388 he entered into one acre of land in Bottisham lode with some companions.[63] Perhaps this was gild land, although it was denied that they held any land in 1389. Thomas Mittilwaye held manorial office in 1386, 1388 and 1389 as inquisitor and ale taster. William Siteler was an inquisitor and ale taster in 1389, and held stock for the Holy Trinity and St Nicholas Gilds as well as Corpus Christi.

Three other men who held gild stock were of high status in Bottisham society. John Skenhale, who held stock for St James's Gild, was a miller. He and two others were twice fined for grinding excessive measures, presumably at profit to themselves,[64] and he was involved in a dispute with his namesake over the money from the sale of some animals.[65] John James, who held stock for All Saints' Gild, was the bailiff of the manor and figures prominently in the court rolls. He was one of the four men named as constables and subcollectors in the 1377 poll tax indenture for Bottisham, as was John Norman, who held stock for Corpus Christi Gild.[66]

The people who held stock were men, and occasionally women, with surplus wealth, as they would be called upon to make payments on the fraternity's behalf when required. This is confirmed by the evidence of the court rolls. The majority of stock-holders were drawn from among the more substantial tenants; those who acted as pledges and were engaged in the land-market;[67] those whom Zvi Razi terms 'Kulaks',[68] who came to be known as 'husbandmen' and 'yeomen' in the fifteenth and sixteenth centuries.

The gilds reflected the hierarchies of their communities. Those men with the highest office in the gilds also held high office outside. To their role in the gild they brought their personal authority. Their power and status was confirmed, as with John James, by external authority; by the lord of the

63 PRO, SC2/155/53, land transaction, fo 3r.
64 PRO, SC2/155/53, fos 3r, 5r.
65 PRO, SC2/155/53, fo 3v.
66 PRO, E179/81/34/11.
67 P.D.A. Harvey, *Manorial Records*, British Record Association no. 5, Gloucester 1984, 50.
68 Z. Razi, 'Family, Land and Village Community in Later Medieval England', *P&P* xciii, 1981, 3–36; C. Dyer, 'The Social and Economic Background to the Rural Revolt of 1381', in *The English Rising of 1381*, ed. R.H. Hilton and T. Aston, Cambridge 1984, 9–24, esp. 17–18.

manor through his position as bailiff; and by national government through his part in the collection of the poll tax. The overlapping responsibilities carried by gild officers reveal the gilds as another facet of local government in rural communities, and as additional instruments of social control for members of the village elite, through their authority over gild brethren.

There are six Cambridgeshire villages for which 1377 poll tax indentures naming subcollectors survive and for which there are also names of gild officers in 1389. In three of these villages the names of the officials correspond: in Bottisham, in neighbouring Swaffham Bulbeck, where Robert Hamond was a stock-holder for the gild of the Nativity of the Virgin,[69] and in Chesterton where Reginald Smythe gave an acre of land to the gild of the Assumption of the Virgin.[70]

In 1377 the collection of the poll tax in the town of Cambridge itself was administered by six men, one of whom was John Blaunkepayne, burgess and sometime mayor of the town and one of the founders of Holy Trinity Gild, Holy Trinity Church.[71] This was perhaps the wealthiest and most prestigious gild in Cambridge in 1389. Where the collection of the tax at a county level was concerned other burgesses and founders of the Holy Trinity Gild were involved. John Gybon senior was a collector in 1377 and an assessor in 1379; and Richard Maystreman of Barnwell was an assessor and collector in 1381.[72] Other Cambridge gildsmen who administered the poll tax at a county level were Robert de Brigham, burgess and founder of the Purification Gild, Great St Mary's Church, a collector in 1379, and John de Colvylle, skinner, founder of St Katherine's Gild, St Benet's Church and brother of the Annunciation Gild of St Botolph's Church, a reassessor of the tax in 1381.[73] At an earlier date Mary Bateson was able to tie in the names of St Mary's Gild brethren with the borough subsidy roll of 1314/15 to show that they were among the substantial burgesses of the town.[74] In cross-referencing the poll tax data with the gild returns of 1389, the pattern is the same.

Elsewhere in the county, Roger, Lord de Scales, the son of a substantial benefactor of the Assumption Gild, Haslingfield, was a reassessor in 1379,[75] and William Everard of Parsondrove, a founder of the Assumption Gild at Leverington was associated with the collection in 1381.[76] Leverington and its

69 W.M. Palmer, 'A List of the Cambridgeshire Subsidy Rolls 1250–1625' in *East Anglian N. & Q.*, new series xii, 1907–8, see Appendix no. xi, 'The Cambridgeshire Poll Taxes', esp. 257; PRO, C47/38/33(1–4).

70 PRO, E179/192/4a/5; C47/38/15.

71 PRO, E179/81/41; C47/38/10; J. Milner Gray, *Biographical Notes on the Mayors of Cambridge*, Cambridge 1922, 11–17.

72 Fenwick, 'The English Poll Taxes', 284–6; PRO, C47/38/10.

73 Fenwick, 'The English Poll Taxes', 284–6; PRO, C47/38/9, 7, 8.

74 Bateson, 151–7.

75 G.E. Cokayne, *The Complete Peerage* xi, R-S, London 1949, 499–507.

76 Fenwick, 'The English Poll Taxes', 284–6, 285 Pokedrove = Parsondrove; PRO, C47/38/25.

hamlet Parsondrove were adjacent to Wisbech. Important men living in Wisbech and its satellite settlements acted in conjunction in the administration of the area for the Bishop of Ely and in other aspects of local government. Given the importance of the towns of Wisbech in the liberty of Ely and of Cambridge in the shire, it is not surprising that their inhabitants were closely involved in the county administration of the poll tax. By tracing the senior members of the gilds or fraternities, the pattern already seen in the rural community of Bottisham is reproduced: that of prominent men undertaking leading roles in a number of institutions.

Gild and Gentry

Although the gentry and aristocracy were not generally members of gilds or fraternities, it had become fashionable for them to join those of regional or national importance by the later fourteenth century. The gild of Corpus Christi in Cambridge, one of the two gilds to found the college of Corpus Christi, had Henry Duke of Lancaster as alderman in 1352, under whom it secured the licence for its collegiate foundation.[77] Thomas de Eltisley, Chaplain to the Archbishop of Canterbury, had interested members of the royal family and nobility in the project, notably Queen Philippa.[78] The gilds were able to found their college and in return, their chief benefactor Henry Duke of Lancaster became alderman. He was succeeded in that office by his son-in-law John of Gaunt.[79] As a result of their patronage other members of the Court joined.[80] The register of the fraternity of the Holy Trinity and Saints Fabian and Sebastian at St Botolph without Aldersgate, London, recorded the membership of gentry and officials of the Court in the early fifteenth century along with craftsmen and traders.[81]

In 1420 John Ingaldesthorp, knight of Swaffham Bulbeck and Burgh in Cambridgeshire, left 100s to the Holy Trinity Gild of Lynn in Norfolk. In 1519 Thomas Lovell, gentleman of Enfield, Middlesex and Chesterton, Cambridgeshire, requested his executors to send 8*s* 4*d* to the alderman of the Holy Trinity Gild, Lynn, for his exequies with twelve priests according to the rules of the fraternity. This was in addition to exequies to be held at every

77 *VCH Cambs*. iii, 371–6.

78 J. Josselin, *Historiola Collegii Corporis Christi et Beatae Maniae Cantabrigiae*, ed. J. Willis, Publns. Camb. Antiq. Soc. xvii, Cambridge 1880, 5–10.

79 Bateson, xxiii–xxvi.

80 J.P. Rushe, 'The Origin of St Mary's Gild and its Connection with Corpus Christi College', *Proc. Camb. Antiq. Soc.* xvi, 1911–12, 20–52; C.P. Hall, 'The Gild of Corpus Christi and the Foundation of Corpus Christi College: An Investigation of the Documents' in P. Zutshi, ed. *Medieval Cambridge: Essays on the Pre-Reformation University*, Cambridge 1993, 65–91.

81 P. Basing, ed., *Parish Fraternity Register: Fraternity of the Holy Trinity, Saints Fabian and Sebastian in the Parish of St Botolph Without Aldersgate*, London Record Society xviii, London 1982, xxi–xxv.

charterhouse in England at a cost of 20*s* each and 40*s* at the mother house in France.[82]

Inclusion in the registers of prominent fraternities ensured commemoration after death. Where evidence exists of gentry patronage of minor gilds, in their own areas of influence, the motivation is more complex. There are various documents associated with the fraternity or gild of the Assumption of the Blessed Mary in Haslingfield. The 1389 certificate names four men: Alderman William Sterne and Richard Bond, gild officials, and Robert de Scales and Master John of Offord.[83] The certificate is written in French but contains a Latin transcription of the 1344 mortmain licence.[84] This was purchased by the third Lord Robert de Scales who was important in the King's service at this time, and later fought in the first division at Crécy.[85] He endowed the fraternity with a messuage and fifty acres of land to maintain a perpetual chaplain to celebrate mass daily in the new chapel of the Virgin, for the souls of the King and his ancestors and of Robert de Scales, Master John of Offord and their parents. In 1344 John of Offord was Archdeacon of Ely and keeper of the Privy Seal. He later became Chancellor and was Archbishop-elect of Canterbury when he died of the plague in 1349.[86] It seems to have been not uncommon for the aristocracy or gentry to have endowed chantries for themselves in this way. The entry following the Haslingfield licence in the 1344 Patent Rolls shows John Giffard endowing a chantry run by a warden and brethren in the church of St Andrew of Cochestok for similar purposes.[87] In 1520 and 1521, Robert Smythe and Thomas Wyth, gentlemen, left lands and tenements to the gild of the Holy Trinity, Wisbech. These were to fund perpetual obits and the salary of one of the four gild chaplains, who was also to keep a school at which their souls were remembered daily in prayers.[88]

In the 1327 lay subsidy, William Sterne, alderman of the Assumption Gild, Haslingfield, paid 3*s* 3½*d*. He was the seventh wealthiest of 42 tax-payers there. The list was headed by Lady Isabella de Scales, who paid 16*s* 10*d*, more than twice as much as anyone else. Richard Bond, the other gild official, paid 9*d*; the lowest sum paid was 6*d*.[89] The fact that these two men were tax-payers is indicative of their high status in the village community.

82 PRO, Prob 11/2b/48, fo 379, 1420 will of John Ingaldesthorp; Prob 11/20/22, fos 16r and v, 1519 will of Thomas Lovell.

83 PRO, C47/38/24.

84 PRO, C66/211, membrane 14, 18 Edward III, part i; C66/212, membrane 37, 18 Edward III, part ii.

85 Cokayne, *The Complete Peerage* xi, 501–2.

86 *Dictionary of National Biography* xiv, ed. L. Stephen and S. Lee, Oxford 1921–2, 901–2.

87 PRO, C66/212, membrane 57, 18 Edward III, part ii.

88 PRO, Prob 11/20/8, fos 55v, 56r and v; Prob 11/20/24, fos 190v–92r.

89 *Cambridgeshire and the Isle of Ely Lay Subsidy 1327*, ed. C.H. Evelyn-White, reprinted from *East Anglian N. & Q.*, new series x–xii, 1903–8 no date or place of publication, 32–33.

In 1392–3 two further mortmain licences were granted for endowments in Haslingfield, one for the gild of the Nativity of the Virgin, and one for a perpetual chantry for five men: Henry Smythe, Peter Kelman, William Lovell, knight, John Marable, chaplain, and John Uphawe.[90] It is not possible to trace the men named in these two documents in the manorial bailiff's accounts of the following year,[91] although there was a Richard Bond, possibly of the same family as the previous Richard Bond. He held eight acres of land belonging to the Nativity Gild and a further eight acres together with a certain John Pryfote, belonging to the chantry.[92] From this and the fifty acres given to the Assumption Gild by Robert de Scales, it is clear that these religious endowments were important to the economic balance of the village and to the individuals who held them.

In these instances members of the aristocracy and gentry were patronising already existing organs of local government. Endowing a perpetual chantry was an uncertain enterprise. Robert de Scales' actions were prudent as the Assumption Gild outlived his family.[93] In return for their services the gilds gained enhanced status, endowments and the benefits of the chaplain. This raises a further issue: the gilds were not in any legal sense corporations, but certain of their activities and the expectations upon them required them to act as such: a point which will be discussed later.

The Gild as a Microcosm of Society

1. *Hierarchy and discipline*

A gild was a microcosm of society, oligarchic in structure. When members named in the statutes as founders, benefactors, officers and stock-holders are traced in other documents, they are found to be wealthy yeomen and burgesses drawn from among those of high social and economic status in the towns and villages where they lived. As well as gild office, sometimes in more than one gild, they held other local positions of responsibility, as churchwardens, manorial officers, jurors and taxation officials. This was partly practical: in a society where cash flow was a chronic problem and few people, especially in rural areas, had much surplus wealth, there was only a small number of men and women who could easily realise the value of the sums entrusted to them, when payments were necessary.[94]

Election procedures ensured the perpetuation of oligarchy. The verb *eligere*

90 PRO, C66/335, membrane 15; C66/335, membrane 30; 16 Richard II, part i.

91 CCRO, L19/36 Bailiffs Account, 18 Richard II, Haslingfield manor belonging to St Mary's Abbey, York.

92 PRO, C66/335, membranes 15, 30.

93 Cokayne, *The Complete Peerage* xi, 507. The Scales family died out in the male line in 1460; the gild was not dissolved until 1547.

94 See chs 2 and 5 for the case of Harry and Johanna Cressewell.

is used where the election of officers is described in the statutes. This does not mean 'to elect' in the current sense of the word, but 'to choose' or 'to select'.

According to the statutes, there were two main types of gild. In 1389, 27 (45%) of the gilds mention only one officer, generally the *custos*, translated as 'warden' or 'guardian', a term used for churchwardens as well.[95] The warden was assisted by a group of stock-holders. At Bottisham and Swaffham Bulbeck the warden and between two and eight other men divided between them goods worth from 10*s* to 64*s* 10½*d*. Some men held goods for more than one gild.[96] It was predominently rural gilds which were organised in this way, and some may have been little more than lights, like that of St Christopher March which left accounts for 1472–1525.[97] Such groups left no details of their election procedures, except for St James' Gild at Dullingham. The statutes of 1517 declared that the outgoing alderman should choose the next aldermen and the outgoing steward, the next steward.[98]

The second type of gild, found predominently in the urban communities of Cambridge and Wisbech, had a more elaborate structure. Duties were divided among a number of officers. The *custos*, known variously as the alderman or the *magister* in Cambridge, a name borrowed from college terminology, was joined by two, sometimes four *scabini* or *skymini*.[99] Once again the names varied from gild to gild. Their function, like that of the stock-holders, was primarily financial. The sums in their hands were larger than in rural areas, generally one or two pounds.[100] It was their task to keep the keys to the gild chest and with the master or alderman to present annual accounts.

In 1389, twelve gilds had an officer called the *decanus* or dean, also known as the *apparitor*, *promotor*, *bedell*, or *belleman*, which give an indication of his tasks. The *apparitor* of the Purification Gild, Great St Mary's Church, Cambridge, was

> to inform brethren of funeral services, meetings and other gatherings; to preside over the offices of the dead; and to organise the torches and the carrying of the dead body to the church.[101]

95 W.E. Tate, *The Parish Chest*, Cambridge 1951, 83.

96 PRO, C47/38/3(1–7), 33(1–4).

97 CCRO, P116/1/4; P11/5/1–2. In Bassingbourne churchwardens' accounts, light wardens held similar sums.

98 CUL, MM1 47, Baker Mss., vol. 36, item 16, 161–2, 1517 St James' gild statutes Dullingham.

99 Reynolds, *Kingdoms and Communities*, 24–32 for discussion of *scabini*.

100 BL Add. Ms. 5846, pp. 5–13; CUL, MM1 36, Baker Mss., vol. 25, item 10, 361–66, 367–71; in the three 15th-century gilds of Cambridge stock-holders held 40*s* each. CCRO, X/28, 1535 two obligations binding four men in all to return up to 40*s* each to the Purification Gild, Great St Mary's, Cambridge. J.F. Williams, 'A Medieval Squabble', *Proc. Camb. Antiq. Soc.* liv, 1961, 109–11, Robert Palmer held 19*s* of gild money which he was unable to pay back.

101 PRO, C47/38/9.

The dean of the Assumption Gild at Leverington near Wisbech was

> to collect all the pennies due to the gild as decided after the mornspeech [annual meeting] from year to year; to offer [alms] for the soul of any brother of the fraternity who dies; and to light and tend the lamps of the said gild hanging in the chapel.[102]

The office was similar to that of parish verger or bedell. In gilds where there was only one officer, he carried out these tasks.[103]

In 1389, ten gilds also had a clerk. The duties of the clerk of the Purification Gild, Great St Mary's Church, Cambridge, were

> to write the names of new brethren, the accounts, the receipts, to write and collect the expenses and fines imposed, and to make payments according to the form described below to poor brothers and sisters.[104]

The duties of the clerk and dean were onerous and were recompensed with a small salary ranging from ½*d* from each new member to 6*s* 8*d* a year or exemption from gild dues.[105] The clerk to St Katherine's Gild, St Benet's Church, Cambridge, was Walter Sutton, a public notary and diocesan official. He was exempt from gild dues and was paid 4*d* by each new member. His presence both reflected the gild's status and brought it added prestige.[106] Most gilds probably relied on the literacy skills of their chaplain, or paid someone for a specific task when writing was necessary.

The warden, the stock-holders, the dean and the clerk, like chairperson, treasurer and secretary, correspond to the committee structure of present-day societies.[107] The statutes of the gilds with this more elaborate structure provide clear evidence of oligarchies perpetuating themselves. At the main annual meeting on the patronal feast, the accounts were heard and new officers 'elected'. The alderman of the Holy Trinity Gild, Holy Trinity Church, Cambridge, chose seven brethren, who in their turn chose the next year's officers. The master, two aldermen and eight brethren of the Purification Gild, Great St Mary's Church, Cambridge, chose the new clerk and apparitor. The clerk and apparitor in the presence of all the brethren then chose the new master and aldermen.[108] It is interesting to note that

102 PRO, C47/38/5.

103 PRO, C47/38/33(1), 35, are two examples of this; the three 15th-century Cambridge gilds also had deans.

104 PRO, C47/38/9.

105 PRO, C47/38/37, ½*d*; C47/38/10, 6*s* 8*d*; C47/38/6, 7, 9, 10 exemptions.

106 PRO, C47/38/7.

107 Reynolds, *Kingdoms and Communities*, 78.

108 PRO, C47/38/10, 9. This type of procedure was also followed by the three 15th-century Cambridge gilds for which statutes survive.

the election of churchwardens and subordinate light wardens for these two Cambridge churches proceeded along almost identical lines.[109]

In its statutes St Katherine's Gild, St Benet's Church, Cambridge, made explicit the principle behind this method of appointment. The officers were chosen by 'majorem et seniorem partem confratrum', 'The Great and the Good among the Brethren'.[110] Two Wisbech gilds at this time claimed to hold 'liberam ellecionem' or 'free elections'. The phrase remains opaque: it is not known whether this meant one man, one vote. In any case, it makes little difference as the two gilds involved, St Peter's and Holy Trinity, were composed already of the '*majorem et seniorem partem*' of the town.[111]

The authority of the alderman and other officers was as much symbolic as it was real; long-established patterns of collective activity too ancient, as Susan Reynolds points out, to have been influenced by thirteenth-century Aristotelian democratic ideas, were based on two principles: the authority of the assembly of the people, and of its appointed leader.[112] Late medieval feudal society and the culture of chivalry, although distant from all but the most sophisticated gentlemen and women, rested on the assumption that the King would govern on the advice of the great and the good in the realm: so it was with the alderman in the gild.[113] Church teachings and other patterns of knowledge, such as the zodiac, described an ordered universe in which all things and all men had their place.[114] Gild structure and ceremonial at its most developed reflected these assumptions.

The dignity of office was safeguarded by a system of fines on those who refused to accept their 'election'. In the fourteenth and fifteenth centuries this was an urban phenomenon written into the statutes of gilds in Cambridge, Wisbech and Ely. In the sixteenth century the statutes of the rural St James' Gild, Dullingham, also contained such a clause. For St Peter's Gild, Holy Trinity Church, Ely, refusal of office cost the alderman 13*s* 4*d* (one mark), the wardens 6*s* 8*d* (half a mark), and the dean 3*s* 4*d* (a quarter mark); for Corpus Christi Gild, St Peter's Church, Ely, fines were 1*s* for the alderman and 6*d* for the wardens and dean.[115] In Dullingham the alderman forfeited 6*s* 8*d* and every cater [caterer?] 3*s* 4*d*. In Lichfield, those who refused to serve as master of St Mary's Gild were expelled.[116] In an urban context penalties were

109 F.A. Gasquet, *Parish Life in Medieval England*, London 1906, 104–5 for Great St Mary's; *VCH Cambs*. iii, 125 for Holy Trinity.

110 PRO, C47/38/7.

111 PRO, C47/38/41, 43.

112 Reynolds, *Kingdoms and Communities*, 5; Dawson, *A History of Lay Judges*, 35–39, the folk-moot and its leaders; R.W. and A.J. Carlyle, *The History of Medieval Political Theory in the West*, 6 vols, Edinburgh 1903–36, esp. vol. iii, 1915.

113 Carlyle, *History of Medieval Political Theory* iii, ch. vi.

114 E.M.W. Tillyard, *The Elizabethan World Picture*, Harmondsworth 1963.

115 PRO, C47/38/23(1), 21.

116 *The Gild of St Mary Lichfield, Being Ordinances of the Gild of St Mary and Other Documents*, ed. F.J. Furnivall, EETS, Extra Series no. cxiv, London 1920, 15.

imposed on those who refused borough office, because expense and inconvenience outweighed remuneration and prestige. This has been linked, although not conclusively, to the economic decline of towns in the later Middle Ages.[117]

The alderman's symbolic role was expressed through ritual on official occasions. On behalf of all the brethren he made offerings at the patronal festival and at funerals: at funerals and commemorative rites he distributed alms to the poor. He led the gild in procession, presided over feasts and between one and four annual meetings or morn-speeches, where the accounts and the oaths of new entrants were heard, elections made, disputes and breaches of the statutes judged, and cases of poverty assessed for assistance. He also granted dispensation for absence from such events. The 1379 inventory of jewels of Holy Trinity Gild, Wisbech, included badges and belts, possibly worn by the alderman and officers on special occasions.[118] Further evidence of elaborate ritual is found in the three fifteenth-century Cambridge statutes. At the Annual General Meeting held after the anniversary mass the alderman was to have 'for his drink and his guests a gallon of ale; and each master a potell [half a gallon]; and the clerk a potell; and the dean a quart of ale'.[119] After a 'common drinking' only the officers were allowed to remain in the hall once the alderman had risen. Entry to this private part of the proceedings was forbidden to ordinary brothers and sisters on penalty of 2 pounds of wax. At every 'morowe speeche' the dean was to deliver the 'yerde' to any man who would not obey the alderman nor keep silence. If the culprit would not receive the 'yerde' he too was to pay 2 pounds of wax.

It is necessary to make a distinction between the symbolic and the real power of the alderman and other officers. In 1389, 47 (78%) gilds gave some indication of where responsibility for decision-making lay. This was apportioned differently from gild to gild, and does not divide neatly along urban-rural lines. Although quite clearly an oligarchy, a gild was not an autocracy. In general the alderman and officers acted with some degree of consensus from the membership, as one would expect from other customary forms of government. In nine gilds in Ely, Wisbech and in rural Chesterton and Swaffham Bulbeck, sisters are specifically mentioned as being party to the decision-making process, although it is possible that this was not the case elsewhere.

It is also necessary to examine how far the alderman and other officers were accountable to the membership of the fraternity for the fulfilment of their duties, especially in financial affairs. The Dean of the Holy Cross Gild, St Peter's Church, Ely, was fined 2*d* for every member he failed to call to

117 J.I. Kermode, 'Urban Decline? The Flight from Office in Late Medieval York', *EcHR* xxxv, 1982, 179–98.

118 WCR1, p. 2.

119 BL Add. Ms. 5846, pp. 5–13; CUL MM1 36, Baker Mss., vol. 25, item 10, pp. 361–6, 367–71.

meetings.[120] The wardens of the four gilds in Swaffham Bulbeck were to be faithful to gild promises and the two aldermen of the Purification Gild, Great St Mary's, Cambridge, swore an oath on the gospels at their election.[121] All Saints' Gild, St Peter's Church, Ely, required all gild works to be done without fraud and at Stretham the gild of the Nativity of Our Lady stated that those who acted by fraud or falsehood while holding office were to leave the gild.[122] It was customary for stock-holders to find pledges and in 14 (23%) gilds to present annual accounts. The stock-holders of St Peter's Gild, Holy Trinity Church, Ely, were to bring the goods and place them on the table before all the brethren: 'et tunc omnes qui habent aliqua catalla gilde opportabunt illa et ponent super mensam coram omnibus fratribus gilde'.[123] Certain Cambridge statutes recorded fines for officers who did not return gild property, and the prosecution of pledges in order to retrieve it.[124] Thus, on paper at least, there was some redress against unscrupulous officers of both urban and rural gilds.

Due to their social position, both within the gild and outside, the officers used the gild as an organ of social control.[125] The stability of medieval society was based on successful self-regulation by all the social groups from which it was constructed, like many other institutions, for example the gild merchant, one of the roles of the lesser gilds and fraternities was to act as a court. Seven urban gilds in Cambridge and Wisbech provided for the internal resolution of disputes between members under the arbitration of the alderman and his deputies. Only when internal arbitration had failed were brethren allowed to appeal to Common or Canon Law, on consent of the alderman and brethren.

In 1389, 26 (43%) gilds, and also the three fifteenth-century gilds, imposed certain standards of behaviour on their brethren. In general these were obedience to the alderman and statutes, payment of dues and attendance at meetings, services and funerals, unless formally excused. Fines of a few pence or a pound of wax to the light for their breach were imposed by 21 gilds altogether. Most, but not all, of these gilds were in Cambridge or Wisbech. The statutes of urban gilds placed greater emphasis on patrolling the behaviour of members 'quibus dicta fraternitas possit scandalizari', 'by which the fraternity might be brought into disrepute'.[126] Like the ecclesiastical courts fraternities punished

120 PRO, C47/38/24.

121 PRO, C47/38/33(1–4), 9.

122 PRO, C47/38/20, 32.

123 PRO, C47/38/23(1).

124 PRO, C47/38/6, 10; Williams, 'A Medieval Squabble', shows that in at least one case legal action was taken to retrieve property.

125 B.R. McCree, 'Religious Gilds and Regulation of Behaviour in Late Medieval Towns', in *People, Politics and Community in the Later Middle Ages*, ed. J. Rosenthal and C. Richmond, Gloucester 1987, 108–22.

126 PRO, C47/38/41, 43.

gambling, general malice and promiscuity.[127] Gambling was particularly frowned upon: it would have stretched credit, created debt and possibly a need for charitable support. A bad reputation could have affected the 'good name' of other brethren, particularly if they were involved in joint economic activity. Such clauses were probably less necessary in country areas where the tight-knit community of village or hamlet would have provided a greater degree of social control.

2. *Collective identity*

The collective identity of a gild or fraternity was affirmed through the pomp and pageantry of ritual, both religious and secular.[128] Obligation to attend the celebration of feasts and solemn meetings was re-enforced, like suit of court, through fines imposed by the officers.[129] Brethren were exhorted to bear brotherly love for one another. The statutes of St Giles' Gild, Tydd St Giles read: 'in primis constituimus et ordinamus quod nos fratres predicti sumus in perfecta caritate et voluntate et unanimi assensu pro salute anime,'[130] 'firstly we agree and ordain that we the brothers are in perfect charity and good will and with a common aim, the salvation of the soul'. Fraternal love did not always come easily. Animosity and violence played their part in gild life. At times they threatened to overwhelm proceedings, necessitating the intervention of the alderman to restore order. Any member of St Peter's Gild, Holy Trinity Church, Ely, who '*maliciose*' or wilfully disrupted the feast day, was fined 2 pounds of wax.[131] Other statutes concerned flouting the authority of the alderman, disrupting meetings, drawing blood through violence, and even seeking to leave the gild without good reason.[132] Social harmony was the ideal, but in practice was rather harder to attain.

The ultimate price for disobedience was expulsion. Eight gilds employed this penalty in 1389. Some features of the statutes are shadows of ancient antecedents; like legal codes, practice had evolved leaving archaic elements still present in the text. This is particularly the case in the statutes which define collective identity, where there are similarities with surviving Anglo-Saxon statutes. Expulsion originally related to outlawry: the fact that no man could survive on his own, except as part of a group, although by this time it was more to protect the group's good name. In 1389, 12 (20%) gilds required

127 M. Spufford, 'Puritanism and Social Control?' in *Order and Disorder in Early Modern England*, ed. A. Fletcher and J. Stevenson, Cambridge 1985, 41–57.

128 S. Lindenbaum, 'Rituals of Exclusion: Feasts and Plays of English Religious Fraternities', unpublished paper 1990; D. Wallace, 'Aspects and Limits of Associational Form', Section 2 of a new book on Chaucer, relating the company of the prologue to the gild structure, unpublished Ms. 1992. I am grateful to these two scholars for lending me these unpublished works.

129 Toulmin Smith, xxi.

130 PRO, C47/38/35.

131 PRO, C47/38/21(1).

132 PRO, C47/38/41, 43.

new brethren to take an oath before the assembled company, a rite of passage which conferred both a new role and new obligations. Brethren of the gilds in Bottisham and Swaffham Bulbeck agreed to keep gild promises, but were not bound by oath, thus keeping a wary eye on the government whose writ enquired into 'oaths, gatherings, feasts and meetings'. Four Cambridge gilds swore the oath on the Gospels to re-enforce the solemnity and also, perhaps, to advertise their ownership of expensive religious texts. The fifteenth-century Cambridge gilds also had oaths. The oath affirmed the solidarity and coherence of the group. One of its requirements in seven urban gilds, those from Cambridge and Wisbech in the fourteenth and fifteenth centuries, was to keep gild secrets and to conceal gild orders. St Katherine's Gild, St Andrew's Church, Cambridge, only gave charity to brethren who had kept gild secrets.[133] The oath was still significant, at least in the towns of the later fourteenth century, or the government would not have been interested in its subversive potential. It is questionable, however, whether oaths had the same force by the later fifteenth and sixteenth centuries, when there is much evidence of multiple gild membership.

The Gild as a Corporate Body

The emphasis on personal loyalty was to protect the corporate identity of the gild and its status in the community. Although the legal concept of the corporation was not yet fully developed, the history of corporate bodies in the Middle Ages was antecedent to this. Martin Weinbaum states: 'Incorporation therefore is one of the substantial and lasting contributions which medieval boroughs make to the growth of English institutions.'[134] The history of the gilds must certainly be added as a footnote to this process. Susan Reynolds argues that medieval law did not develop a concept of legal personality before 1300. Mortmain legislation may have been a catalyst, first enacted at about the same time throughout western Europe.[135] In 1279, when it was first enacted in England, it enabled the Crown to tax lands passing into the 'dead hand' or '*mort main*' of the church. In 1391 it brought gifts to boroughs, town corporations and gilds within its scope. Finally, in 1532, it was made applicable to gifts to the parish.[136] The concept of the corporation, therefore, developed parallel to many other local government institutions from 1300 onwards, and more importantly in this context, parallel to the most intense period of medieval gild foundation.

133 PRO, C47/38/6.
134 M. Weinbaum, *The Incorporation of Boroughs*, Manchester 1937, 17.
135 S. Reynolds, 'The Idea of the Corporation in Western Christendom before 1300' in *Law and Social Change in British Society*, ed. J.A. Guy and H.G. Beale, Royal Historical Society Studies in History xl, London 1984, 27–33.
136 S. Raban, *Mortmain Legislation and the English Church*, Cambridge 1982, 170.

There is no question that gilds, both rural and urban, did act as legal personalities when pursuing their affairs. In 1526 William Walsh of Great Shelford left

> to my eldest daughter Mary 5 marks and a great brass pot, to Anne my daughter 5 marks; and the 10 marks to be delivered to the Aldermen of St Anne's and Our Lady gilds, who are to bring in every year the stock and increase and take of every noble 4*d* for the gild's advantage till they be married, and if they die before, 5 marks to remain to the gild and 5 to my wife.[137]

Walsh had invested the girls' dowries in the gilds until such time as they were married. Further evidence of their corporate identity is their proprietorship of gildhalls, stocks of animals, tenure of land and other assets. Although the writ of 1388 requested details of 'lands, tenements, rents and possessions',[138] remarkably little evidence of gild property was produced in the returns. It seems more likely that wherever possible its existence was concealed. Although six Cambridgeshire gilds admitted to having lands, only the Assumption Gild, Haslingfield, had a mortmain licence. The other five held land by a variety of means to avoid such a necessity. The three gilds in Chesterton held land by court roll and by mortgage. Two brethren had assigned a rood and an acre of land to the gild of the Nativity of the Virgin at Stretham. Presumably this meant that they held it on the gild's behalf. Lands with buildings and their appurtenances and three acres of marshland belonging to the Holy Trinity Gild, Wisbech, were held in fee simple by various brethren including Adam Reynolds, a chaplain as feoffees.[139]

In the fifteenth century the brotherhood or fraternity of Gamlingay appears in rentals and surveys as a distinct entity holding lands in its own right. In the terrier of 1470, three messuages, a headland, and seven other parcels of land are listed under its name.[140] In the rental of 1483, a yard and ten acres, a close, a tenement and a messuage are mentioned.[141] By 1505 it had a gildhall, malt mill, messuages, crofts, and over 60 acres of land.[142]

In the town of Wisbech, as in rural Gamlingay, Haslingfield and Bottisham, the pattern is confirmed of an oligarchy of wealthy and substantial men holding office in both manor and gild. John Halman senior, a founder of Holy Trinity Gild, was also alderman of St John Baptist's Gild.[143] Simon Pocdyche, a founder of Holy Trinity Gild and one of the four *scabini* in 1379, was also

137 Palmer, 350.
138 Toulmin Smith, 128.
139 PRO, C47/38/24, 13, 14, 15, 32, 43.
140 Merton College, Oxford, Gamlingay rentals no. 5458, Terrier 1470.
141 Merton College, Oxford, Gamlingay rentals, no. 5461, rental c.1500 (almost certainly c.1483).
142 *VCH Cambs*. v, 83.
143 PRO, C47/38/43, 39.

alderman of St Peter's Gild.[144] Adam Mareys, a feoffee of marshland and a *scabinus* of Trinity Gild, was a juror of Wisbech court leet in 1378, and in the same year Martin Myles, a new entrant, was elected head of a tithing group.[145] At the 1389 court leet, Laurence Cooper, alderman of the Purification Gild, was elected bailiff and ale taster for Wisbech South Bank.[146] The Everard family, minor gentry in the area, one of whom, William Everard, was founder of the Assumption Gild, Leverington, and associated with poll tax collection in 1381, also featured in Wisbech court rolls, elected as officers concerned with various aspects of town life.[147]

Of the six men and four wives named in the 1453 mortmain licence purchased for the sum of 20 marks to endow the chantry of the Trinity Gild, two, the alderman John Masse and Simon Lombe, were leet jurors. Three of them, John Masse, his wife Alicia, and Emma, wife of William Belman, and two other jurors, John Elwyn and John Hunt, a thatcher, later left bequests to the Trinity Gild by will.[148]

The Trinity Gild claimed to have been founded in 1379, the date of its first surviving accounts, but according to these it already had 69 members and a flourishing part in Wisbech religious, social and economic life.[149] There were no further entries in the gild book until 1423, but it can be presumed that it continued to play a significant role in the town. By the mid-fifteenth century it supported a number of chaplains and poor almsmen and a gildhall with paid staff.[150] In 1463 a bailiff was appointed to administer its lands, which continued to accumulate into the sixteenth century: they amounted to almost 800 acres in 1549. By that time the gild also supported a grammar school, a number of chapels and the upkeep of banks and ditches.[151] Its corporate status was set out in the chantry licence purchased from the King in 1453.

> Concedimus per presentes quod predicti Aldermannus fratres et sorores fraternitatis sive gilde predicte, sint per se unum corpus et una communitas perpetua et corporata in re et in nomine, habeantibusque successionem perpetuam et commune sigillum pro negociis fraternitatis sive gilde illius imperpetuum futuris.

144 PRO, C47/38/43, 41; WCR1, p. 2.

145 PRO, C47/38/43; WCRl, p. 1r; CUL, EDR/C8/56.

146 PRO, C47/38/40; CUL, EDR/C8/64.

147 PRO, C47/38/25; CUL, EDR/C8/56, 64.

148 PRO, C66/478, 32 Henry VI, membrane 23, 1453; CUL, EDR/C9/1–3, esp. 3; PRO, Prob 11/5/14, fos 112r, v, 113r, 1466 will of John Masse; ECC HK2791/A/96, fos 34r, v, 35r, 1454 will of Alicia, wife of John Masse; ECC HK2791/A/202, fo 57v, 1458 will of Emma, wife of William Belman; PRO, Prob 11/7/22, fos 167r, v, 1484 will of John Elwyn; ECC HK2791/A/187, fo 54v, 1457 will of John Hunt, thatcher.

149 WCR1, p. 1.

150 WCR1, p. 2, a *hostiarius* administered the hall; PRO, C66/478 mentions almsmen and women and one chaplain, Robert Barbour.

151 WCR1, pp. 136–8, 1451 Terrier of lands; *VCH Cambs*. iv, 256.

[We grant by these present [letters] that the Alderman, brothers and sisters of the fraternity or gild, may be of themselves, one body and one community, perpetual and incorporated, in fact and in name, and may have perpetual succession and a common seal for the business of the fraternity or gild in perpetuity.]

Martin Weinbaum states that *communitas* or collective identity was the fundamental prerequisite for incorporation, which the Trinity Gild clearly had already in 1379. Other characteristics present in incorporated institutions included perpetual succession, the power to hold lands and a common seal, all confirmed here.[152]

At Wisbech the Holy Trinity Gild made the natural progression in 1547 from leading fraternity to town corporation. It is interesting to note that the statute of incorporation provided for the new body to be overseen by the churchwardens.[153] This transition was smoothed by the patronage of the bishop, unwilling to lose a useful agency for the administration of his northern township. This same body continued to fund the grammar school, the upkeep of banks and ditches, and other public works as before. At neighbouring King's Lynn, the new corporation, formerly Trinity Gild, similarly converted the chapel above the charnel-house into a school and funded a lectureship in place of the thirteen chaplains supported before the Reformation.[154]

The pattern is the same in many of the smaller towns and villages of Cambridgeshire. The parish took over those functions and assets of the gilds which were central to community life. At Haslingfield the chapel of the Assumption Gild in the churchyard became a school room, and at Whittlesford, the gildhall was successfully hidden from the commissioners for concealed lands by the parish, using it as a workhouse, poorhouse, and schoolroom, until it was eventually sold in 1966.[155]

The dissolution of the gilds and the confiscation of their possessions undoubtedly fractured local economic religious and social life to the impoverishment of their communities. However, with respect to the control of local affairs, to the advantage of local elites, both gentry and those comparatively neglected at the level below gentry, the question is: how much did the Reformation change?

152 PRO, C66/478; F.J. Gardiner, *A History of Wisbech and Neighbourhood*, Wisbech 1898, 18, illustration of seal; Weinbaum, *The Incorporation of Boroughs*, 44, 18.

153 WCR1, pp. 107–8; *VCH Cambs*. ii, 92, 320–7; iv, 256–60.

154 F. Blomefield, *An Essay Towards a Topography of the County of Norfolk* viii, London 1808, 501; King's Lynn Museum, 'The Town Scene': selected topographical material from the King's Lynn Borough Charters, King's Lynn 1973, 34.

155 *VCH Cambs*. v, 238; vi, 272.

7

Epilogue: 1547 and After

This study has traced gradual changes in local government over the period from about 1350 to 1558, and within that framework the role of the gilds in religious, economic, social and political life. Information on these groups, existing at the interface of various facets of late medieval life, provides important insights into the society.

These gilds, whose activities focused on the parish churches of the rural villages and towns of Cambridgeshire and elsewhere, were neither entirely religious nor entirely secular in scope. Because of this, few of their records survived the impact of the Reformation: they were hard to categorise; possibly superstitious; concerned with obsolete institutions; not required to prove title to land; and likely to contain details of assets which the government sought to confiscate. Their records either perished due to neglect, or were deliberately destroyed, like those at Godmanchester burnt by Henry Frere.[1] Apart from chance survivals, our insights into their form and functions have been obtained obliquely from what was written by various authorities.

It was central government authority which, between 1545 and 1547, initiated the process by which all gilds, colleges, chantries and hospitals were abolished and their goods confiscated.[2] Reformation historians have placed this in the context of recent events, the Henrician Reformation, government financial difficulties, and the desire of the Edwardian administration to further the cause of English Protestantism. However, when investigations are extended back beyond the artificial periodisation imposed by historians, this is seen also to be the continuation of a far longer-term process.

As J.P. Dawson's work, *A History of Lay Judges*, shows, the history of collective institutions is one of increasing governmental control. From the sixth century onwards the anxiety of governments in various parts of Europe about the autonomy of self-regulating groups is recorded in the periodic

1 A. Kreider, *English Chantries: The Road to Dissolution*, Cambridge, Massachusetts 1979, 158. Considering the increased numbers of churchwardens' accounts and other parish records surviving from the second half of the 15th century on, it is likely that gild records were also produced in increased quantities.

2 Kreider, *English Chantries*, esp. chs 7 and 8.

attempts to curb their activities.[3] In England this anxiety instigated the royal survey of 1388–9 and later the dissolution of gilds and other groups in 1547–9.

Gilds were essentially conservative in religious terms. They existed to augment divine service in churches and chapels, to remember the dead, and to organise charity and collective self-help for those who were living. It was their very orthodoxy which made them susceptible to suspicion and attack as the potential focus for opposition to Protestant religious change.

However, it was perhaps their autonomy which was more of a threat to the newly uniform Tudor parish. From this point of view it is no surprise that the fenlands of Cambridgeshire and surrounding East Anglian counties, with their long tradition of gild activity and other manifestations of collective self-government, should become a later stronghold of non-conformity.[4] Tudor legislation sought to bring under central government control those organs of local government which were perceived as too independent: those descended from the vill of ancient times. Christopher Kitching demonstrates that the motive for closing many of the free chapels was their autonomy.[5] So it was with the gilds also. Helen Cam shows that the vill was just as much the forerunner of the sixteenth-century parish as the religious unit of that name.[6] Parish legislation of the sixteenth century was the culmination of medieval developments which united a multiplicity of local jurisdictions into one, the parish, simplifying the line of control from central government and rationalising the powers thus devolved under national legislation.

Although craft gilds fall outside the scope of this study, it is interesting to note some comparisons. Over the course of the Middle Ages their powers were eroded by increasing royal control over trade. By the fourteenth and fifteenth centuries they were subordinate in importance to borough councils,[7] and it was not the craft, but the fraternity, or religious and social, side of their corporate identity, that was more important to members' lives.[8] The abolition of religious activities and confiscation of related assets in 1547, may well have been significant in precipitating their seventeenth-century demise. On

3 J.P. Dawson, *A History of Lay Judges*, Cambridge, Massachusetts, 1960.

4 R.H.C. Davis, 'East Anglia and the Danelaw', *TRHS*, 5th series v, 1955, 23–39; D.M. Palliser, 'Popular Reactions to the Reformation during the Years of Uncertainty', in *The English Reformation Revised*, ed. C. Haigh, Cambridge 1987, 94–113, esp. 112; P. Collinson, *The Elizabethan Puritan Movement*, Oxford 1990, 223.

5 C.J. Kitching, 'Church and Chapelry in Sixteenth Century England', *SCH* xvi, 1979, 281.

6 H. Cam, 'The Community of the Vill', in *Medieval Studies Presented to Rose Graham*, ed. V. Ruffner and A.J. Taylor, Oxford 1950, 1–14.

7 N. Fryde, 'Gilds in England Before the Black Death', *Vorträge und Forschung* xxix, 1985, 225; H. Swanson, 'The Illusion of Economic Structure: Craft Gilds in Late Medieval Towns', *P&P* cxxi, 1988, 29–38.

8 Swanson, 'The Illusion of Economic Structure', 38.

the continent, royal intervention in the working of the craft gilds in fifteenth-century Spain led there to their decline and disappearance.[9]

The changed ideological climate of Counter-Reformation Catholic Europe also imposed new forms on local collective activity through the re-modelling of confraternities under stricter church control, thereby limiting their secular roles. These changes must be seen as the parallel of those presided over in England by the Tudors. However, as in England, local elites sought to retain their ascendance over local affairs by shifting their influence to new or newly powerful institutions. Angelo Torre outlines this process for eighteenth-century Piedmont.[10] There, local oligarchies gained control of brotherhoods, originally begun to foster new religious devotions, in order to consolidate their hold on local society. In so far as possible, they used these to mediate national and regional government initiatives to their own advantage.

In Cambridgeshire and, it may be inferred, elsewhere in England, office-holding in a range of local institutions was concentrated in the hands of a small oligarchy, generally yeomen or husbandmen under the patronage of local gentry.[11] On the abolition of the gilds and chantries in 1547 such people concentrated their energies on those institutions which remained, particularly the parish, where their jurisdiction had been substantially augmented over the previous decades. With the legislation of Elizabeth's reign, particularly the Poor Laws of 1598 and 1601, a familiar pattern re-established itself: that of a local oligarchy of substantial tenant-farmers holding public office, now as overseers of the highways, the Poor Law, parish constables and churchwardens, under the patronage of the gentry in their role as Justices of the Peace. This oligarchy evolved into vestries and select vestries and, as in times before, did their best to organise local events to their own satisfaction and profit.[12]

To explore the continuities between the eras pre- and post-Reformation is not to deny that the Reformation brought about immense social and religious change. As John Craig's work shows, it brought tension and division to small market towns in East Anglia, although interestingly their oligarchies tended to fragment into conservative and reformist groupings along pre-existing fissures.[13] This is probably what occurred in smaller communities. In social

9 J. Klein, 'Medieval Spanish Gilds', in *Facts and Factors in Economic History*, ed. E.F. Gay, Cambridge, Massachusetts, 1932, 164–88; K. Wrightson and D. Levine, *Poverty and Piety in an English Village*, New York 1979, 7–13.

10 A. Torre, 'Village Ceremonial Life and Politics in Eighteenth Century Piedmont', in *Disciplines of Faith*, ed. J. Obelkevich, L. Roper and R. Samuel, London 1987, 194–207.

11 Westlake, 128; K. Wrightson, *English Society 1580–1660*, London 1982, part ii, esp. 225–6.

12 W.E. Tate, *The Parish Chest*, Cambridge 1951, 14–18.

13 J. Craig, 'A Tale of Two Boroughs: Protestantism and Conflict in the Towns of Thetford and Bury St Edmunds', paper given at Professor Collinson's seminar, Cambridge 22 Nov. 1990; J. Craig, 'Reformation, Politics and Polemics in 16th-Century East Anglian Market Towns', Ph.D. Cambridge 1992; Palliser, 'Popular Reactions', 105–7.

terms as well as religious, the Reformation was an opportunity for those who were impatient for change. In Gamlingay, for example, two of the wealthiest yeomen families, the Apthorps and the Russells, were poised ready to elevate themselves into the gentry with the purchase of monastic and chantry land.[14]

Although the Reformation brought increased social opportunities, especially for the wealthier sectors of the population, for others, particularly the poorer sectors, it was a disaster: it abolished the multiple foci for devotional and social activity which gilds, lights and other groups for those too poor to join the gilds had formerly provided. The polarities of church and chapel could not replace that. John Guy states:

> The Vestry meeting of the Elizabethan parishes never adequately discharged the social functions of the late medieval gilds and religious confraternities and there may have been a significant rise in impiety among ordinary people.[15]

Moral restraint and obedience to authority once fostered by gilds and other associations were gone. With medieval frames of reference abolished, the well-to-do and the middling sort, newly armed with puritan ideology, fought the age-old vices of the poor, particularly bastardy and other breaches of the moral or social order.[16]

Groups such as gilds which had expressed late medieval Catholic devotional practices failed to return in Mary I's reign. Its time-span was too short to reinstate traditional worship, by comparison with the generation or so which had passed since Catholicism had begun to be dismantled; furthermore, the economic and administrative effects of the abolitions of 1547 were of major significance. There is no Cambridgeshire evidence for resistance to the abolitions, but much for the attempted concealment of goods from confiscation: pots and pans, cows and lands disappeared into the communities which had donated them.[17] Dr Palmer cites distribution of herrings at the gildhall in Great Linton as the only Cambridgeshire evidence for revived interest in gilds during Mary I's reign.[18] Elsewhere, for example, in Cornwall and London, one or two gilds were re-established, but not on the same scale as before.[19]

14 J. Brown, *Gamlingay: Six Hundred Years of Life in An English Village*, London 1989, 83–84.

15 J. Guy, *Tudor England*, Oxford 1990, 292.

16 M. Spufford, 'Puritanism and Social Control?', in *Order and Disorder in Early Modern England*, ed. A. Fletcher and J. Stevenson, Cambridge 1985, 41–57; Wrightson, *English Society*, ch. 6; Wrightson and Levine, *Terling*, chs 4 and 5; *Continuity and Change: Personnel and Administration of the Church in England 1500–1642*, ed. F. Heal and R. O'Day, Leicester 1976.

17 Palmer, 367–70 for example Bassingbourne; C. Kitching, 'The Quest for Concealed Lands in the Reign of Elizabeth I', *TRHS*, 5th series xxiv, 1974, 63–78.

18 Palmer, 352.

19 J. Mattingley, 'The Medieval Parish Gilds of Cornwall', *Journal of the Royal Institution of Cornwall*, new series x, 1989, 290–329, Appendices 1–3; Westlake, 135.

Once confiscated, stocks of land, animals and goods built up by preceding generations in the period of economic prosperity following the Black Death could not be immediately re-constituted. As Christopher Hill says: 'Under Mary "the Crown" was unable to undo the economic consequences of the Reformation.'[20] The overall failure of the gilds to return, and indeed the very limited revival of Catholicism achieved by Mary I, must be seen within this broader economic context.

On the evidence of wills from about 1544, there was a marked decline, and indeed from 1547 to 1556, a complete discontinuation, of bequests for traditional Catholic devotional practices. There was also the reduction, to a very minimal level, of bequests to enterprises such as church repairs and maintenance of the highways. All these causes had previously been widely supported. Anxieties about confiscation were presumably responsible for this effect. The tentative re-establishment of such activities is expressed by John Oliver of Elsworth in his will of 1557: 'I give to the beginning of a common stock if the neighbours will go about such a purpose, a quarter of barley.'[21] In the longer term, the changes of the Reformation era contributed to the transformation of late medieval Catholicism from a broadly based popular religion into a minority confessional faith. Continuities between pre- and post-Reformation periods must be sought in local government rather than on a religious level. In a society where there was an increasing distinction between the religious and secular spheres, the gilds, as an embodiment of a medieval collective culture which straddled this boundary, were rendered obsolete. The Reformation ended the need for gild administration of medieval Catholic devotional and commemorative practices. In their provision of internal discipline, charity for members and social amenities for their communities, they were superseded by the parish.[22] However, it must be remembered that the strength and vitality of the sixteenth- and seventeenth-century parish reflect the powerful contribution made by the late medieval laity to its rise.

20 C. Hill, *Puritanism and Revolution*, London 1958, 37.

21 ACE (4/1/16), 1557 will of John Oliver.

22 C.M. Barron, 'The Parish Fraternities of Medieval London', in *The Church in Pre-Reformation Society*, ed. C.M. Barron and C. Harper-Bill, Woodbridge 1985, 13–37, esp. 35–37.

Appendix: Table of 1389 Returns and Other Extant Gild Statutes for Cambridgeshire

L, F, E = Latin, French and English document

PRO C47/38/3(1) L	Founded: Time without memory	Holy Trinity Gild	Holy Cross/ Trinity Church	Bottisham
C47/38/3(2) L	*ditto*	Nativity BVM	*ditto*	*ditto*
C47/38/3(3) L	*ditto*	Corpus Christi	*ditto*	*ditto*
C47/38/3(4) L	*ditto*	All Saints'	*ditto*	*ditto*
C47/38/3(5) L	*ditto*	St Nicholas	*ditto*	*ditto*
C47/38/3(6) L	*ditto*	St Peter	*ditto*	*ditto*
C47/38/3(7) L	*ditto*	St James	*ditto*	*ditto*
C47/38/4 L	1379	Annunciation BVM	Great St Mary's Church	Cambridge
C47/38/5 L	1384 (+ previous activity)	Assumption (formerly Nativity) BVM	Holy Trinity Church	*ditto*
C47/38/6 L	1385	St Katherine	St Andrew the Great	*ditto*
C47/38/7 L	1379/80	St Katherine	St Bene't's Church	*ditto*
C47/38/8 L	1378	Annunciation BVM	St Botolph's Church	*ditto*
C47/38/9 L	1386 (+ previous activity)	Purification BVM	Great St Mary's Church	*ditto*
C47/38/10 L	1384 (+ previous activity)	Holy Trinity	Holy Trinity Church	*ditto*
C47/38/11 L	—	Holy Trinity	Great St Mary's Church	*ditto*
C47/38/12(a)F	1384/5	Holy Trinity	St Mary's (Convent Church)	Chatteris
C47/38/12(b)F	1346/7	Holy Sepulchre	St Peter's Church	*ditto*

C47/38/13 L	1336	Resurrection	St Andrew's Church	Chesterton
C47/38/14 L	1377/8 (+ previous activity)	St Katherine	*ditto*	*ditto*
C47/38/15 L	1377/8	Assumption BVM	*ditto*	*ditto*
C47/38/16 L	Time without memory	St Katherine	All Saints' Church	Elm
C47/38/17 L	—	Assumption BVM	Chapel of St Mary (Lady Chapel)	Ely
C47/38/18 L	1331	All Saints	St Mary's Church	Ely
C47/38/19 L	1378	St John Baptist	*ditto*	*ditto*
C47/38/20 L	1375 (+ previous activity)	All Saints'	St Peter's Church	*ditto*
C47/38/21 L	—	Corpus Christi	*ditto*	*ditto*
C47/38/22 L	—	St John Baptist	*ditto*	*ditto*
C47/38/23(1)L	c.1309 (or earlier)	St Peter Apostle	Holy Trinity Church	*ditto*
C47/38/23(2)L	c.1289 (or earlier)	St Etheldreda	*ditto*	*ditto*
C47/38/23(3)L	c.1376 (or earlier)	St Katherine	*ditto*	*ditto*
C47/38/23(4)L	c.1374 (or earlier)	Holy Cross	St Peter's Church	*ditto*
C47/38/23(5)L	c.1358 (or earlier)	Holy Trinity	*ditto*	*ditto*
C47/38/24F+L	1343 (+ previous activity)	Assumption BVM	Chapel of St Mary	Haslingfield
C47/38/25 L	1386 (+ previous activity)	Assumption BVM	Chapel of St Mary	Leverington
C47/38/26(1)L	1378	Corpus Christi	St Andrew/ George Church	Littleport
C47/38/26(2)L	1378	St George	*ditto*	*ditto*
C47/38/26(3)L	1382/3	St Mary	*ditto*	*ditto*
C47/38/26(4)L	1380/1	St John Baptist	*ditto*	*ditto*

C47/38/27 L	Time without memory	St Wendreda	Chapel (now church) of St Wendreda	March
C47/38/28 F	Lately begun	Assumption BVM	St Peter's & Paul's Church	Pampesworth (now Pampisford)
C47/38/29(1)F	*ditto*	Holy Cross	St Mary's Church	Sawston
C47/38/29(2)F	*ditto*	Nativity of St John Baptist	*ditto*	*ditto*
C47/38/29(3)F	*ditto*	Nativity BVM	*ditto*	*ditto*
C47/38/30 L	c.1359 (or earlier)	Nativity of St John Baptist	St Mary's Church	Stowe Cum Quye
C47/38/31 L	1350	Corpus Christi	St James's Church	Stretham
C47/38/32 L	1344	Nativity BVM	St James's Church	Stretham
C47/38/33(1)L	Time without memory	Holy Cross	St Mary's Church	Swaffham Bulbeck
C47/38/33(2)L	*ditto*	St Margaret	*ditto*	*ditto*
C47/38/33(3)L	*ditto*	All Saints	*ditto*	*ditto*
C47/38/33(4)L	*ditto*	Nativity BVM	*ditto*	*ditto*
C47/38/34 L	1385/6	Holy Cross	Chapel of Holy Cross	Tydd St Giles
C47/38/35 L	1386/7	St Giles	St Giles's Church	*ditto*
C47/38/36 L	Post primam pestilenciam	Assumption BVM	*ditto*	*ditto*
C47/38/37 F	Lately begun	St John Baptist	St Andrew/ Mary's Church	Whittlesford
C47/38/38 L	—	Corpus Christi	St Peter & Paul's Church	Wisbech
C47/38/39 L	1384	St John Baptist	*ditto*	*ditto*
C47/38/40 L	1387	Purification BVM	*ditto*	*ditto*
C47/38/41 L	1327/8	St Peter Apostle	*ditto*	*ditto*
C47/38/42 L	—	St Thomas Archbishop & Martyr	*ditto*	*ditto*

C47/38/43 L	1379	Holy Trinity	*ditto*	*ditto*
C47/46/462 L	—	Holy Trinity	St Michael & All Angels	Caldecote
BL Add. Ms. 5846, fos 4–8 L+E	1431	St Clement		Cambridge
CUL, MM1 36 Baker Mss. vol. 25, pp. 361–6 L+E	1448	St Peter & Paul		*ditto*
pp. 367–71 L+E	1473	All Saints		*ditto*
[NB Other copies of the above three documents are extant]				
CUL, MM1 47 Baker Mss. vol. 36, pp. 161–2 E	1517	St James's Gild		Dullingham

Bibliography

Manuscripts

Cambridge

Cambridge University Library

Cambridge University Library Muniments

CUL, MM1 36, Baker Mss. vol. 25, Item 10, pp. 361–6, statutes of the gild of Saints Peter & Paul, St Peter's Church, Cambridge, 1448; pp. 367–71, statutes of the gild of All Saints, All Saints' Church, Cambridge, 1473.

CUL, MM1 47, Baker Mss. vol. 36, Item 16, pp. 161–2, statutes of the gild of St James, Dullingham, 1517.

Wills proved under the peculiar jurisdiction of the vice-chancellor of Cambridge University, original wills 1521–58 (38 wills).

Ely Diocesan Archives

Episcopal Consistory Court of Ely, original wills, boxes 1–9, 1485, 1503–58 (953 wills); registered copy wills, microfilm EPR HK2791, Liber A, 1449–59 (263 wills).

Archdeaconry Court of Ely, original wills, boxes 1–4, 1545–58 (373 wills); registered copy wills, microfilm EPR VLP427, 1513–22 (29 wills).

EDR C8/56 (R2) Wisbech Court Leet 1378; EDR C8/64 (12–13 RII) Wisbech Court Leet 1389; EDR C9/1–3, Wisbech Court Leet 1452/3.

Cambridgeshire County Record Office, Cambridge Branch

P11/5/1–2, Churchwardens' Accounts, parish of Bassingbourne, Saints Peter & Paul 1490–1540.

P20/24/1–7, records of 19th-century gilds, Cambridge.

P22/5/1, Churchwardens' Accounts, Holy Trinity Church, Cambridge 1504–58. P22/5/15, Accounts of St Katherine's Gild, Holy Trinity Parish 1514–37.

P116/1/4, pp. 131–7, Accounts of St Christopher's stock, church of St Wendreda the Virgin, March 1472–1525.

L19/36, Bailiff's Account, Haslingfield, 18 Richard II (1394/5)

X/28, Cambridge City Records, two obligations to the gild of the Purification of the Virgin, 1535.

King's College Cambridge

Wills proved under the peculiar jurisdiction of King's College Cambridge, registered copy wills, Ledger Book 1, 1449–1558 (39 wills).

London

British Library

Additional Ms. 5846, pp. 5–13, statutes of the gild of St Clement, St Clement's Church, Cambridge, 1431.
Egerton Ms. 2886, Account of the book of the gild of the Blessed Virgin Mary, Boston, Lincolnshire, 1514–25.
Harleian Ms. 4795, register of the gild of Corpus Christi, Boston, Lincolnshire, 1335 on.

Public Record Office

C47/38–46, returns or certificates made to the King by all gilds in the kingdom in 1389 in obedience to a writ issued by the Cambridge Parliament (1388).
C47/38/3–43, returns from Cambridgeshire.
C47/46/462, return from Caldecote, Cambridgeshire (drawn to my attention by Margaret Condon, too late to be included in the statistics for this project).
C66/211, 18 Edward III, Part I, membrane 14, 1344/5, Chantry licence granted to the gild of the Assumption of the Virgin, Haslingfield, deleted.
C66/211, 18 Edward III, Part II, membrane 37, 1344/5, Chantry licence to the same.
C66/335, 16 Richard II, Part I, membrane 15, 1392/3, Chantry licence granted to the gild of the Nativity of the Virgin, Haslingfield.
C66/335, 16 Richard II, Part I, membrane 30, 1392–3, Chantry licence granted to a group of feoffees, on behalf of the souls of five men, Haslingfield.
C66/478, 32 Henry VI, membrane 23, 1453, Chantry licence granted to the Trinity Gild, Wisbech.
DL38/5, four Chantry certificates for Cambridgeshire.
E179/81/34/11, poll tax indenture, Bottisham.
E179/81/41, 4 Richard II, poll tax account for Cambridge Borough.
E179/192/4a/5, poll tax indenture, Chesterton.
PCC Prob 11, records of the Prerogative Court of Canterbury, registered copy wills, 1383–1558, registers 1–42a, Rous–Welles & register F sampled according to key parishes (214 wills).
SC2/155/53, fos 1–5, Bottisham Court Rolls: Honour & General Courts, 10–17, 21, 22, Richard II, 1386/7–1393/4, 1397/8, 1398/9.

Oxford

Merton College Oxford

Gamlingay Rentals 5458–5461, 1470–c.1483.
Gamlingay Court Rolls, 5489–5491, views of frankpledge 1502–1511.

Wisbech

Wisbech and Fenland Museum

Wisbech Corporation Records, vol. 1, The Register of Holy Trinity Gild, Wisbech 1379–1547.

Microfilm 8, Item 1, Leverington Church Accounts, St Leonard's Church, 1497–1600.

Primary Printed Sources

Ault, W.O. *Private Jurisdiction in England*, Newhaven 1923

Barron, C.M. & Roscoe, J. 'The Medieval Parish of St Andrew Holborn: Light Wardens' Accounts 1477–8', in *London Topographical Record*, ed. A.L. Saunders, xxix, 1980, 55–59

Blomefield, F. *An Essay towards a Topography of the County of Norfolk* viii, London 1808

Cambridge Gild Records, ed. Mary Bateson, *Publns Camb. Antiq. Soc.* xxxix, Cambridge 1903

Cambridgeshire and the Isle of Ely Lay Subsidy 1327, ed. C.H. Evelyn-White (reprinted from *East Anglian N & Q* new series, x–xii, 1903–8, no date or place of publication)

Cheshire, J.G. 'William Dowsing's Destructions in Cambridgeshire', *Cambs. & Hunts. Arch. Soc.* iii, 1914, 77–91

Churchwardens' Accounts of St Mary the Great Cambridgeshire 1504–1635, ed. J.E. Foster, *Publns Camb. Antiq. Soc.* xxxv, Cambridge 1935

Clark, J.W. 'On the Charitable Endowments of the University called Chests', *Proc. Camb. Antiq. Soc.* xi, 1903–6, 78–101

Councils and Synods: with other Documents Relating to the English Church ii ed. F.M. Powicke and C.R. Cheney, Oxford 1964

Diplomatarium Anglicum Aevi Saxonici, ed. B. Thorpe, London 1865

Erasmus, D. *Pilgrimages to St Mary of Walsingham and St Thomas of Canterbury*, ed. J. Gough Nichols, London 1849

Evelyn-White, C.H. 'Cambridgeshire and the Isle of Ely, Lay Subsidy for the Year 1327', *East Anglian N & Q*, new series x–xii, 1903–8, vol x, pp. 1–3 et seq.

Foster, J.E. 'On Charters granted by Ramsay Abbey to the Fraternity of the Holy Sepulchre', *Proc. Camb. Antiq. Soc.* ix, 1894–8, 367–70

Gerchow, J. *Die Gedenküberlieferung der Angelsachsen mit einem Katalog der Libri Vitae und Necrologien*, Berlin, New York 1988, and review in *Research on British History in the Federal Republic of Germany 1983–8*, ed. F. Rexroth, London 1990, 25–26

The Gild of St Mary Lichfield, being Ordinances of the Gild of St Mary and Other Documents, ed. F.J. Furnivall, EETS, Extra Series, cxiv, London 1920

Gross, C. *The Gild Merchant: A Contribution to British Municipal History*, 2 vols, Oxford 1890, reissued 1927

Hussey, A., ed., *Kent Obit and Lamp Rents*, Ashford 1936

Josselin, J. *Historiola Collegii Corporis Christi et Beatae Mariae Cantabrigiae*, ed. J. Willis, *Publns Camb. Antiq. Soc.* xvii, Cambridge 1880

Langland, W. *Piers the Ploughman*, translated by J.F. Goodridge, Harmondsworth 1975

The Lay Subsidy of 1334, ed. R.E. Glasscock, British Academy Records of Social and Economic History ii, London 1975

Map, W., *De Nugis Curialium*, translated by M.R. James etc., Cymmrodorion Record Series ix, London 1923

More, T. *A Dyalogue of Syr Thomas More Knyght*, London 1529

Muskett, J.J. 'Cambridgeshire Church Goods', *East Anglian N & Q*, new series vi–x, 1895–1904, vol. vi, pp. 145–49 et seq.

Orme, N. 'The Kalendar Brethren of the City of Exeter', *Report and Transactions of the Devonshire Association for the Advancement of Science, Literature and Art* cix, 1977, 153–69

Owen, D.M. *The Making of King's Lynn: A Documentary Survey*, British Academy Records of Social and Economic History, new series, ix, London 1984

Palmer, W.M. 'A List of the Cambridge Subsidy Rolls 1250–1695 with Appendices', *East Anglian N & Q*, new series vii–xiii, 1897–1910, vol. vii, pp. 362–36 et seq.; esp. vol. xii, 1907–8, 218–19 et seq. 'Appendix no. xi: The Cambridgeshire Poll Taxes'; vol. xiii, 1909–10, 90–93 et seq. 'Appendix no. xii: The Clerical Poll Tax of 1379 in Cambridgeshire'

———. 'Churchwardens' Bills or Returns for the Deanery of Barton for Michaelmas 1554', *Cambs. & Hunts. Arch. Soc.* v, 1937, 257–65

———. 'Fifteenth-Century Visitation Records of the Deanery of Wisbech', *Proc. Camb. Antiq. Soc.* xxxix, 1938–9, 69–75

———. 'Village Gilds of Cambridgeshire', *Cambs. & Hunts. Arch. Soc.* i, 1902, 330–402, and separately printed Ely, 1904

Parish Fraternity Register: Fraternity of the Holy Trinity and Saints Fabian and Sebastian in the Parish of St Botolph Without Aldersgate, ed. P. Basing, London Record Society xviii, London 1982

Proceedings before the Justices of the Peace in the Fourteenth and Fifteenth Centuries Edward III-Richard III, ed. B. Putnam, London 1938

Raven, J.J. 'A Parish House for Church Ales and Other "Drynkynggs" ', *East Anglian N & Q*, new series vi, 1895–6, 49–50

Records of the Borough of Chesterfield, ed. P. Riden and J. Blair, vol. v, Chesterfield 1980

Remling, L. *Bruderschaften in Franken: Kirchen und Sozialgeschichtliche Untersuchungen zum Spätmittelalterlichen und Frühneuzeitlichen Bruderschaftswesen*, Wurzburg 1986

Rosser, A.G. 'The Gild of St Mary and St John the Baptist, Lichfield: Ordinances of the late Fourteenth Century', *Staffordshire Record Society Collections for a History of Staffordshire*, 4th series xiii, 1988, 19–26

Rye, W. 'The Order of Funerals, Ringings etc. at Norwich', *East Anglian N & Q*, new series ii, 1887–8, 389–92

Sayles, G.O. 'The Dissolution of a Gild at York in 1306', *EHR* lv, 1940, 83–98

Sparvel-Bayly, J.A. and King, H.W. 'Records Relating to the Gild or Fraternity of Jesus in Prittlewell', *Transactions of Essex Archaeological Society*, new series ii, 1884, 153–64

Stubbs, W. *Select Charters Illustrative of English Constitutional History*, 1st edition Oxford 1870, 9th edition Oxford 1913

The Tibetan Book of the Dead, ed. W.Y. Evans-Wentz,Oxford 1957, 3rd edition paperback 1960

Toulmin Smith, J., ed. *English Gilds*, EETS, original series xl, London 1870, reprinted 1892
The Transcript of the Churchwardens' Accounts of Tilney All Saints Norfolk 1443–1589, ed. A.D. Stallard, London 1922
Vetus Liber Archidiaconi Eliensis, ed. Rev. C.L. Feltoe, *Publns Camb. Antiq. Soc.* xlviii, Cambridge 1917
Walberswick Churchwardens' Accounts AD 1450–1499, ed. R.M. Lewis, no date but Preface 1947
The Westminster Chronicle, ed. L.C. Hector and B. Harvey, Oxford 1982

Secondary Sources

Adam, P. *La Vie Paroissale en France au XIV Siècle*, Paris 1964
Ariès, P. *L'Homme devant la Mort*, Paris 1977, translated as *The Hour of our Death*, New York 1981
———. *Western Attitudes towards Death*, Baltimore 1974
Arnold-Forster, F. *Studies in Church Dedications, or England's Patron Saints*, 3 vols, London 1899
Aston, M. 'Segregation in Church', *SCH* xxvii, 1990, 237–94
Atkinson, T.D. 'On the Gilds of Cambridgeshire', *Proc. Camb. Antiq. Soc.* ix, 1894–8, 385–90
Ault, W.O. 'Manor Court and Parish Church in Fifteenth-Century England', *Speculum* xlii, 1967, 53–67
———. 'The Village Church and the Village Community in Medieval England', *Speculum* xlv, 1970, 197–215
d'Avray, D.L. *Death and the Prince: Memorial Preaching before 1350*, Oxford 1994
Banker, J.R. *Death in the Community: Memorialisation and Confraternities in an Italian Commune in the Late Middle Ages*, Athens, Georgia 1989
Barron C.M. 'The Parish Fraternities of Medieval London' in *The Church in Pre-Reformation Society*, ed. C.M. Barron and C. Harper-Bill, Woodbridge 1985, 13–27
Barron C.M. and Harper-Bill C., eds., *The Church in Pre-Reformation Society*, Woodbridge 1985
Bean, J.M.W. *The Decline of English Feudalism 1215–1540*, Manchester 1968
Beier, A.L. *The Problem of the Poor in Tudor and Early Stuart England*, London 1983
Beresford, M.W. *The Lay Subsidies, Parts 1 and 2, 1290–1334 and after 1334: The Poll Taxes of 1377, 1379 and 1381*, Bridge Place near Canterbury 1963
Bennett, J. 'Conviviality and Charity in Medieval and Early Modern England', *P&P* cxxxiv, 1992, 3–41
Beveridge, W. 'Westminster Wages in the Manorial Era', *EcHR*, 2nd series viii, 1955–6, 118–35
Black, A. *Gilds and Civil Society in European Political Thought from the Twelfth Century to the Present*, London 1984
Blair, J. 'Religious Gilds as Landowners in the Thirteenth and Fourteenth Centuries: the Example of Chesterfield', in *The Medieval Town in Britain*, ed. P. Riden, Cardiff 1980, 35–49

Bloch, M. and Parry, J. *Death and the Regeneration of Life*, Cambridge 1982

Boggis, R.J.E. *Praying for the Dead: An Historical Review of the Practice*, London 1913

Bond, F. *Dedications and Patron Saints of English Churches: Ecclesiastical Symbolism: Saints and Their Emblems*, London 1914

———. *Screens and Galleries in English Churches*, London 1908

Bossy, J. 'Blood and Baptism: Kinship, Community and Christianity in Western Europe from the Fourteenth to the Seventeenth Centuries', *SCH* x, 1973, 129–43

———. *Christianity in the West 1400–1700*, Oxford 1985

———. *The English Catholic Community 1570–1850*, London 1975; paperback 1979

———. 'Holiness and Society', *P&P* lxxv, 1977, 119–37, review article

———. 'The Mass as a Social Institution 1200–1700', *P&P* c, 1983, 29–61

———. 'Some Elementary Forms of Durkheim', *P&P* xcv, 1982, 3–18

le Bras, G. *Etudes de Sociologie Religieuse*, 2 vols, Paris 1955–6

———. 'Les Confréries Chrétiennes: Problèmes and Propositions', *Revue Historique du Droit Français et Etranger*, series 4 xix–xx, 1940–1, 310–63

Bredero, A.H. *Le Moyen Age et le Purgatoire*, *Revue d'Histoire Ecclescastique* lxxviii, 1983, 429–52

Brigden, S. 'Religion and Social Obligation in Early Sixteenth Century London', *P&P* ciii, 1984, 67–112

———. 'Youth and the English Reformation', *P&P* xcv, 1982, 37–67

Britton, E. *The Community of the Vill*, Toronto 1977

Brown, J. *Gamlingay: 600 Years of Life in an English Village*, London 1989

Buckatzsch, E.J. 'The Geographical Distribution of Wealth in England 1086–1843: An Experimental Study of Certain Tax Assessments', *EcHR*, 2nd series iii, 1950–1, 180–202

Burgess, C. ' "A Fond Thing Vainly Invented": an Essay on Purgatory and Pious Motive in Late Medieval England', in *Parish, Church and People: Local Studies in Lay Religion in England 1350–1750*, ed. S. Wright, London 1988, 56–84

———. 'A Service for the Dead: the Form and Function of the Anniversary in Late Medieval Bristol', *Transactions of Bristol and Gloucester Archaeological Society* cv, 1987, 183–211

———. 'The Benefactions of Mortality: The Lay Response in the Late Medieval Urban Parish', in *Studies in Clergy and Ministry in Medieval England*, ed. D.M. Smith, York 1991, 65–86

———. 'By Quick and By Dead: Wills and Pious Provision in Late Medieval Bristol', *EHR* ccccv, 1987, 837–58

———. 'For the Increase of Divine Service: Chantries in the Parish in Late Medieval Bristol', *JEH* xxxvi, 1985, 46–65

Burgess, C. and Kümin, B. 'Penitential Bequests and Parish Regimes in Late Medieval England', *JEH* xliv, 1993, 610–30

Burke, P. *Popular Culture in Early Modern Europe*, London 1978

Burrell, H.J.E. and Montagu Benton, G. 'The English Alabaster Carvings of Cambridgeshire, with Special Reference to Fragmentary Examples at Wood Ditton Church', *Proc. Camb. Antiq. Soc.* xxxiv, 1934, 78–83

Cam, H.M. 'The Community of the Vill', in *Medieval Studies Presented to Rose Graham*, ed. V. Ruffner and A.J. Taylor, Oxford 1950, 1–14

Camporesi, P. *The Fear of Hell: Images of Damnation and Salvation in Early Modern Europe*, Oxford 1991
Carlyle, R.W. and A.J. *The History of Medieval Political Theory in the West*, 6 vols, Edinburgh 1903–36
Catto, J. 'Religious Change under Henry V', in *Henry V: The Practice of Kingship*, ed. G.L. Harriss, Oxford 1985, 97–115
Champion, B. 'The Gilds of Medieval Beverley', in *The Medieval Town in Britain*, ed. P. Riden, Cardiff 1980, 51–66
Chiffoleau, J. *La Comptabilité de l'Au-delà: Les Hommes, La Mort et la Religion 1320–1480*, Rome 1980
Christian, W.A. *Apparitions in late Medieval and Renaissance Spain 1399–1523*, Princeton 1981
———. *Local Religion in Sixteenth Century Spain*, Princeton 1981
Clanchy, M.T. *From Memory to Written Record*, London 1979
Clay, R.M. *The Medieval Hospitals of England*, London 1909
Cobbett, L. 'The Hospitals of St John the Baptist and St Mary Magdalene at Ely', *Proc. Camb. Antiq. Soc.* xxxvi, 1935, 58–75
Coleman, D.C. 'Review: W.K. Jordan, Philanthropy in England', *EcHR*, 2nd series xiii, 1960–1, 113–15
Collinson, P. *The Birthpangs of Protestant England: Religious and Cultural Change in the Sixteenth and Seventeenth Centuries*, London 1988
———. *The Elizabethan Puritan Movement*, London 1967
Cook, G.H. *English Collegiate Churches of the Middle Ages*, London 1959
———. *Medieval Chantries and Chantry Chapels*, London 1963, original edition 1947
Coornaert, E. 'Les Ghildes Médiévales (Ve – XIVe Siècles) Définition – Évolution', *Revue Historique* cxcix, 1948, 22–55, 208–43
Cowley, P. *The Church Houses: Their Religious and Social Significance*, London 1970
Cox, J.C. *Churchwardens' Accounts*, London 1913
Cox, J.C. and Harvey, A. *English Church Furniture*, London 1907
Darby, H.C. *Domesday England*, Cambridge 1977
———. 'The Domesday Geography of Cambridgeshire, *Proc. Camb. Antiq. Soc.* xxxvi, 1934–5, 35–57
———. *The Domesday Geography of Eastern England*, Cambridge 1971
———. *The Medieval Fenland*, Cambridge 1940, 2nd edition 1974
Darby, H.C., Glasscock, R.E., Sheail, J. and Versey, G.R. 'The Changing Geographical Distribution of Wealth in England: 1086–1334–1525', *Journal of Historical Geography* v, 1979, 247–62
Davis, N.Z. 'The Sacred and the Body Social in Sixteenth Century Lyons', *P&P* xc, 1981, 40–70
———. *Society and Culture in Early Modern France: Eight Essays*, Oxford 1987
———. 'Some Tasks and Themes in the Study of Popular Religion' in *The Pursuit of Holiness in Late Medieval and Renaissance Society*, ed. C. Trinkaus and H.A. Oberman, Leyden 1974, 307–36
Davis R.H.C. 'East Anglia and the Danelaw', *TRHS*, 5th series v, 1955, 23–29
Dawson, J.P. *A History of Lay Judges*, Cambridge, Massachusetts, 1960
Dewindt, E.B. *Land and People in Holywell Cum Needleworth*, Toronto 1972
Dickens, A.G. *The English Reformation*, London 1964

Dinn, R. 'Baptism, Spiritual Kinship and Popular Religion in Late Medieval Bury St Edmunds', *Bulletin of John Rylands Library* lxxii, 1990, 93–106

Dobson, R.B. 'The Foundation of Perpetual Chantries by the Citizens of Medieval York', SCH iv, 1967, 22–38

Duby, G. *William Marshall: The Flower of Chivalry*, London 1986

Duffy, E. *The Stripping of the Altars: Traditional Religion in England c.400–1580*, Yale 1992

P. Duparc, 'Confraternities of the Holy Spirit and Village Communities in the Middle Ages' in *Lordship and Community in Medieval Europe*, ed. F.L. Cheyette, New York 1975, original edition 1968

Durkheim, E. *The Elementary Forms of the Religious Life*, translated by J.W. Swain, 2nd edition London 1976

Dyer, C. 'The Social and Economic Background to the Rural Revolt of 1381', in *The English Rising of 1381*, ed. R.H. Hilton and T. Aston, Cambridge 1984, 9–24

———. *Standards of Living in the Later Middle Ages*, Cambridge 1989

Eliade, M. *The Myth of the Eternal Return*, Princeton 1965

Finucane, R.C. 'Sacred Corpse: Profane Carrion: Social Ideas and Death Rituals in the Later Middle Ages', in *Mirrors of Mortality: Studies in the Social History of Death*, ed. J. Whaley, London 1981, 40–60

Flynn, M. *Sacred Charity: Confraternities and Social Welfare in Spain 1400–1700*, London 1989

Fraser, J.G. *The Golden Bough*, London 1890

Fryde, N. 'Gilds in England before the Black Death', *Vorträge Und Forschung* xxix, 1985, 215–29

Galpern, A.N. *The Religions of the People in Sixteenth-Century Champagne*, Cambridge, Massachusetts, 1976

Gardiner, F.J. *A History of Wisbech and Neighbourhood*, Wisbech 1898

Gasquet, Abbot F.A. *Parish Life in Medieval England*, London 1908

Gerchow, J. 'Bruderschaften im Spätmittelalterlichen Freiburg im Breisgau', *Freiburger Diozesanarchiv 3*, cxiii, 1993, 5–74

———. 'Memoria als Norm: Aspekte Englischer Gildenstatuten des 14 Jahrhunderts', in *Memoria in der Gesellschaft des Mittelalters*, ed. D. Geuenich and O.G. Oexle, Göttingen 1994

———. 'Trinkstuben, Zünfte und Bruderschaften: Die Freiburger Genossenschaften im Mittelalter', in *Geschichte der Stadt Freiburg im Breisgau*, ed. H. Haumann and H. Schadek, Stuttgart 1995, forthcoming

Gierke, O. *Community in Historical Perspective: A Translation of Selections from Das Deutsche Genossenschaftsrecht (The German Law of Fellowship)* translated by M. Fisher and ed. A. Black, Cambridge 1990

———. *Political Theories of the Middle Ages*, translated with an introduction by F.W. Maitland, Cambridge 1922

Given-Wilson, C. *The English Nobility in the Late Middle Ages: The Fourteenth Century Political Community*, London 1987

Godfrey, W.H. *The English Almshouse*, London 1955

le Goff, J. *The Birth of Purgatory*, Chicago 1984

Gottfried, R.S. *Bury St Edmunds and the Urban Crisis 1290–1539*, Princeton 1982

Gutton, J.-P., 'Confraternities, Curés and Communities in Rural Areas of the Diocese of Lyons under the *Ancien Régime*', in *Religion and Society in Early Modern Europe*, ed. K. Von Greyerz, London 1984, 202–11

Guy, J.A. and Beale, H.G., ed. *Law and Social Change in British Society*, Royal Historical Society Studies in History 40, London 1984
Haigh, C. 'Anti-Clericalism and the English Reformation', *History* lxviii, 1983, 391–407
———. (ed.) *The English Reformation Revised*, Cambridge 1987
———. *English Reformations: Religion, Politics and Society under the Tudors*, Oxford 1993
———. *Reformation and Resistance in Tudor Lancashire*, Cambridge 1975
Haigh, D. *The Religious Houses of Cambridgeshire*, Cambridge 1988
Hailstone, E. *The History and Antiquities of the Parish of Bottisham and the Priory of Anglesey in Cambridgeshire, Publns Camb. Antiq. Soc.* xiv, Cambridge 1873 and Supplement xvi, 1878
Hall C.P. 'The Gild of Corpus Christi and the Foundation of Corpus Christi College', in *Medieval Cambridge: Essays on the Pre-Reformation University*, ed. P. Zutshi, Woodbridge 1993, 65–71
Hampson, E.M. *The Treatment of Poverty in Cambridgeshire 1597–1834*, Cambridge 1924
Hanawalt, B.A. 'Keepers of the Lights: Late Medieval English Parish Gilds', *Journal of Medieval and Renaissance Studies* xiv, 1984, 21–37
———. *The Ties that Bound: Peasant Families in Medieval England*, Oxford 1986
Hanawalt, B.A. and McCree, B. 'The Guilds of "Homo Prudens" in Late Medieval England', *Continuity and Change* vii, 1992, 163–79
Harper-Bill, C. *The Pre-Reformation Church in England 1400–1530*, London 1989
Hatcher, J. *Plague Population and the English Economy 1348–1530*, London 1977
Harvey, P.D.A. *Manorial Records*, British Record Association v, Gloucester 1984
Heal, F. 'The Idea of Hospitality in Early Modern England', *P&P* cii, 1984, 66–93
Heath, P. *The English Parish Clergy On the Eve of the Reformation*, Toronto 1969
Henderson, J. *Piety and Charity in Late Medieval Florence*, Oxford 1994
Hicks, M. 'Chantries Obits and Almshouses: the Hungerford Foundations 1325–1478', in *The Church in Pre-Reformation Society*, ed. C.M. Barron and C. Harper-Bill, Woodbridge 1985, 123–42
———. 'The Piety of Margaret, Lady Hungerford', *JEH* xxxviii, 1987, 19–38
Hill, C. *Puritanism and Revolution*, London 1958
Hilton, R.H. *The English Peasantry in the Later Middle Ages*, Oxford 1975
———. 'Peasant Movements in England before 1381', *EcHR*, 2nd series ii, 1949, 117–36
Holmes, G.A. *The Estates of the Higher Nobility in Fourteenth Century England*, Cambridge 1957
Homans, G.C. *English Villagers of the Thirteenth Century*, Cambridge, Massachusetts, 1941
Horden, P. 'The Confraternities of Byzantium', *SCH* xxiii, 1985–6, 25–45
Hörger, H. 'Organisational Forms of Popular Piety in Rural Old Bavaria, Sixteenth to Nineteenth Centuries', in *Religion and Society in Early Modern Europe 1500–1800*, ed. C. Von Greyerz, London 1984, 212–20
Huizinga, J. *The Waning of the Middle Ages*, London 1924, Harmondsworth 1955
James, M. 'Ritual, Drama and Social Body in the Late Medieval English Town', *P&P* xcviii, 1983, 3–29

James, M.R. 'On the Wall Paintings in Willingham Church', *Proc. Camb. Antiq. Soc.* ix, 1894–8, 96–101

Johnston, A.F. 'The Guild of Corpus Christi and the Procession of Corpus Christi in York', in *Medieval Studies* xxxviii, 1976, 372–403

———. 'The Plays of the Religious Guilds of York: The Creed Play and the Pater Noster Play', *Speculum* l, 1975, 55–90

Jones, W.R. 'English Religious Brotherhoods and Medieval Lay Piety: The Inquiry of 1388–9', *The Historian* xxxvi, 1974, 646–59

Jordan, W.K. *The Charities of London 1480–1660: The Aspirations and Achievements of the Urban Society*, London 1960

———. *The Charities of Rural England: The Aspirations and Achievements of the Rural Society*, London 1961

———. *Philanthropy in England 1480–1660: A Study of the Changing Patterns of English Social Aspirations*, London 1959

Kermode, J.I. 'Urban Decline? The Flight from Office in Late Medieval York', *EcHR*, 2nd series xxxv, 1982, 179–98

Kettle, A. 'City and Close: Lichfield in the Century before the Reformation', in C.M. Barron and C. Harper-Bill, eds, *The Church in Pre-Reformation Society*, Woodbridge 1985, 158–69

Keyser, C.E. 'On Mural Paintings and Other Coloured Decorations at Chippenham Church, Cambridgeshire', *Proc. Camb. Antiq. Soc.* vi, 1884–8, 321–29

Kitching, C.J. 'Church and Chapelry in Sixteenth Century England', *SCH* xvi, 1979, 279–90

———. 'The Quest for Concealed Lands in the Reign of Elizabeth I', *TRHS*, 5th series xxiv, 1974, 63–78

Klein, J. 'Medieval Spanish Gilds', in *Facts and Factors in Economic History*, ed. E.F. Gay, Cambridge, Massachusetts, 1932, New York 1967, 164–88

Kramer, S. *The English Craft Gilds: Studies in their Progress and Decline*, New York 1927

Kreider, A. *English Chantries: The Road to Dissolution*, Cambridge, Massachusetts, 1979

Kubler-Ross, E. *Death: The Final Stage of Growth*, Englewood Cliffs, New Jersey 1975

———. *On Death and Dying*, New York 1969

Leff, G. *Heresy in the Middle Ages: The Relation of Heterodoxy to Dissent c.1250–1450*, 2 vols, Manchester 1967

Lobel, M.D. *The Borough of Bury St Edmunds*, Oxford 1935

Loggon, S. *A History of the Brotherhood or Guild of the Holy Ghost in the Chapel of the Holy Ghost near Basingstoke in Hampshire*, Reading 1742

Lovatt, R. 'Two Collegiate Loan Chests in Late Medieval Cambridge', in *Medieval Cambridge: Essays on the Pre-Reformation University*, ed. P. Zutshi, Woodbridge 1993, 129–65

MacCulloch, D. 'The Myth of the English Reformation', *Journal of British Studies* xxx, 1991, 1–19

Mackenney, R. *Tradesmen and Traders: The World of the Gilds in Venice and Europe c.1250–1650*, London 1987

Malet-Lambert, Rev. J. *Two Thousand Years of Gild Life*, Hull 1891

Maitland, F.W. *Township and Borough*, Cambridge 1898

Martin, G.H. 'The English Borough in the Thirteenth Century', *TRHS*, 5th series xiii, 1963, 123–44
Mason, E. 'The Role of the English Parishioner 1100–1500', *JEH* xxvii, 1976, 17–29
Mattingley, J. 'The Medieval Parish Guilds of Cornwall', *Journal of the Royal Institution of Cornwall*, new series x, 1989, 290–329
Mauss, M. *The Gift: Forms and Functions of Exchange in Archaic Societies*, London 1966
McCree, B.R. 'Charity and Gild Solidarity in Late Medieval England', *Journal of British Studies* xxxii, 1993, 195–225
———. 'Religious Gilds and Regulation of Behaviour in Late Medieval Towns', in *People, Politics and Community in the Later Middle Ages*, ed. J. Rosenthal and C. Richmond, Gloucester 1987, 108–22
McDannell, C. and Lang, B. *Heaven: A History*, Yale 1988
McHardy, A. 'Careers and Disappointments in the Late Medieval Church: some English Evidence', *SCH* xxvi, 1989, 111–30
———. *The Church in London*, London Record Society xiii, London 1977
McIntosh, M.K. *Autonomy and Community: The Royal Manor of Havering 1300–1500*, Cambridge 1986
———. 'Local Change and Community Control 1465–1500', *Huntingdon Library Quarterly* xlix, 1986, 219–42
———. 'Local Responses to the Poor in Late Medieval and Tudor England', *Continuity and Change* ii, 1988, 209–45
———. 'Social Change and Tudor Manorial Elites', *Law and Social Change in British Society*, ed. J.A. Guy and H.G. Beale, Royal Historical Society Studies in History 40, London 1984, 73–85
McMurray-Gibson, G. *The Theater of Devotion: East Anglian Drama and Society in the Late Middle Ages*, Chicago 1989
Michaud-Quantin, P. *Universitas: Expression du Mouvement Communautaire dans le Moyen Age Latin*, Paris 1970
Miller, E. *The Abbey and Bishopric of Ely: The Social History of an Ecclesiastical Estate from the Tenth Century to the early Fourteenth Century*, Cambridge 1951
Miller, E. and Hatcher, J. *Medieval England: Rural Society and Economic Change 1086–1348*, London 1978
Milner Gray, J. *Biographical Notes on the Mayors of Cambridge*, Cambridge 1922
Moir, E.A.L. *The Justices of the Peace*, Harmondsworth 1969
Mollat, M. *Les Pauvres Au Moyen Age: Etude Sociale*, Paris 1978
Moorman, J.R.H. *Church Life in England in the Thirteenth Century*, Oxford 1945
Obelkevich, J., Roper, L. and Samuel, R. *Disciplines of Faith*, London 1987
Oexle, O.G. 'Conjuratio et Ghilde dans l'Antiquité et dans le Haute Moyen Age: Remarques sur la Continuité des formes de la Vie Sociale', *Francia* x, 1982, 1–19
———. 'Conjuratio und Gilde im Frühen Mittelalter: Ein Beitrag zum problem der Sozialgeschichtlichen Kontinuität Zwischen Antike und Mittelalter', *Vorträge Und Forschung* xxix, 1985, 151–214
———. 'Die Mittelalterliche Zünfte als Forschungsproblem: ein Beitrag zur Wissenschaftsgeschichte der Moderne' in *Blätter für Deutsche Landesgeschichte* cxviii, 1982, 1–77
———. 'Gilden als soziale Gruppen in Der Karolingerzeit' in *Das Handwerk in*

Vor- und Frühgeschichtlicher Zeit, Teil i, Historische und Rechtshistorische Beitrage und Untersuchungen zur Frühgeschichte der Gild, ed. H. Jankuhn et al., Göttingen 1981, 284–354
Owen, D.M. 'Chapelries and Rural Settlement: An Examination of some of the Kesteven Evidence', in *Medieval Settlement: Continuity and Change*, ed. P.H. Sawyer, 1976, 66–71
———. *Church and Society in Medieval Lincolnshire*, Lincoln 1971
———. *Ely Records: A Handlist of the Records of the Bishop and Archdeacon of Ely*, Cambridge 1971
Page, F.M. 'The Customary Poor Law of three Cambridgeshire Manors', *Cambridge Historical Journal* iii, 1929–31, 125–33
Palmer, W.M. 'The Hospitals of St John the Baptist and St Mary Magdalene at Ely', *Proc. Camb. Antiq. Soc.* xxxvi, 1935, 76–108
Palliser, D. 'Popular Reactions to the Reformation during the Years of Uncertainty', in *The English Reformation Revised*, ed. C. Haigh, Cambridge 1987, 94–113
Pantin, W.A. *The English Church in the Fourteenth Century*, Cambridge 1955
Pearson, Rev. J.B. 'The Assessments of Cambridgeshire 1291–1889', *Proc. Camb. Antiq. Soc.* viii, 1891–4, 283–91
———. 'On the Cambridgeshire Subsidies', *Proc. Camb. Antiq. Soc.* ix, 1894–8, 120–37
Pevsner, N. *The Buildings of England: Cambridgeshire*, Harmondsworth 1954
Pfaff, R.W. 'The English Devotion to St Gregory's Trental', *Speculum* xlix, 1974, 75–90
———. *New Liturgical Feasts in Later Medieval England*, Oxford 1970
Phelps-Brown, H. and Hopkins, S. *A Perspective of Wages and Prices*, London 1981
Phythian-Adams, C. *The Desolation of a City: Coventry and the Urban Crisis of the Late Middle Ages*, Cambridge 1979
———. 'Ceremony and the Citizens: The Communal Year at Coventry', in *Crisis and Order in English Towns 1500–1700*, ed. P. Clark and P. Slack, London 1972, 57–85
———. *Local History and Folklore: A New Framework*, London 1975
Pirenne, H. *Economic and Social History of Medieval Europe*, translation, London 1936
Platt, C. *The Parish Churches of Medieval England*, London 1981
Pollard, G. 'Medieval Loan Chests in Cambridge', *BIHR* xvii, 1939–40, 113–29
Poos, L. *A Rural Society After the Black Death: Essex 1350–1525*, Cambridge 1991
Pound, J. *Poverty and Vagrancy in Tudor England*, London 1971
Power, Eileen, 'English Craft Gilds in the Middle Ages', *History* iv, 1919–20, 211–14
Pullan, B. *Rich and Poor in Renaissance Venice: The Social Institutions of a Catholic State to 1620*, Oxford 1971
Raban, S. *Mortmain Legislation and the English Church 1279–1500*, Cambridge 1982
Raftis, J.A. *The Estates of Ramsay Abbey*, Toronto 1957
———. *Tenure and Mobility: Studies in the Social History of the Medieval English Village*, Toronto 1964
Razi, Z. 'Family, Land and Village Community in Later Medieval England', *P&P* xciii, 1981, 3–36

Reynolds, S. 'The Idea of the Corporation in Western Christendom before 1300', in *Law and Social Change in British Society* ed. J.A. Guy and H.G. Beale, Royal Historical Society Studies in History 40, London 1984, 27–33
———. *An Introduction to the History of English Medieval Towns*, Oxford 1977
———. *Kingdoms and Communities in Western Europe 900–1300*, Oxford 1984
Richards, P. *The Medieval Leper and his Northern Heirs*, Cambridge 1977
Richmond, C. 'Religion and the Fifteenth-Century English Gentleman', in *The Church, Politics and Patronage in the Fifteenth-Century*, ed. R.B. Dobson, Gloucester 1984, 193–208
Riden, P., ed., *The Medieval Town In Britain*, Cardiff 1980
Rosenthal, J. *The Purchase of Paradise: Gift Giving and the Aristocracy 1307–1485*, London 1972
Rosser, A.G. 'The Anglo-Saxon Gilds', in *Minsters and Parish Churches: The Local Church in Transition 950–1200*, ed. J. Blair, Oxford 1988, 31–33
———. 'Communities of Parish and Guild in the Late Middle Ages', in *Parish Church and People: Local Studies in Lay Religion 1350–1750*, ed. S. Wright, London 1988, 29–55
———. 'The Essence of Medieval Urban Communities: The Vill of Westminster 1200–1540', *TRHS*, 5th series xxxiv, 1984, 91–112
———. 'The Town and Gild of Lichfield in the Late Middle Ages', *Transactions of the South Staffordshire Archaeological and Historical Society* xxvii, 1985–6, 39–47
Rubin, M. *Charity and Community in Medieval Cambridge*, Cambridge 1987
———. *Corpus Christi: The Eucharist in Late Medieval Culture*, Cambridge 1991
———. 'Corpus Christi Fraternities and Late Medieval Piety', *SCH* xxiii, 1985–6, 97–109
Rushe, Rev. J.P. 'The Origin of St Mary's Gild and its Connection with Corpus Christi College', *Proc. Camb. Antiq. Soc.* xvi, 1911–12, 20–52
Russell, J.C. *British Medieval Population*, Albuquerque 1948
Scarisbrick, J.J. *The Reformation and the English People*, Oxford 1984
Scharrer, W. *Laienbrüderschaften in der Stadt Bamberg vom Mittelalter bis zum Ende des Alten Reiches – Geschichte, Brauchtum, Kultobjekte*, Bamberg 1990
Schofield, R.S. 'The Geographical Distribution of Wealth in England 1334–1649', *EcHR*, 2nd series xviii, 1965, 483–510
Scribner, R.W. 'Interpreting Religion in Early Modern Europe', in *European Studies Review* xiii, 1983, 89–105, review article
Sheehan, M.M. *The Will in Medieval England*, Toronto 1963
Siraut, M. 'Accounts of St Katherine's Gild at Holy Trinity Church, Cambridge 1514–1537', *Proc. Camb. Antiq. Soc.* lxvii, 1977, 111–21
Slack, P. *The English Poor Law 1531–1782*, London 1990
Smith, R.M. 'Modernisation and the Corporate Medieval Village Community in England: Some Sceptical Reflections', in *Explorations in Historical Geography*, ed. A.R.H. Baker and D. Gregory, Cambridge 1984, 140–79
Spufford, M. *Contrasting Communities: English Villages in Sixteenth and Seventeenth Century Cambridgeshire*, Cambridge 1974, reprinted 1979
———. 'Puritanism and Social Control?', in *Order and Disorder in Early Modern Europe*, ed. A. Fletcher and J. Stevenson, Cambridge 1985, 41–57
Stephenson, C. *Borough and Town: A Study of Urban Origins in England*, Cambridge, Massachusetts, 1935

Strohm, R. *Music in Late Medieval Bruges*, Oxford 1985
Stubbs, W. *Constitional History of England*, 3 vols, Oxford 1874–8, 2nd and 3rd editions 1878–80
Swanson, H. 'The Illusion of Economic Structure: Craft Gilds in Late Medieval Towns', *P&P* cxxi, 1988, 29–48
Swanson, R.N. *Church and Society in Late Medieval England*, Oxford 1989
Tait, J. *The Medieval English Borough: Studies on its Origins and Constitutional History*, Manchester 1936
Tanner, N. *The Church in Late Medieval Norwich 1370–1532*, Toronto 1984
Tate, W.E. *The Parish Chest*, Cambridge 1951
Tenenti, A. 'La Vie et la Mort à Travers l'Art du XVe Siècle', *Cahiers Des Annales* viii, Paris 1952
Thomas, K. *Religion and the Decline of Magic: Studies in Popular Beliefs in Sixteenth Century England*, London 1971
Thompson, J.A.F. 'Piety and Charity in Late Medieval London', *JEH* xvi, 1965, 178–95
Thorold-Rogers, J.E. *A History of Agriculture and Prices in England*, 7 vols, Oxford 1866–1902
Tiernay, B. *Medieval Poor Law: A Sketch of Canonical Theory and its Application in England*, Berkeley and Los Angeles 1959
Tillyard, E.M.W. *The Elizabethan World Picture*, Harmondsworth 1963
Torre, A. 'Village Ceremonial Life and Politics in Eighteenth Century Piedmont', in *Disciplines of Faith*, ed. J. Obelkevich, L. Roper and R. Samuel, London 1987, 194–207
Toussaert, J. *Le Sentiment Religieux en Flandres à la Fin du Moyen Age*, Paris 1963
Trexler, R.C. *Public Life in Renaissance Florence*, New York 1980
Trinkaus, C. and Oberman, H.A. *The Pursuit of Holiness in Late Medieval and Renaissance Religion*, Leyden 1974
Tuck, J.A. 'The Cambridge Parliament 1388', *EHR* lxxxiv, 1969, 225–43
Turner, V. and E. *Image and Pilgrimage in Christian Culture: Anthropological Perspectives*, New York 1978
Unwin, G. *The Gilds and Companies of London*, London 1908, 4th edition with a new introduction by W.F. Kahl 1963
Vale, M.G.A. *Piety, Charity and Literacy among the Yorkshire Gentry 1370–1480*, Borthwick Papers l, York 1976
Van Engen, J. 'The Christian Middle Ages as an Historiographical Problem', *American Historical Review* ixc, 1986, 519–52
Van Gennep, A. *The Rites of Passage*, translated by M.B. Vizedom and G.L. Caffee, London 1977
Ventris, Rev. E. 'Notes upon Chantries and Free Chapels', *Proc. Camb. Antiq. Soc.* i, 1859, 201–40
Victoria History of the County of Cambridge, 9 vols, London 1938–1989, in progress
Vincent, C. *Des Charités Bien Ordonnées: Les Confréries Normandes de la fin du Treizième Siècle au debut du Seizième Siècle*, Paris 1988
Vinogradoff, P. *The Growth of the Manor*, London and New York 1904, 2nd edition 1911
Von Greyerz, K., ed. *Religion and Society in Early Modern Europe 1500–1800*, London 1984

Vrijhof, P. and Waardenburg, J. *Official and Popular Religion: Analysis of a Theme for Religious Studies*, The Hague 1979
Walford, C. *Gilds: Their Origins, Constitution, Object and later History*, London 1879, new and enlarged edition 1888
Webb, S. and B. *English Local Government*, 10 vols, London 1906–29
———. *The History of Trade Unionism*, 1st edition London 1894, 2nd edition 1920
Weinbaum, M. *The Incorporation of Boroughs*, Manchester 1937
Weissman, R.F.E. *Ritual Brotherhood in Renaissance Florence*, New York 1982
Wenham, L.P. 'The Chantries, Guilds, Obits and Lights of Richmond, Yorkshire', *York Archaeological Journal* xxxviii, 1952–5, 96–111
Westlake, H.F. *The Parish Gilds of Medieval England*, London 1919
———. 'The Parish Gilds of the Later Fourteenth Century', *Transactions of St Paul's Ecclesiological Society*, viii, 1917–20, 99–110
Whiting, R. *The Blind Devotion of the People: Popular Religion and the English Reformation*, Cambridge 1989
Williams, J.F. 'A Medieval Squabble', *Proc. Camb. Antiq. Soc.* liv, 1960, 109–11
Wood-Leigh, K.L. *Perpetual Chantries in Britain*, Cambridge 1965
Wright, S., ed. *Parish, Church and People: Local Studies in Lay Religion 1350–1750*, London 1988
Wrightson, K. *English Society 1580–1660*, London 1982
Wrightson, K. and Levine, D. *Poverty and Piety in an English Village: Terling 1525–1700*, New York 1979
Wunderli, R. and Broce, E. 'The Final Moment before Death in Early Modern England', *Sixteenth Century Journal* xx, 1989, 259–75
Zutshi, P., ed. *Medieval Cambridge: Essays on the Pre-Reformation University*, Woodbridge 1993

Unpublished Theses

Craig, J.S. 'Reformation, Politics and Polemics in Sixteenth-Century East Anglian Market Towns', Cambridge University Ph.D. 1992
Fenwick, C. 'The English Poll Taxes of 1377, 1379 and 1381: A Critical Examination of the Returns', London University Ph.D. 1983
Sheail, J, 'The Regional Distribution of Wealth in England as indicated in the 1524/5 Lay Subsidy Returns', Ph.D. London 1968

Index